Infrastructure Automation with Terraform

Automate and Orchestrate Your Infrastructure with Terraform Across AWS and Microsoft Azure

Ankita Patil

Mitesh Soni

www.bpbonline.com

Group Product Manager: Marianne Conor

Publishing Product Manager: Eva Brawn

Senior Editor: Connell

Content Development Editor: Melissa Monroe

Technical Editor: Anne Stokes

Copy Editor: Joe Austin

Language Support Editor: Justin Baldwin

Project Coordinator: Tyler Horan

Proofreader: Khloe Styles

Indexer: V. Krishnamurthy

Production Designer: Malcolm D'Souza

Marketing Coordinator: Kristen Kramer

First published: May 2022

Published by BPB Online
WeWork, 119 Marylebone Road
London NW1 5PU

UK | UAE | INDIA | SINGAPORE

ISBN 978-93-55510-907

www.bpbonline.com

Dedicated to

*Mummy-Pappa, Ayush, Anurag, and
Mummy-Pappa (Nandurbar)*
　　　　　　　—Ankita Patil

Vinay Kher
　　　　　— Mitesh Soni

About the Authors

- **Ankita Patil** is a DevOps evangelist. She is passionate learner and practitioner of Agile, DevOps, and Cloud Computing. As a change agent, she tries to bring change in an organization to get the maximum benefits of DevOps and Cloud Technologies. So, she wants to share her knowledge and ensure that IT professionals are trained and empowered to make those changes.

  Ankita has worked on multiple projects and tools for automating the entire software development lifecycle. Her approach has always been to develop a solution using different DevOps tools that would make the Development to Deployment cycle shorter and deliver software to market as quickly as possible. She has knowledge of the development of Java web applications and also has a lot of experience in Hybrid mobile app development. Her tools/technologies stacks include Jenkins, Azure DevOps, GitHub, Bitbucket, Rundeck, AWS Developer tools, and Terraform.

  Ankita is a great lover of art and craft. She likes to paint and sketch while listening to silent retro Bollywood music when she's not working. She likes to watch movies and series to unwind and is a nature lover who likes to visit beaches, lakes, and mountains, exploring new places. Ankita has authored one more book with BPB, titled Hands-On Pipeline as Code With Jenkins.

- **Mitesh Soni** is a DevOps engineer and in love with the DevOps culture and concept. Continuous improvement is his motto in life with existing imperfection. Mitesh has worked on multiple DevOps practices implementation initiatives. His primary focus is the improvement of the existing culture of an organization or a project using Continuous Integration and Continuous Delivery. He believes that attitude and dedication are the biggest virtues that can improve professional as well as personal life. He is experienced in DevOps consulting and enjoys talking about DevOps and CULTURE transformation using the existing practices and about improving them with open-source or commercial tools.

  Mitesh always believes that DevOps is a cultural transformation facilitated by people, processes, and tools. DevOps transformation is a tools agnostic approach. He loves to impart training and share knowledge with the community, and his main objective is to get enough information related to the project in such a way that it helps create an end-to-end automation pipeline.

His favorite tools/services for DevOps practices implementation are Azure DevOps and Jenkins in the commercial and open-source categories, respectively.

In his leisure time, he likes to walk in the garden, click photographs, and cycle. He prefers spending time in peaceful places.

Mitesh has authored the following books with BPB:

- Hands-On Pipeline as Code With Jenkins
- Hands-On Azure DevOps
- Agile, DevOps, and Cloud Computing With Microsoft Azure
- Hands-On Pipeline as YAML With Jenkins

About the Reviewers

❖ **Edgar Maucourant** is a seasoned professional with more than 20 years of experience in IT and development. He started off as a web developer in 1999 and took up various roles, working as an IT expert, a project manager, a teacher, a consultant, a SharePoint expert, a system architect, and a software architect. He also worked for different companies around the world, including big groups, start-ups and middle-sized businesses, both as an employee and as a freelancer. He started working with Azure platforms and services as early as 2010, when it was still called Windows Azure, and he set up a large variety of solutions, including IAAS, PAAS, and SAAS. Recently, he switched to the XR industry as a senior software architect for ModiFace, helping shape the future of Beauty XR and Beauty AI . When he's not in front of his computer , he likes spending time with his wife and kids, reading books, playing music, and tasting new dishes.

❖ **Matt Osborne** is a solutions engineer at Akamai. After graduating from Plymouth University with a degree in Computer Systems and Networks degree in 2006, he worked as a solutions engineer and PHP/C# developer for WiredRed, a video conferencing startup. He then joined Taylor Made Computer Solutions Ltd. as a support desk analyst, working with VMWare, Citrix, Windows OSes, and underlying networking. At Akamai, Matt now specializes in enabling the retail, travel, and hospitality industries to deliver engaging, reliable, and secure digital experiences via a global edge compute platform. He is also part of the developer champion team that guides customers on how best to automate Akamai solutions in their workflows via APIs, CLIs, and infrastructure as code. When Matt's not playing with tech, he loves adventure and has been known to drive three-wheelers around distant countries. He lives in the UK with his partner in adventure, Helen, and their two Russian blue cats.

❖ **Palash Purohit** has more than 6 years of experience in the IT industry working as a DevOps Engineer. His expertise in CI/CD designing and planning has helped projects and teams with DevOps adoption in their SDLC and deliveries. He has worked on multiple technologies like JS frameworks and backend technologies ranging from backend processing to mobile applications and cloud migration programs for major government and bank customers. Palash learned the core principles of DevOps as part of the CoE team, which allowed him to explore a wide range of products/tools spanning all aspects of application lifecycle management. He has onshore client-facing experience in planning and aligning applications with best practices, from branching strategy to deployment strategy, to help teams manage applications more efficiently. He is currently working with a banking firm that focuses on the containerized ecosystem with the latest changes in multi-cloud strategy for container orchestration platforms like self-managed Kubernetes, managed Kubernetes solutions, and Infrastructure-as-Code (IaC), along with configuration management as code. It also focuses on shifting the core applications to microservices architecture and containerized and cloud-native solutions.

Acknowledgements

○ **Ankita Patil**: Mummy and pappa, without your encouragement it would not have been possible for me to be where I am today. I would never miss a chance to say a big thank you.

Anurag, your presence in my life has positively shaped my life and career. Thank you for supporting me in everything that I have wanted to do and for encouraging me to do things that would help me grow in every aspect of life. You understand me, help me progress, and even take care of me like a child. Thank you and I love you a lot□.

Heartfelt thanks to Isha, Ashvanee, Siddharth, Palash, Kaustubh, Priya, Neeraja, and Khalida for always being there in the good and bad days of my life. My journey wouldn't have been so beautiful without you guys.

Mitesh, my guide and mentor always, thank you for giving me the opportunity to co-author this book with you.

Last but not least, I would like to thank the BPB team for giving me the opportunity to write this book for them.

○ **Mitesh Soni:** Vinay Sir, thank you for being there for me. I couldn't have managed things without your help. Thank you for teaching me and inspiring me.

Ruby, all that you are, is all that I'll ever need. Thank you for being there for me and for being part of one of the BEST stories of my life. You are, by far, the most amazing, beautiful, loving, kind, and ANGRY woman in the world. I included that last one so that you know I am being honest!

Special thanks to Gowri-Arya, Sourabh Mishra, Sudeep, Krimali, and Rita.

Ankita, you have always been special, and you inspire me to work hard. Miles to go!

I would like to thank the BPB team for giving me the opportunity to write this book for them.

Preface

DevOps is a culture that includes multiple software development practices that focus on culture change and ensure quality and faster time to market in Application Lifecycle Management. DevOps practices implementation is popular in all customer discussions. At times, it is considered value addition. The combination of people, processes, and tools makes the culture change initiative a reality.

The DevOps pipeline or CI/CD pipeline is a popular term. What does it mean? The pipeline includes different operations in different environments. Continuous Integration (CI) and Continuous Delivery (CD) are some of the most popular DevOps practices. Continuous Integration involves development, code analysis, unit testing, code coverage calculation, and build activities that are automated using various tools. Continuous Delivery is all about deploying your package into different environments so that end users can access it.

There are different ways to create a pipeline/orchestration, including Continuous Integration, Infrastructure as Code, Continuous Delivery, Continuous Testing, Continuous Deployment, Continuous Monitoring, and other DevOps practices. Each open-source or commercial tool provides different ways to create a CI/CD pipeline. Infrastructure as Code is gaining popularity in all organizations as it manages on-premise or on-cloud resources, along with Containers and Kubernetes, effectively and easily.

In this book, we will mainly focus on Terraform and cover Jenkins and Terraform integration in the last few chapters. Terraform is one of the most widely used and popular tools available in the Infrastructure as Code category. Terraform can manage resources across different Cloud Service Providers such as Microsoft Azure, Amazon Web Services, Google Cloud Platform, and so on. It provides an easy way to manage resources using declarative languages.

Jenkins is an open-source automation tool that offers an easy way to set up a CI/CD pipeline for almost any combination of languages, tools, and source code repositories. The Jenkins community offers more than 1,500 plugins that empower Jenkins users to create orchestration by integrating almost all popular tools in different categories.

This book provides a quick and easy way to learn and implement Terraform and CI/CD Pipeline that includes Infrastructure as Code in a step-by-step manner, with screenshots and diagrams to provide visualization. It provides examples for managing resources in Amazon Web Services (AWS) and Microsoft Azure. It also covers sample implementation of DevOps practices such as Continuous Integration, Infrastructure as Code, and Continuous Delivery using a sample project.

Chapter 1 covers recipes that are required as pre-requisites for the remaining chapters, such as Installing and configuring Terraform on Windows using Chocolatey, and Installing and configuring Terraform on Mac, Ubuntu, and CentOS. It also provides step-by-step instructions on Terraform IAC Development and IDE, how to create Microsoft Azure Account, installing and configuring Azure CLI, how to create AWS Account, and how to install and configure AWS CLI.

Chapter 2 explains the importance of Infrastructure as Code and introduces you to the various tools that can be used for implementing IaC. It covers topics such as Terraform Variables, how to use Terraform Functions and Terraform Graphs, and how to understand Terraform Output and export Terraform Output in JSON. It also covers details about Terraform Registry and Terraform States - Desired and Current States. Plus, it explains how to use conditional expressions, how to use Count and Count Index to provision multiple resources, and how to debug the Terraform execution.

Chapter 3 includes recipes related to Provisioners in Terraform, such as how to use Provisioners in Terraform, how to implement remote-exec provisioners and local-exec provisioners, and an overview of Creation-Time and Destroy-Time Provisioners.

Chapter 4 covers recipes related to AWS, such as how to configure AWS Credentials in Terraform files; how to add key-pair to instance; how to create IAM Role, VPC, Security Group, EC2 instance, EC2 instance with Nginx Web Server, Autoscaling Group, Elastic Load Balancer, and EC2 instance with Packer AMI; how to manage, maintain, and validate Terraform Script; how to destroy AWS Infrastructure; and how to implement S3 Buckets and Bucket Policies.

Chapter 5 includes recipes related to Microsoft Azure Cloud, such as using Terraform in Azure Cloud Shell; creating Resource Group, Virtual Network, Network Security Groups, Virtual Machine, Scale set and Availability set for

Virtual Machines; Configuring an App Services and database for Java Web App; Load Balancer; and managing Azure Spring Cloud.

Chapter 6 has recipes related to Terraform Modules, such as creating and distributing custom modules; how to manage production-like infrastructure using Terraform; creating Amazon VPC and EKS cluster using Terraform modules; and overview of Azure network and AKS cluster using Terraform modules.

Chapter 7 walks you through recipes related to Terraform Cloud. This chapter introduces all the areas that encompass the field of Terraform Cloud, Terraform Cloud usage, and its benefits in daily operations. It includes topics like how to perform IaC configuration, and Workspace and Repository and Access Management in Terraform Cloud.

Chapter 8 introduces Jenkins and different types of Pipelines available in Jenkins and teaches you how to integrate Jenkins and Terraform. This chapter will cover topics such as how to deploy Jenkins automation server, Jenkins pipeline – best practices, Terraform in Jenkins declarative pipeline, and how to adopt IaC culture in an organization.

Chapter 9 This chapter will cover the implementation of CI/CD and IaC for a sample project using Terraform. It will include Static Code Analysis using SonarQube, Unit tests execution and code coverage calculation, build package, and creating Terraform plan and resources.

Code Bundle and Coloured Images

Please follow the link to download the
Code Bundle and the *Coloured Images* of the book:

https://rebrand.ly/y2ftpla

The code bundle for the book is also hosted on GitHub at **https://github.com/bpbpublications/Infrastructure-Automation-with-Terraform**. In case there's an update to the code, it will be updated on the existing GitHub repository.

We have code bundles from our rich catalogue of books and videos available at **https://github.com/bpbpublications**. Check them out!

Errata

We take immense pride in our work at BPB Publications and follow best practices to ensure the accuracy of our content to provide with an indulging reading experience to our subscribers. Our readers are our mirrors, and we use their inputs to reflect and improve upon human errors, if any, that may have occurred during the publishing processes involved. To let us maintain the quality and help us reach out to any readers who might be having difficulties due to any unforeseen errors, please write to us at :

errata@bpbonline.com

Your support, suggestions and feedbacks are highly appreciated by the BPB Publications' Family.

Did you know that BPB offers eBook versions of every book published, with PDF and ePub files available? You can upgrade to the eBook version at www.bpbonline.com and as a print book customer, you are entitled to a discount on the eBook copy. Get in touch with us at :

business@bpbonline.com for more details.

At **www.bpbonline.com**, you can also read a collection of free technical articles, sign up for a range of free newsletters, and receive exclusive discounts and offers on BPB books and eBooks.

Piracy

If you come across any illegal copies of our works in any form on the internet, we would be grateful if you would provide us with the location address or website name. Please contact us at **business@bpbonline.com** with a link to the material.

If you are interested in becoming an author

If there is a topic that you have expertise in, and you are interested in either writing or contributing to a book, please visit **www.bpbonline.com**. We have worked with thousands of developers and tech professionals, just like you, to help them share their insights with the global tech community. You can make a general application, apply for a specific hot topic that we are recruiting an author for, or submit your own idea.

Reviews

Please leave a review. Once you have read and used this book, why not leave a review on the site that you purchased it from? Potential readers can then see and use your unbiased opinion to make purchase decisions. We at BPB can understand what you think about our products, and our authors can see your feedback on their book. Thank you!

For more information about BPB, please visit **www.bpbonline.com**.

Table of Contents

CHAPTER 1
Setting Up Terraform

> "Believe in yourself! Have faith in your abilities! Without humble but reasonable confidence in your powers, you cannot be successful or happy."
>
> —*Norman Vincent Peale*

Application delivery and the activities involved in it have changed a lot after cloud computing and DevOps practices gained the attention of different organizations. Everything as code is a new norm where your automation or CI/CD pipeline is also part of version control - pipeline as code. High availability, disaster recovery, and business continuity have become crucial considering the competitive market. Terraform helps us write and execute code to define, deploy, update, and destroy your infrastructure in different cloud environments; hence, we don't need to learn cloud specific tools. Terraform is an open-source Infrastructure as Code tool that codifies cloud APIs into declarative configuration files to make managing different environments easier.

In this chapter, we will install and configure Terraform in different operating systems as well as in Docker container. We will use Docker Desktop to create a container that has Terraform installed on it. We will also understand the details for AWS and Azure accounts and **Command line (CLIs)**. It will help us in the upcoming chapters when using Terraform to create infrastructure in AWS and Microsoft Azure cloud environment.

Structure

We will discuss the following topics in this chapter:

- Installing and configuring Terraform on Windows using Chocolatey
- Installing and configuring Terraform on Mac
- Installing and configuring Terraform on Ubuntu
- Installing and configuring Terraform on CentOS
- Terraform IAC Development and IDE
- Creating Microsoft Azure Account
- Installing and Configuring Azure CLI
- Creating AWS Account
- Installing and Configuring AWS CLI

Objectives

After studying this unit, you should be able to install and configure Terraform in different operating systems or different types of platform, such as Docker container. You should also be able to understand how to create AWS and Azure accounts and installing CLIs.

Installing and configuring Terraform on Windows using Chocolatey

Terraform open-source project and Terraform plugins are written in GO programming language. We can use Terraform to create infrastructure resources across different cloud service providers such as **Amazon Web Services (AWS)** and Azure as well as other cloud deployment models and virtualization platforms. In this book, we are going to use AWS and Microsoft Azure. We will install and configure Terraform, AWS CLI, Azure CLI, and editors. This environment creation will help us write Terraform files to create resources in different cloud platforms.

Chocolatey is a small piece of wonder for all those who hate struggling with the installation of different packages on Windows. It helps make installation easier and can be done from your command-line. Its features include management of dependencies and version control, and it offers ease of use for handling different packages on Windows. Chocolatey is an open-source package management tool, but it has a commercial edition. Chocolatey is in a similar pool of yum, apt, and Homebrew. In simple words, Chocolatey is a Windows Package Manager that makes your life easy with simplicity, efficiency, power, and flexibility.

Note: Terraform doesn't require GO as a pre-requisite for installation or any GO programming skills.

Here are the pre-requisites to install Chocolatey:

- Windows 7+ / Windows Server 2003+

- PowerShell v2+ (the lowest version is v3 for install from this website due to TLS 1.2 requirement)

- .NET Framework 4+ (the installation will attempt to install .NET 4.0 if you do not have it) (the lowest version is 4.5 for install from this website due to TLS 1.2 requirement)

Let's try to install Chocolatey using the following commands:

We will install it with PowerShell:

1. With PowerShell, execute the "**Get-ExecutionPolicy**" command first. Here's the explanation of the output of the execution of this command:

   - If output is restricted, run Set-ExecutionPolicy AllSigned Or Set-ExecutionPolicy Bypass -Scope Process

   If output is **AllSigned**, then go to *Step 2*.

   Visit **https://docs.microsoft.com/en-us/powershell/module/ microsoft.powershell.core/about/about_execution_ policies?view=powershell-7.1** for more details on execution policies.

2. Execute the following command to install Chocolatey. Visit the official website for more details on Chocolatey installation.

```
Set-ExecutionPolicy Bypass -Scope Process -Force; [System.
Net.ServicePointManager]::SecurityProtocol = [System.Net.
ServicePointManager]::SecurityProtocol -bor 3072; iex ((New-
Object System.Net.WebClient).DownloadString('https://chocolatey.
org/install.ps1'))
```

3. Type **choco** or **choco -?**. You are ready to install packages using Chocolatey. Chocolatey is installed in following screenshot:

```
PS C:\WINDOWS\system32> Get-ExecutionPolicy
AllSigned
PS C:\WINDOWS\system32> Set-ExecutionPolicy Bypass -Scope Process -Force; [System.Net.ServicePointManager]::SecurityProtocol = [System.Net.Service
]::SecurityProtocol -bor 3072; iex ((New-Object System.Net.WebClient).DownloadString('https://chocolatey.org/install.ps1'))
Forcing web requests to allow TLS v1.2 (Required for requests to Chocolatey.org)
Getting latest version of the Chocolatey package for download.
Not using proxy.
Getting Chocolatey from https://chocolatey.org/api/v2/package/chocolatey/0.10.15.
Downloading https://chocolatey.org/api/v2/package/chocolatey/0.10.15 to C:\Users\Mitesh\AppData\Local\Temp\chocolatey\chocoInstall\chocolatey.zip
Not using proxy.
Extracting C:\Users\Mitesh\AppData\Local\Temp\chocolatey\chocoInstall\chocolatey.zip to C:\Users\Mitesh\AppData\Local\Temp\chocolatey\chocoInstall
Installing Chocolatey on the local machine
Creating ChocolateyInstall as an environment variable (targeting 'Machine')
  Setting ChocolateyInstall to 'C:\ProgramData\chocolatey'
WARNING: It's very likely you will need to close and reopen your shell
  before you can use choco.
Restricting write permissions to Administrators
We are setting up the Chocolatey package repository.
The packages themselves go to 'C:\ProgramData\chocolatey\lib'
  (i.e. C:\ProgramData\chocolatey\lib\yourPackageName).
A shim file for the command line goes to 'C:\ProgramData\chocolatey\bin'
  and points to an executable in 'C:\ProgramData\chocolatey\lib\yourPackageName'.
```

Figure 1.1: *Install Chocolaty on Windows using PowerShell*

4. Verify environment variables after installing Chocolatey as per the following screenshot. Visit **https://chocolatey.org/install** for advanced installation of Chocolatey.

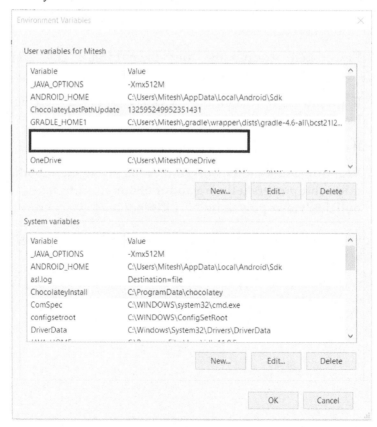

Figure 1.2: *Environment variables*

Note: Terraform is used to efficiently manage compute, storage, and networking resources along with identity- and access-management related features, etc. Terraform can manage resources in cloud Platforms such as AWS, Microsoft Azure, Google cloud, VMware, and so on.

5. Verify the Chocolatey version using the following command:

    ```
    PS C:\> choco --version
    0.10.15
    ```

    Now, we are ready with Chocolatey installation; the next step is to install Terraform.

6. Visit **https://chocolatey.org/packages/terraform** and get more details on the Terraform package and the command to install Terraform using Chocolatey.

Figure 1.3: Installing Terraform using Chocolatey

Now, Terraform version 1.1.6 is available for installation using Chocolatey.

7. Execute the following command in PowerShell to install Terraform as per the following screenshot:

```
choco install terraform
```

```
PS C:\WINDOWS\system32> choco install terraform
Chocolatey v0.10.15
Installing the following packages:
terraform
By installing you accept licenses for the packages.
Progress: Downloading terraform 1.1.6... 100%

terraform v1.1.6 [Approved]
terraform package files install completed. Performing other installation steps.
The package terraform wants to run 'chocolateyInstall.ps1'.
Note: If you don't run this script, the installation will fail.
Note: To confirm automatically next time, use '-y' or consider:
choco feature enable -n allowGlobalConfirmation
Do you want to run the script?([Y]es/[A]ll - yes to all/[N]o/[P]rint): yes

Removing old terraform plugins
File appears to be downloaded already. Verifying with package checksum to determine if it needs to be redownloaded.
Error - hashes do not match. Actual value was 'F76B215F7DBA2556ED3ACAE3B87B1A742D7276D10E8C56F3D27B7515158E63E5'.
Downloading terraform 64 bit
  from 'https://releases.hashicorp.com/terraform/1.1.6/terraform_1.1.6_windows_amd64.zip'
Progress: 100% - Completed download of C:\Users\Mitesh\AppData\Local\Temp\chocolatey\terraform\1.1.6\terraform_1.1.6_windows_amd64.zip
(18.12 MB).
Download of terraform_1.1.6_windows_amd64.zip (18.12 MB) completed.
Hashes match.
Extracting C:\Users\Mitesh\AppData\Local\Temp\chocolatey\terraform\1.1.6\terraform_1.1.6_windows_amd64.zip to C:\ProgramData\chocolatey
\lib\terraform\tools...
C:\ProgramData\chocolatey\lib\terraform\tools
 ShimGen has successfully created a shim for terraform.exe
 The install of terraform was successful.
  Software installed to 'C:\ProgramData\chocolatey\lib\terraform\tools'

Chocolatey installed 1/1 packages.
 See the log for details (C:\ProgramData\chocolatey\logs\chocolatey.log).
```

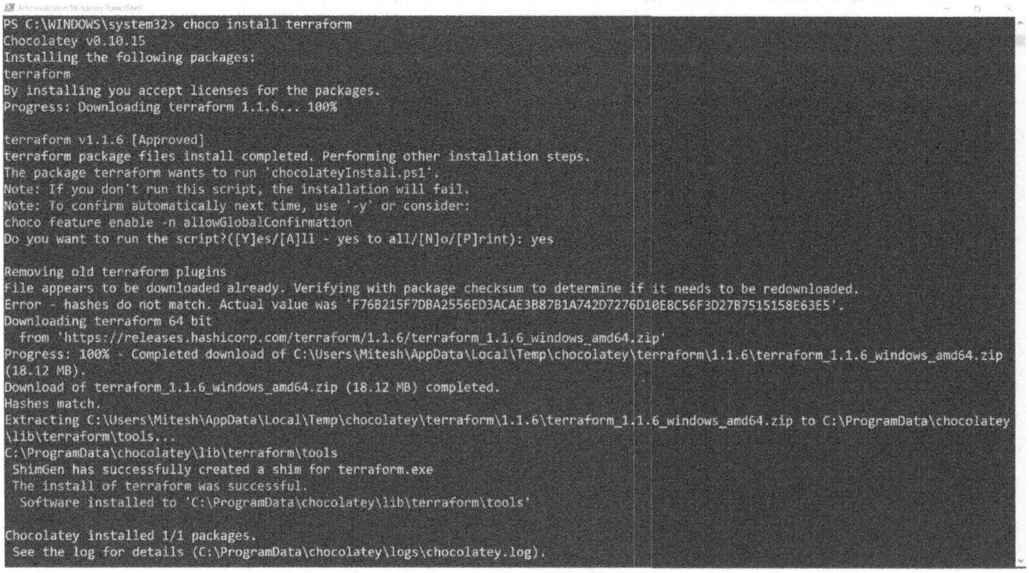

Figure 1.4: Install Terraform using Chocolatey

Note: Infrastructure as code tools like Terraform help you to create infrastructure that is consistent, repeatable, and predictable even if you run it multiple times. Same Code = Same Output!

In the next section, we will look at how to install Terraform in macOS.

Installing and configuring Terraform on Mac

There are two ways to install Terraform on macOS: manually and via the HomeBrew package manager; both are detailed below. Let's see how to install Terraform manually:

1. We will download the installable file for macOS from **https://www.terraform.io/downloads.html**.

2. Extract terraform installation file.

3. Open your **.bash_profile** file available in the root folder; create a profile if it is not available in your system. Create new **bash_profile** with the **touch .bash-profile** command.

4. Edit the file and add the folder to where you've chosen to extract the Terraform binary export **PATH=$PATH:~/terraform**.

```
1. export PATH="$PATH:~/terraform
```

5. Save the **.bash_profile** file.

6. Restart your terminal.

7. Enter the source **.bash_profile** command to use the bash profile with the new terraform-folder as an executable binary path.

8. Verify the installation with the **terraform -version** command.

   Let's see how to install terraform on Mac using HomeBrew. Download and install it from **https://brew.sh**. Add homebrew to the **$PATH** variable.

The following table lists the steps and the commands.

Description	Command
Install the HashiCorp tap, a repository of all our Homebrew packages.	`brew tap hashicorp/tap`
Install Terraform with `hashicorp/tap/ terraform`	`brew install hashicorp/tap/ terraform`
Update and install.	`brew upgrade hashicorp/tap/ terraform`
Verify the installation with the command.	`terraform -version`

Table 1.1: *Commands to install Terraform on macOS*

Note: Terraform helps to create "Disposable Environments" such as QA, Pre-Prod, or Production. The same Terraform script can be used to create multiple environments with minor changes in the type of resources required for a specific environment.

In the next section, we will explore how to install Terraform in Ubuntu/Debian operating system.

Installing and configuring Terraform on Ubuntu/Debian

Let's see how to install Terraform manually; we will download the installable file for Ubuntu/Debian from **https://www.terraform.io/downloads.html**.

1. Install zip with the following command:

    ```
    sudo apt-get install zip -y
    ```

2. Unzip the Terraform download with the following command:

    ```
    unzip terraform*.zip
    ```

3. Let's move it to **/usr/local/bin**. (This is where we can keep system programs and libraries that are not available with standard distribution, and usually, they are binary executables).

4. Verify the installation with the **terraform -version** command.

Let's see how to install terraform on Ubuntu/Debian with apt-get. The following table lists the steps with their description and the commands.

Add the HashiCorp GPG key.	`curl -fsSL https://apt.releases.hashicorp.com/gpg	sudo apt-key add -`
Add the official HashiCorp Linux repository.	`sudo apt-add-repository "deb [arch=amd64] https://apt.releases.hashicorp.com $(lsb_release -cs) main"`
Update and install.	`sudo apt-get update && sudo apt-get install terraform`
Verify the installation with the command	`terraform -version`

Table 1.2: Commands to install Terraform on Ubuntu/Debian

Note: Terraform is cloud-agnostic, and it also supports custom solutions. Terraform allows the same configuration to be used to manage resources across multiple providers in the multi-cloud scenario.

In the next section, we will cover how to install Terraform in CentOS/RHEL/Amazon Linux operating system.

Installing and configuring Terraform on CentOS/RHEL/Amazon Linux

Let's see how to install Terraform using *yum*; *yum* is the tool to install software packages from official Red Hat repositories as well as third-party repositories. The following table lists the steps with description and the commands.

Install yum-config-manager to manage your repositories	`sudo yum install -y yum-utils`
Use yum-config-manager to add the official HashiCorp Linux repository	`CentOS/RHEL: sudo yum-config-manager --add-repo` https://rpm.releases. hashicorp.com/RHEL/hashicorp.repo `Amazon Linux: sudo yum-config-manager --add-repo` https://rpm.releases. hashicorp.com/AmazonLinux/hashicorp.repo
Install	`sudo yum -y install terraform`
Verify the installation with the command	`terraform -version`

Table 1.3: Commands to install Terraform on CentOS/RHEL/Amazon Linux

In the next section, we will discuss how to install Terraform in a Docker container. We will use Docker Desktop.

Terraform in Docker

Docker Desktop is an easy-to-install community version for Windows and Mac. It is designed to run on Windows 10 (Professional or Enterprise 64-bit or Home 64-bit with WSL 2) and Mac 10.14 or newer. Docker Desktop helps you build and share containerized applications. It is available for free and supports both Linux and Windows Docker containers.

Docker Desktop has the following components:

- Docker Engine
- Docker CLI client
- Docker Compose
- Notary
- The latest version of Kubernetes
- Credential Helper

Following are the steps to install Docker Desktop for Mac.

1. To install Docker Desktop for Mac, visit **https://docs.docker.com/docker-for-mac/install/**.

2. To install Docker Desktop for Windows, visit **https://docs.docker.com/docker-for-windows/install/**.

3. Once Docker Desktop is installed, the objective is to install Terraform in Docker Container.

Here, we will install Terraform in Ubuntu Container. Hence, pull Ubuntu image using the **docker pull ubuntu:latest** command and verify it with docker images command once it is downloaded successfully:

```
F:\1.DevOps\2022\Terraform 1.1.6\Chapter 1\Code>docker pull
ubuntu:latest

latest: Pulling from library/ubuntu

08c01a0ec47e: Pull complete

Digest: sha256:669e010b58baf5beb2836b253c1fd5768333f0d1dbcb834f7c07a4d-
c93f474be

Status: Downloaded newer image for ubuntu:latest

docker.io/library/ubuntu:latest


F:\1.DevOps\2022\Terraform 1.1.6\Chapter 1\Code>docker images
```

REPOSITORY	TAG	IMAGE ID	CREATED	SIZE
jenkinsci/blueocean	latest	d76a171ee820	2 weeks ago	582MB
ubuntu	latest	54c9d81cbb44	2 weeks ago	72.8MB
sonarqube	latest	4ac4842c584e	3 weeks ago	520MB
docker	dind	1a42336ff683	4 weeks ago	233MB
docker/getting-started	latest	26d80cd96d69	2 months ago	28.5MB

We have downloaded ubuntu images, next step is to confirm it in Docker Desktop.

1. Let's open Docker Desktop in Windows and verify the image downloaded.

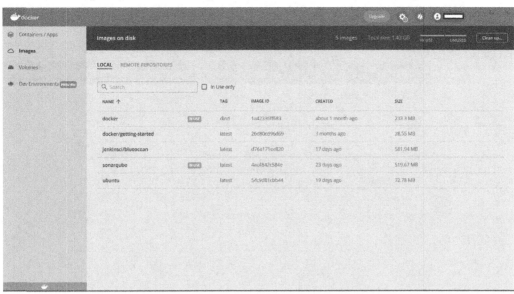

Figure 1.5: Ubuntu image in Docker Desktop

Note: Infrastructure always evolves over the duration of the project. In the case of Infrastructure as Code, code remains in the repository, such as Git. All the versions of Infrastructure Code evolve in the repository; hence, it is easier to walk through the changes over time.

2. The following is the dockerfile to utilize Ubuntu image and create an image that has terraform installed in it. It will install all the required packages to install Terraform, and finally, it will install Terraform in Docker Image, which can be utilized to create Docker Instances with Terraform available on it.

```
FROM ubuntu:latest

ENV TERRAFORM_VERSION=1.1.6

RUN apt-get update && apt-get -y install sudo && apt-
get -y install curl && apt-get -y install gnupg && apt-
get -y install software-properties-common && curl -fsSL https://
apt.releases.hashicorp.com/gpg | sudo apt-key add - && sudo apt-
add-repository "deb [arch=amd64] https://apt.releases.hashicorp.
com $(lsb_release -cs) main" && sudo apt-get update && sudo apt-
get install terraform
```

3. Create a dockerfile with the preceding script. Use the **`docker build -t terraform:v1.1.6`** . command to create an image that has terraform installed in it.

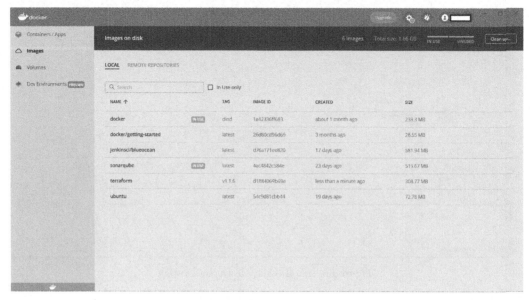

Figure 1.6: Terraform image in Docker Desktop

4. Use **`docker run -it --name terraform116 terraform:v1.1.6 /bin/bash`** to execute a command in the container created from the terraform image.

5. Verify that the Terraform version is 6.

```
F:\1.DevOps\2022\Terraform 1.1.6\Chapter 1\Code>docker build -t terraform:v1.1.6 .
[+] Building 608.0s (6/6) FINISHED
 => [internal] load build definition from Dockerfile                         0.7s
 => => transferring dockerfile: 478B                                         0.0s
 => [internal] load .dockerignore                                           2.9s
 => => transferring context: 2B                                             0.2s
 => [internal] load metadata for docker.io/library/ubuntu:latest           0.0s
 => [1/2] FROM docker.io/library/ubuntu:latest                              0.7s
 => [2/2] RUN apt-get update && apt-get -y install sudo && apt-get -y install curl && apt-get -y install gnupg && apt-get -y i  601.1s
 => exporting to image                                                      2.9s
 => => exporting layers                                                     2.8s
 => => writing image sha256:d1884069b69e2e074657bbd5e5304286aa7c8b231db3167fd295d93f174da421  0.1s
 => => naming to docker.io/library/terraform:v1.1.6                         0.1s

Use 'docker scan' to run Snyk tests against images to find vulnerabilities and learn how to fix them

F:\1.DevOps\2022\Terraform 1.1.6\Chapter 1\Code>docker run -it --name terraform116 terraform:v1.1.6 /bin/bash
root@4cbd8df63636:/# terraform -version
Terraform v1.1.6
on linux_amd64
root@4cbd8df63636:/#
```

Figure 1.7: Verify Terraform version

6. Then, go back to the Docker Desktop screen and verify the logs. A recent command execution log is available.

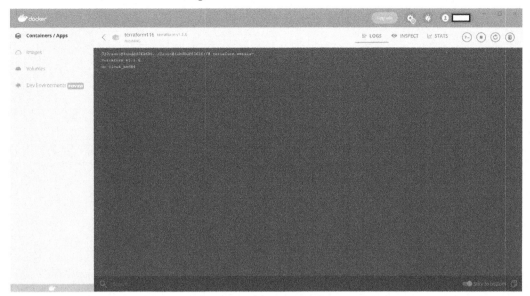

Figure 1.8: Docker Desktop container logs

7. Click on the **INSPECT** link to verify environment variables in the running Terraform container.

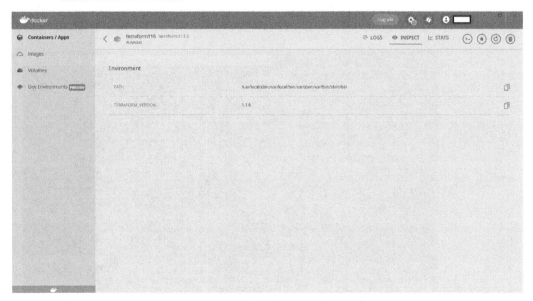

Figure 1.9: Docker Desktop container environment

8. Click on the **STATS** link to get details on CPU usage, memory usage, disk, and network related details.

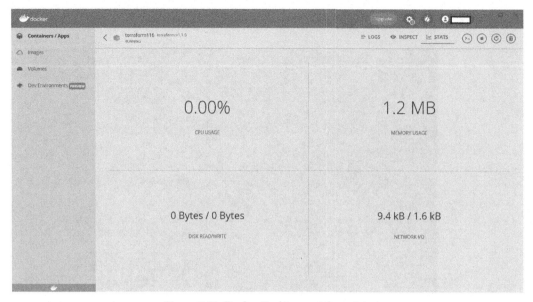

Figure 1.10: Docker Desktop container stats

9. Execute another command in a container using a command prompt, and verify the logs in the Docker Desktop screen.

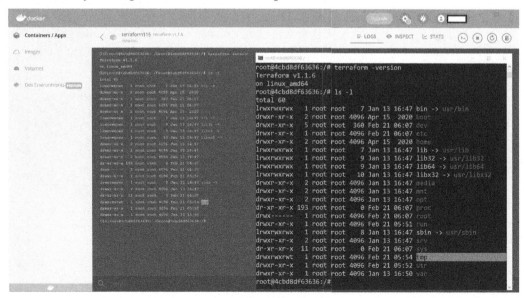

Figure 1.11: Logs

In the next section, we will create an AWS account for the Free tier.

Creating an AWS Account

AWS free tier has more than 85 products. There are three categories of free products available with AWS:

Category	Description
Always free	Do not expire and are available to all AWS customers
12 months free	Available for 12-months following your initial sign-up date to AWS
Trials	Short-term free trial offers after you activate the services

Table 1.4: *AWS free tier*

Let's verify Free tier services in AWS management console.

1. Go to **https://aws.amazon.com/free/?all-free-tier.sort-by=item. additionalFields.SortRank&all-free-tier.sort-order=asc** and verify all the products based on the offers available in free trial.

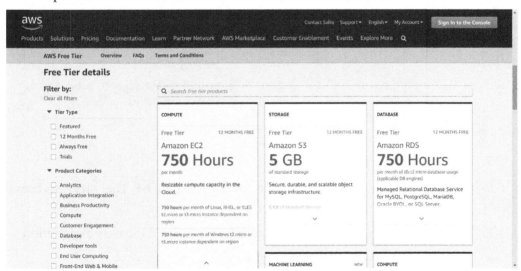

Figure 1.12: *Tier type and products*

2. Visit **https://aws.amazon.com/free** to create an account for free tier.

3. Click on **Create a Free Account**.

4. On the page Sign up for AWS and provide email address and credentials.

Explore Free Tier products with a new AWS account.

To learn more, visit aws.amazon.com/free.

Sign up for AWS

Email address
You will use this email address to sign in to your new AWS account.

[   ]@outlook.com

Password

••••••••••••••

Confirm password

••••••••••••••

AWS account name
Choose a name for your account. You can change this name in your account settings after you sign up.

m[   ]

Continue (step 1 of 5)

Figure 1.13: Sign up for AWS free tier

5. Fill in the contact information.

6. Click on **I have read and agree to the terms of the AWS Customer Agreement**.

7. Provide billing information, and complete it with OTP-based registration.

8. Confirm your identity.

9. Select a support plan - Basic support – Free. (Not all services that we have used in this book comes under free tier, e.g., Amazon EKS is not covered in free tier. You can get more details about AWS free tier at **https://aws.amazon. com/free/**.)

Congratulations

Thank you for signing up for AWS.

We are activating your account, which should only take a few minutes. You will receive an email when this is complete.

Go to the AWS Management Console

Sign up for another account or contact sales.

Figure 1.14: *Successful signup*

10. Log in to **AWS Management Console - console.aws.amazon.com**, as shown here:

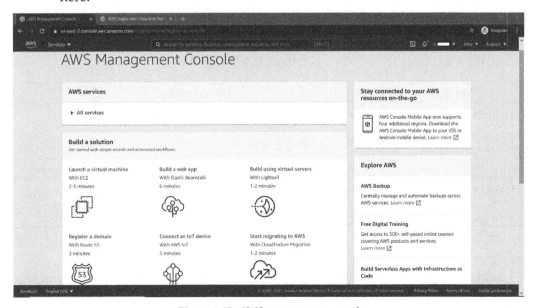

Figure 1.15: *AWS management console*

Now, you become a root user. Root user has administrator access, which can become a security issue. At this point, we can create multiple user accounts that have limited access using **Identity and Access Management (IAM)**.

In the next section, we will install and configure AWS CLI.

Installing and Configuring AWS CLI

The **AWS Command Line Interface (AWS CLI)** helps you to interact with AWS services using commands in your command prompt or shell. Why is it useful, and why is it popular?

This is because AWS CLI is an open-source tool. You can execute commands and achieve all your objectives just like with the AWS management console.

You can use the following to execute AWS CLI commands:

- Windows command prompt
- Linux shells
- Windows PowerShell
- Cloud virtual machines with PuTTY or SSH

You can manage and maintain the following services using AWS CLI:

- AWS Administration
- AWS Management
- AWS Access functions
- New AWS IaaS features and services (at launch or within 180 days of launch)

The AWS CLI is available in two versions, listed as follows:

Version	Description
Version 2.x	- Current version - Generally available release - The objective is to use it in production environments
Version 1.x	- Previous version - Available for backward compatibility

Table 1.5: AWS CLI version

The objective of installing and configuring AWS CLI is automation; it helps manage AWS resources using command line.

> **Note: It is difficult to manage large-scale architecture with traditional infrastructure management activities: the time to market gets hit due to the time taken in providing infrastructure to the team for deployment. It is a slow and manual process that invites manual errors. There are multiple tools or services provided by specific cloud service providers, but it has a steep learning curve and vendor lock-in.**

You can either choose to download the AWS CLI package for your own OS from the website (**https://aws.amazon.com/cli/**) or follow the steps listed below to use the Chocolately package manager to keep thing organised on Windows.

Let's install AWS CLI using Chocolatey. Visit **https://chocolatey.org/packages/awscli** to get more details and execute choco install awscli.

```
PS C:\WINDOWS\system32> choco install awscli  Chocolatey v0.10.15

Installing the following packages:

awscli

By installing you accept licenses for the packages.

Progress: Downloading awscli 2.1.28... 100%


awscli v2.1.28 [Approved]

awscli package files install completed. Performing other installa-
tion steps.

The package awscli wants to run 'chocolateyinstall.ps1'.

Note: If you don't run this script, the installation will fail.

Note: To confirm automatically next time, use '-y' or consider:

choco feature enable -n allowGlobalConfirmation

Do you want to run the script?([Y]es/[A]ll - yes to all/[N]o/[P]rint): yes


File appears to be downloaded already. Verifying with package check-
sum to determine if it needs to be redownloaded.

Hashes match.

Hashes match.

Installing awscli...

awscli has been installed.

 awscli may be able to be automatically uninstalled.

Environment Vars (like PATH) have changed. Close/reopen your shell to
```

see the changes (or in powershell/cmd.exe just type `refreshenv`).

The install of awscli was successful.

 Software installed as 'MSI', install location is likely default.

Chocolatey installed 1/1 packages.

 See the log for details (C:\ProgramData\chocolatey\logs\chocolatey.log).

Configure AWS CLI with the following command. For obtaining key ID and secret key, you'll need to access the **Identity and Access Management (IAM)** service in the AWS Console; access your default account and select the **Security Credentials** tab:

PS C:\Users\Mitesh\3.Hands-onn Terraform> aws configure

AWS Access Key ID [None]: ********************Y

AWS Secret Access Key [None]: *****************XYZ

Default region name [None]: ap-south-1

Default output format [None]:

In the next section, we will create a Microsoft Azure free account.

Creating a Microsoft Azure Account

Microsoft Azure free tier provides popular services free for 12 months. Additionally, 25+ services are always free, and it provides $200 credit to use in your first 30 days.

1. Visit **https://azure.microsoft.com/free**, as shown here:

Figure 1.16: Azure free services

2. Click on **Start free**.

3. Accept the agreement.

4. Complete identity verification by phone: select **Phone**, and you will receive the verification code.

5. Verify the code.

6. Complete identity verification by card.

7. Click on **Sign up**.

Microsoft Azure free tier has more than 85. There are three categories of free products available with Azure.

Always free	25+ services
12 months free	Popular free services
₹14,500 credit	Explore Azure for 30 days

Table 1.6: *Azure free tier*

TIP: Visit https://azure.microsoft.com/en-in/free/#12-months-free for more details about the services that are free for 12 months. Refer to *figure 1.17:*

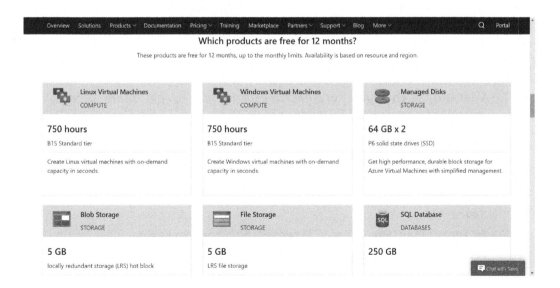

Figure 1.17: *12 months of free services*

In the next section, we will install and configure Azure CLI.

Installing and configuring Azure CLI

The **Azure command-line interface** (**Azure CLI**) helps you interact with Microsoft Azure services using commands in your command prompt or shell. Why is it useful, and why is it popular?

It is because it is available across Azure services. You can execute commands and achieve all your objectives just like the Azure Management Portal.

You can use the following to execute Azure CLI commands:

- Azure cloud shell
- Windows command prompt
- macOS terminal
- Linux shells
- Windows PowerShell
- Cloud virtual machines with PuTTY or SSH

The objective of installing and configuring Microsoft Azure CLI is automation: it helps manage Microsoft Azure resources using command line.

You can either choose to download the Azure CLI package for your own OS from the website (**https://docs.microsoft.com/en-us/cli/azure/?view=azure-cli-latest**) or follow the steps listed below to use the Chocolately package manager to keep things organised on Windows.

Let's install Microsoft Azure CLI using Chocolatey:

1. Visit **https://chocolatey.org/packages/azure-cli** to get more details and execute **choco install azure-cli.**

   ```
   PS C:\WINDOWS\system32> choco install azure-
   cli                                                        C-
   hocolatey v0.10.15
   Installing the following packages:
   azure-cli
   By installing you accept licenses for the packages.
   Progress: Downloading azure-cli 2.20.0... 100%

   azure-cli v2.20.0 [Approved]
   azure-cli package files install completed. Performing other instal-
   lation steps.
   ```

The package azure-cli wants to run 'chocolateyInstall.ps1'.

Note: If you don't run this script, the installation will fail.

Note: To confirm automatically next time, use '-y' or consider:

choco feature enable -n allowGlobalConfirmation

Do you want to run the script?([Y]es/[A]ll - yes to all/[N]o/[P]rint): yes

Downloading azure-cli

 from 'https://azcliprod.blob.core.windows.net/msi/azure-cli-2.20.0.msi'

Progress: 100% - Completed download of C:\Users\Mitesh\AppData\Local\Temp\chocolatey\azure-cli\2.20.0\azure-cli-2.20.0.msi (50.01 MB).

The download of azure-cli-2.20.0.msi (50.01 MB) completed.

Hashes match.

Installing azure-cli...

azure-cli has been installed.

 azure-cli may be able to be automatically uninstalled.

Environment Vars (like PATH) have changed. Close/re-open your shell to

 see the changes (or in powershell/cmd.exe just type `refreshenv`).

 The install of azure-cli was successful.

 Software installed as 'msi', install location is likely default.

Chocolatey installed 1/1 packages.

 See the log for details (C:\ProgramData\chocolatey\logs\chocolatey.log).

Did you know the proceeds of Pro (and some proceeds from other

 licensed editions) go into bettering the community infrastructure?

Your support ensures an active community, keeps Chocolatey tip top,

 plus it nets you some awesome features!

 https://chocolatey.org/compare

PS C:\WINDOWS\system32>

2. Use the **az login** command to configure Azure CLI. It will open a browser where you need to log in with Microsoft Azure credentials with a valid subscription.

> **Note: Infrastructure as Code (IaC) provides ease of use and enables you to quickly manage different resources. Consistency is key to the IaC approach. We can use all the benefits of programming, such as conditions and loops, to create repeatable infrastructure across different cloud platforms.**

3. You will get a response as shown here:

```
You have logged into Microsoft Azure!

You can close this window, or we will redirect you to the Azure
CLI documents in 10 seconds.
```

4. In Powershell or in Terminal (Mac/Linux), verify the output after successful login:

```
PS C:\Users\Mitesh> az login
 The default web browser has been opened at https://login.
microsoftonline.com/common/oauth2/authorize. Please contin-
ue the login in the web browser. If no web browser is avail-
able or if the web browser fails to open, use device code flow-
 with `az login --use-device-code`.

You have logged in. Now let us find all the subscriptions to whic
h you have access...
[
  {
    "cloudName": "AzureCloud",
    "homeTenantId": "XXXXXXXX-XXXX-XXXX-XXXX-XXXXXXXXXXXXX",
    "id": " XXXXXXXX-XXXX-XXXX-XXXX-XXXXXXXXXXXXX",
    "isDefault": true,
    "managedByTenants": [],
    "name": "Free Trial",
    "state": "Enabled",
    "tenantId": " XXXXXXXX-XXXX-XXXX-XXXX-XXXXXXXXXXXXX ",
```

```
      "user": {
        "name": "user1.XXXXXXXX@XXXXXX.com",
        "type": "user"
      }
    }
  ]
```

5. Use the **az account show** command to get the details of a subscription.

In the next section, we will explore editors that can be used to create Terraform scripts.

Terraform IAC Development and IDE

Terraform is a powerful tool to automate and orchestrate one of the most popular practices of DevOps culture: Infrastructure as Code. It is important to have an IDE that helps you in the process, and we will discuss a few of them here.

Atom

Atom is a free and open-source text editor available at **https://github.com/atom**. It has simple auto-completion functionality to view and insert possible options in the editor using tab or enter. By default, the autocomplete system will search 'search item'in the currently open file.

1. Go to **https://atom.io** and download Atom to install it.

2. Use **AtomSetup.exe** for 32-bit and **AtomSetup-x64.exe** for 64-bit systems to install Atom.

3. The next step is to install the language-terraform package in Atom from **https://atom.io/packages/language-terraform** or Open Atom Editor, search fo language-terraform package, and install it, as shown here:

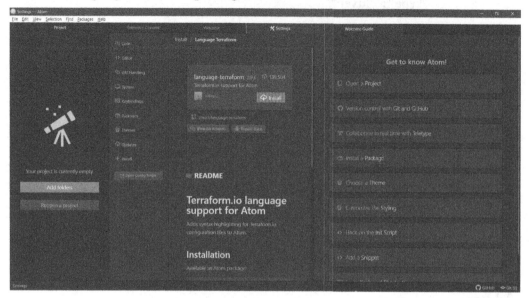

Figure 1.18: Terraform package for Atom

Note: Infrastructure as Code has benefits like reusability, visibility, stability, and scalability.

Let's download code from **https://github.com/terraform-aws-modules/terraform-aws-eks/** and check one of its Terraform files in Atom editor. Open a TF file to check whether the recently installed language-terraform Atom package is working, and format it to make it more readable, as shown in the following figure:

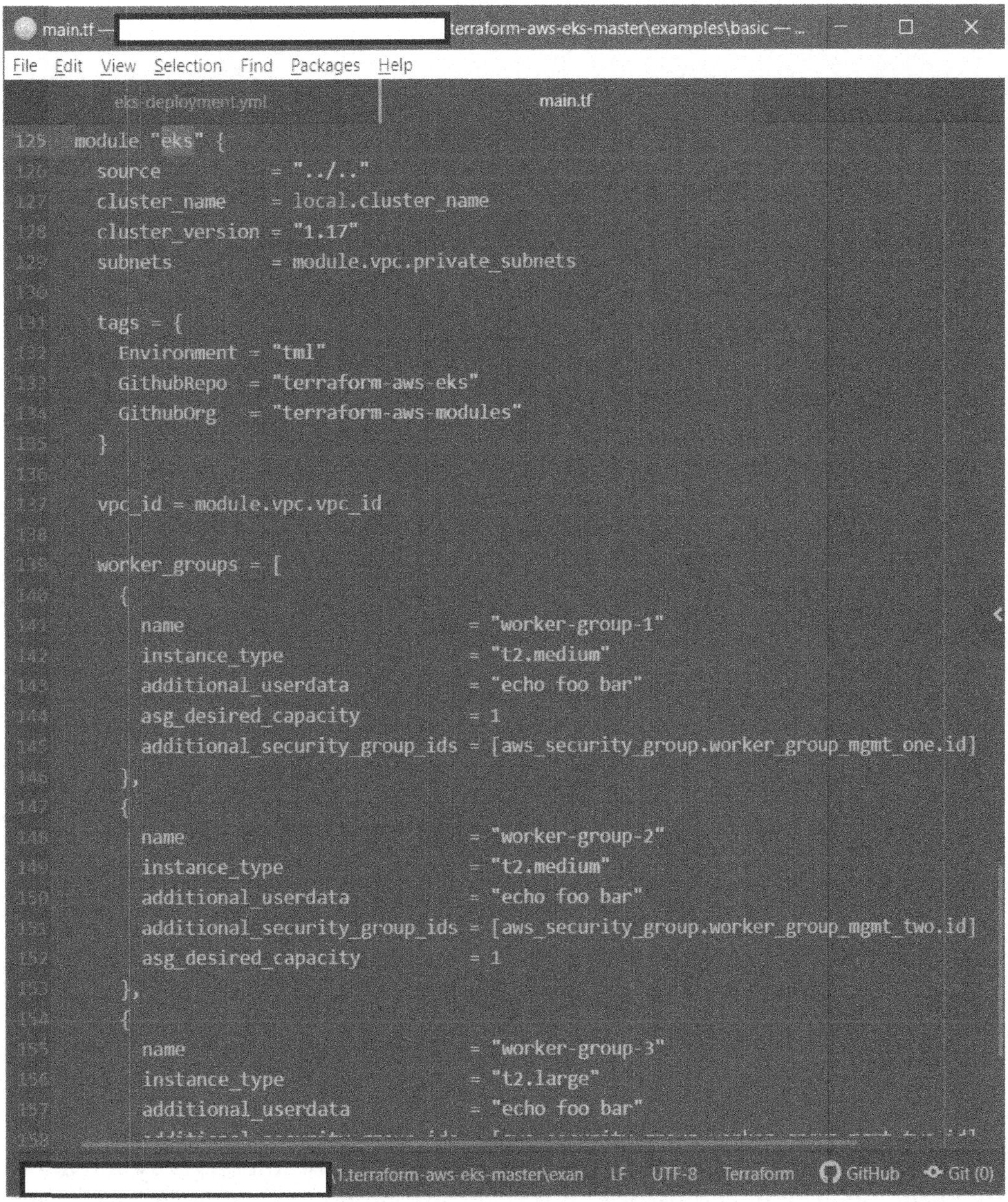

```
125  module "eks" {
126      source              = "../.."
127      cluster_name        = local.cluster_name
128      cluster_version     = "1.17"
129      subnets             = module.vpc.private_subnets
130
131      tags = {
132        Environment = "tml"
133        GithubRepo  = "terraform-aws-eks"
134        GithubOrg   = "terraform-aws-modules"
135      }
136
137      vpc_id = module.vpc.vpc_id
138
139      worker_groups = [
140        {
141          name                          = "worker-group-1"
142          instance_type                 = "t2.medium"
143          additional_userdata           = "echo foo bar"
144          asg_desired_capacity          = 1
145          additional_security_group_ids = [aws_security_group.worker_group_mgmt_one.id]
146        },
147        {
148          name                          = "worker-group-2"
149          instance_type                 = "t2.medium"
150          additional_userdata           = "echo foo bar"
151          additional_security_group_ids = [aws_security_group.worker_group_mgmt_two.id]
152          asg_desired_capacity          = 1
153        },
154        {
155          name                          = "worker-group-3"
156          instance_type                 = "t2.large"
157          additional_userdata           = "echo foo bar"
158
```

Figure 1.19: *Terraform script in Atom editor*

Note: The command terraform plan generates an execution plan that will be worked upon once terraform apply will be used.

In the next section, we will go through the details about Visual Studio Code.

Visual Studio Code

Visual Studio Code is a lightweight and powerful source code editor. It is available for Windows 7, 8, 10, Debian, Ubuntu, macOS 10.10+, Red Hat, Fedora, and SUSE. It provides built-in support for JavaScript, TypeScript, and Node.js, and it also supports programming languages like Java, Python, PHP, and Go.

Let's look at the steps to install Terraform package in VS code:

1. VS Code is a free code editor. You can visit **https://code.visualstudio.com/ docs/setup/setup-overview** and install VS Code based on your operating system.

2. Open Visual Studio Code and click on **Extensions** (refer to *figure 1.20*).

3. Search for Terraform package and install it.

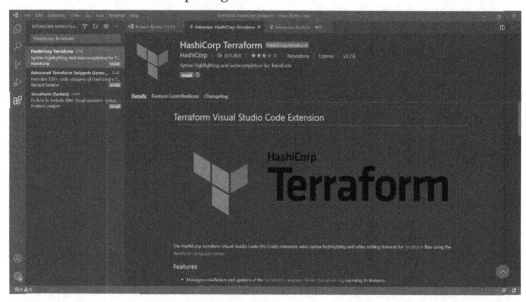

Figure 1.20: Terraform Visual Code extension

> **Note: Terraform helps in Disaster Recovery and Fault Tolerance by having a defined blueprint of cloud-based infrastructure stored in version control; it can be easily executed, enabling a copy of infrastructure to be spun up quickly and reliably.**

Let's download a piece of sample Terraform code from **https://github.com/Azure/ terraform-azurerm-aks** and check one of its files in Visual Studio Code editor. Open any terraform script available in the downloaded directory, and you should find it formatted nicely in Visual Studio Code, as shown in the following screenshot:

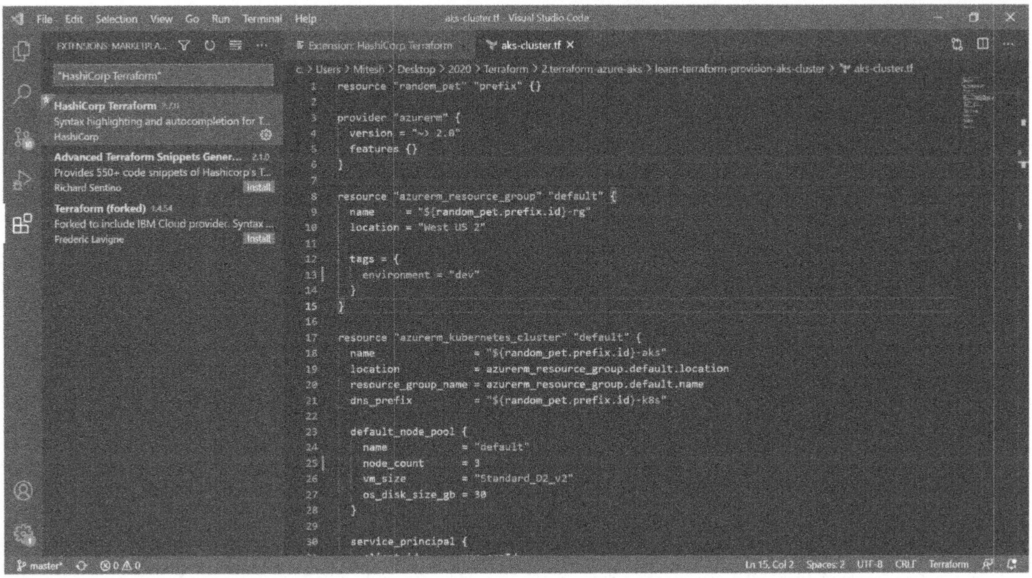

Figure 1.21: *Terraform script in VS Code Editor*

We've covered two popular IDEs for use with Terraform, but there are other IDEs in the wild, such as Notepad or Notepad++. Ultimately, it's a personal choice!

Conclusion

In this chapter, you understood how to install Terraform in different operating systems, such as Windows (using Chocolatey), Ubuntu, CentOS, RedHat, MacOS, and so on. You also installed Terraform in Docker Container using Docker Desktop. Additionally, this chapter walked you through creating AWS and Azure accounts and installing CLIs for both providers. You also learned about Code Editors that can be utilized while working with Terraform.

In the next chapter, we will cover the basics of Terraform, such as Terraform Variables, Terraform Functions, Terraform Output, and Conditional expressions.

Points to remember

- Terraform is used to efficiently manage compute, storage, and networking resources along with identity- and access- management related features, etc.

- Infrastructure as code tools like Terraform help you to create infrastructure that is consistent, repeatable, and predictable even if you run it multiple times. Same Code = Same Output!

- Terraform helps to create "Disposable Environments" such as QA, Pre-Prod, or Production.

- Terraform is cloud-agnostic, and it also supports custom solutions.

- Terraform allows the same configuration to be used to manage resources across multiple providers in the multi-cloud scenario.

Multiple choice questions

1. **State True or False: Terraform doesn't require GO as a pre-requisite for installation or any GO programming skills.**

   a. True

   b. False

2. **State True or False: Terraform can manage resources in cloud Platforms such as AWS, Microsoft Azure, Google cloud, VMware, and so on.**

   a. False

   b. True

3. **State True or False: The command terraform plan generates an execution plan that will be worked upon once terraform apply will be used.**

   a. True

   b. False

Answers

1. a
2. b
3. a

Questions

1. What is Infrastructure as Code?

2. Why Terraform is popular in IaC category for DevOps Practices implementation?

3. Which are the popular tools as Terraform script editor?

## CHAPTER 2

Terraform Basics and Configuration

Terraform is an open source *"Infrastructure as Code"* tool by *HashiCorp* and is written in the GO language.

Terraform is an infrastructure automation tool that uses high-level configuration language previously called **HashiCorp Configuration Language** (HCL) to describe the desired state of the infrastructure on multiple cloud or on-premise environment. From this configuration, Terraform then generates a plan to reach the desired state and then executes the plan for infrastructure provisioning. Currently, Terraform is one of the most popular open-source, cloud-agnostic **Infrastructure-as-code** (IaC) tool because it uses simple syntax, provisions infrastructure across multiple cloud and on-premises, and safely re-provisions infrastructure for any configuration changes. Terraform is mostly used by DevOps engineers to automate the infrastructure creation.

In this chapter, we will go through Terraform workflow and then cover the basic concepts of Terraform. We will learn how to create Terraform configuration using Terraform basic concepts like variables, in-built functions, expressions, and output. We will also understand and configure Amazon S3 and Dynamo DB to manage and lock Terraform state while working with large teams. We will learn the concept of **count** and **for_each** to avoid duplication of Terraform code for the creation of multiple resources having the same resource type with different configuration.

Structure

We will discuss the following topics in this chapter:

- Terraform introduction and its workflow
- Terraform language
- Terraform registry
- Terraform provider
- Terraform resources
- Terraform variables
- Terraform functions
- Terraform resource graph
- Terraform output
- Exporting Terraform Output in JSON
- Terraform states - desired and current states
- Terraform expressions
- Provisioning multiple resources
- Debugging the Terraform execution

Objectives

After studying this chapter, you will understand the terraform workflow and its basic concepts like registry, provider, and resources. You will also be able to use terraform variables, output, and functions to make the code more configurable. You will be able to understand the concept of terraform graph and terraform state management. This chapter aims to provide you with the basic knowledge about Terraform and its configurations for provisioning multiple resources in your infrastructure.

Terraform workflow

Terraform core workflow consists of lifecycle stages init, plan, apply, and destroy. These stages are executed as commands to perform the operation expected by them.

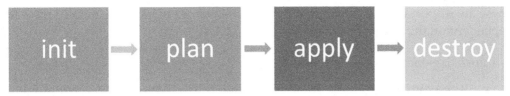

Figure 2.1: *Terraform workflow*

Here's the description and command for the execution of these stages in the Terraform workflow:

- **Terraform init** runs a number of initialization tasks to enable Terraform for use in the current working directory. This is usually executed only once per session.

  Command:

  ```
  # Initialize Terraform

  $ terraform init
  ```

- **Terraform plan** compares the desired Terraform state with the current state in the cloud and builds and displays an execution plan for infrastructure creation or destruction. This command is just for the creation of a plan for you to verify/review the work done by you and your teammates; it does not change the deployment. So, you can update the Terraform configuration if the plan is not as per your requirements.

  Command:

  ```
  $ terraform plan
  ```

- **Terraform apply** executes the plan that is created, comparing the current and desired states. This will create or destroy your resources, which means it potentially changes the deployment by adding or removing resources based on changes in the plan. Terraform apply will run the plan command automatically to execute the most recent changes. However, you can always tell it to execute a specific terraform plan command by providing a plan file.

  Command:

  ```
  $ terraform apply
  ```

- **Terraform destroy** will delete all resources that are created/managed by the Terraform environment you are working in.

  Command:

  ```
  $ terraform destroy
  ```

These are important sets of commands that you cannot work without, and they are dependent on the sequences shown in *figure 2.1*.

Terraform has the following advantages:

- It helps in infrastructure orchestration and provisioning, not just configuration management.

- It provides immutable infrastructure where we can change the configuration smoothly.

- Terraform helps manage dependencies. For example, the order of blocks, resources etc. doesn't necessarily matter; TF helps work that out for itself.

- Terraform supports multiple providers such as AWS, Azure, Oracle, and GCP.

- It is easily portable to other providers.

- Terraform language is easy to understand and is a **configuration language.**

In this chapter, you will learn about Terraform language, providers, resources, variables, and output variables and understand how to define them in Terraform configuration in detail.

Terraform language

All the configuration written in Terraform language is the heart of the Terraform workflow and also Terraform's primary user interface. Terraform Configuration Language previously was also called HCL.

It is a declarative language, so you just need to provide the details related to the infrastructure you want to create. Terraform itself figures out how to create the infrastructure when you execute the code.

The main purpose of the Terraform language is to declare resources that need to be created in your infrastructure, which may also be called **infrastructure objects**. Features similar to other languages exist to make the code more customizable and make defining the resources convenient.

A configuration may consist of multiple files and directories. Code in the Terraform language is stored in plain text files (called **configuration files**) with the `.tf` and `.tf.json` file extensions.

Each Terraform configuration has its root module, which has `.tf` files. A collection of `.tf` or `.tf.json` files together in a directory is considered as a module in Terraform. A Terraform module may have subdirectories with Terraform configuration files, but only the top-level configuration files in a directory are part of that module. The sub-directories are treated as separate modules.

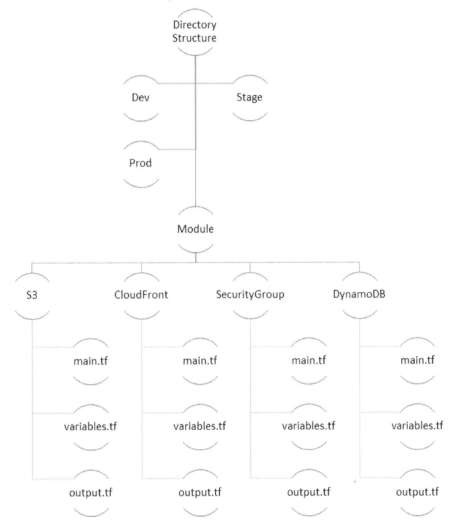

Figure 2.2: *Terraform modules*

Terraform language consists of only a few basic elements called **building blocks**, shown in the following syntax:

```
<BLOCK TYPE> "<BLOCK LABEL>" "<BLOCK LABEL>" {
  # Block body
  <IDENTIFIER> = <EXPRESSION> # Argument
}
```

Let's create an example using these building blocks to create an AWS EC2 instance:

```
resource "aws_instance" "example" {
  ami           = var.image_ami
  instance_type = "t2.micro"
}
```

Blocks are containers of various types; in our example, it is a **resource**. These containers are for other content, usually for the configuration of some kind of object, like a **resource**. These Blocks require the following inputs:

- Zero or more labels (we have two labels in the example: "**aws_instance**" and "**example**").

- A body that contains any number of arguments (like **ami** and **instance_type**, which are basic inputs required to create EC2 instance). Arguments assign a value to a name; arguments value can contain expressions combining or just referencing other values.

- Nested blocks (if needed).

In a Terraform configuration file, most of Terraform's features are controlled by top-level blocks. Terraform considers only implicit and explicit relationships between the resources when it determines the order of operations.

We will look at the most important concepts of Terraform language in the next sections of this chapter, which will help you create readable, easy-to-understand, and customizable code for your infrastructure creation.

You can use any code editor to write the Terraform configuration, but we would recommend using Visual Studio Code for your terraform development as it provides you with the editor along with the terminal to execute Terraform CLI commands.

Terraform registry

Terraform registry is like a hub to get all the reusable components for providers and modules. There are around 928 providers and 5525 modules, and some of them are verified by HashiCorp (organisation of the product Terraform). The URL to Terraform registry is **https://registry.terraform.io/**. When you go to this URL through a browser, you should land on a web page as shown in the following screenshot:

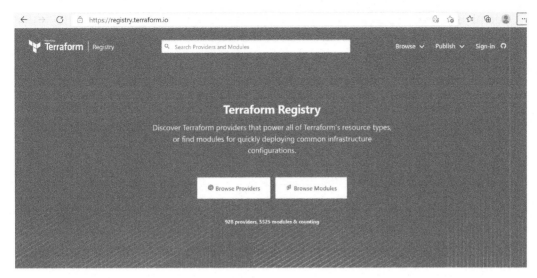

Figure 2.3: Terraform registry

You can log in using the **Sign-in** option in the top-right corner with GitHub icon. If you already have a GitHub account, you can sign in and publish new modules and providers to the Terraform registry or create a GitHub account for future use.

Then, you can see that there are two options to browse on the Terraform registry page: one for providers and another for modules. We will look at the providers in detail in the coming sections of this chapter, and we will explore modules in *Chapter 6, Terraform Modules*.

Terraform registry provides official, verified, and community-tier providers for free in our Terraform configuration. Providers are plugins that implement resource types. AWS, Azure, and Google are examples of providers.

There are plenty of modules that make our work easier: just plug in the common modules to your Terraform code, and you can save plenty of time and energy to create the use-case you want. Terraform registry modules are for quickly deploying the common infrastructure configurations. This was a brief overview of the Terraform registry. Now, let's look at the Terraform provider.

Terraform provider

Terraform is used to create infrastructure on different cloud platforms, so it requires a plugin to interact with these remote platforms.

Before starting with the actual development of Terraform code, we need to provide the configuration for the provider where we want to configure our infrastructure. Then, Terraform will install the plugins required for that particular provider.

A set of resource types and/or data sources are added by each provider that Terraform can manage. Implementation of each resource type is done by a provider; Terraform cannot manage any kind of infrastructure without a provider.

Most providers support a specific infrastructure platform, either cloud or self-hosted. AWS, AZURE, Google, and Kubernetes are some of the widely used providers.

Here are the steps required to use any provider in your Terraform configuration:

1. Declare the providers so that Terraform can install them.

2. Configure the providers.

3. Use dependency lock file to tell Terraform to use a specific set of provider version (optional).

Now, let's look at this process in detail, starting with the declaration of the required provider.

Declaring provider in Terraform code

Each Terraform module must have a declaration for the required providers. Only then can Terraform install the provider in the '**terraform init**' command. After installation, Terraform can use this provider to create infrastructure in that cloud environment, for example, **aws** in the following code snippet. The required providers are declared in a **required_providers** block, which consists of the local name to be used in the module, source location where the provided would be available for download, and the version as shown in the following example:

```
terraform {

  required_providers {

    aws = {

      source = "hashicorp/aws"

      version = "3.35.0"

    }

  }

}
```

The **required_providers** block is nested inside a Terraform block (which can also contain other settings). Each new argument in the **required_providers** blocks a separate provider. However, in our example, we have only one provider with a local name AWS, and the value is an object with the following elements:

- **Source**: The global source address for the provider you intend to use; in the preceding example, it is **hashicorp/aws**. It consists of part **[<HOSTNAME>/]<NAMESPACE>/<TYPE>**. We ignore hostname if we are using Terraform public registry for the provider, so the correct value in the example would have been **registry.terraform.io/hashicorp/aws**.

- **Version**: A version is a constraint that specifies a subset of available provider versions that the module is compatible with.

Note: Platforms like AWS issue new versions of the Provider, so they may alter the way certain resources operate or add/remove data types. It can sometimes be a good idea to define the version of the provider you would like to use as it can help prevent your code from breaking unexpectedly!

Now, let's look at how to configure these providers.

Configuring the provider

Each root module should have its provider configuration, for which we will declare the following provider block in the Terraform code:

```
provider "aws" {

  region = <AWS REGION>

  access_key = <your AWS ACCESS KEY>

  secret_key = <Your AWS SECRET KEY>

}
```

The name given in the provider **aws** is the local name that we declared in the **required_providers** earlier in the Terraform block.

The body of the provider block (between { and }) contains arguments for the configuration specific to the provider. Most arguments are defined by the provider itself; in the preceding example, **region**, **access_key** and **secret_key** are specific to the AWS provider.

We can also use the expressions in these values of configuration arguments of the providers (i.e. above provider block). That said, these expression values should be available before this configuration is done. If we do not provide the required value, Terraform will ask you for it in the command-line during the execution of Terraform plan or apply commands.

Dependency lock file

The dependency lock file is a file named **.terraform.lock.hcl**, and it belongs to the whole configuration, including separate modules. It is a lock file for the Terraform caches of various items in the **.terraform** subdirectory in your working directory.

This lock file is created or updated by Terraform automatically when we execute the **Terraform init** command.

When Terraform init is installing the required providers for a configuration, Terraform considers both the version in the configuration and the selections of the version recorded in the lock file.

If "**terraform init**" makes changes to the lock file, Terraform will mention that as part of its logs, as shown on line 10 in the following logs:

```
C:\Users\Ankita\Terraform\Provider>terraform init

Initializing the backend...

Initializing provider plugins...

- Finding hashicorp/aws versions matching "3.35.0"...

- Installing hashicorp/aws v3.35.0...

- Installed hashicorp/aws v3.35.0 (signed by HashiCorp)

Terraform has created a lock file .terraform.lock.hcl to record the provider
so that Terraform can guarantee to make the same selections by default
when you run "terraform init" in the future.

Terraform has been successfully initialized!

You may now begin working with Terraform. Try running "terraform plan" to
see any changes that are required for your infrastructure. All Terraform
commands should now work.

If you ever set or change modules or backend configuration for Terraform,
rerun this command to reinitialize your working directory. If you forget,
other
```

When you see the "**Terraform has made some changes to the provider** ..." message, you should always check your version control system to review the changes Terraform has made to the file during init. If they are changes that you made intentionally to upgrade your providers, then you can send them to the source control repository.

This lock file is important for any provider-related changes that can cause issues if the lock file is not maintained in the source control repository.

This is how we declare, configure, and maintain providers in Terraform.

Terraform resources

In the Terraform language, Terraform resources are the most important element and can also be described as the basic building block of Terraform. Each resource block is an infrastructure object, like compute instances, virtual networks, or any higher-level components.

Declaring resource

The syntax for declaring the resource is as follows:

```
resource <"RESOURCE TYPE"> <"LOCAL NAME"> {

    argument = "value"

}
```

A resource block declares a resource of a given type with a given local name. The name is used to refer to this resource within the same module, but it cannot be referred to from outside that module's scope.

The resource type and name together serve as an identifier for a given resource and so, they must be unique within a module. The following is an example of creating an AWS EC2 instance by declaring the resource:

```
resource "aws_instance" "example" {

    ami           = "ami-0aef57767f5404a3c"

    instance_type = "t2.micro"

}
```

In the example, we have "**aws_instance**" as the resource type and "**example**" as the name of the resource. The **ami** and **instance_type** arguments are required for the creation of the EC2 instance.

Within the body, i.e., between curly braces, are the arguments required for the resource itself. Most arguments in this section depend on the resource type, and in this example, both the **ami** and **instance_type** arguments are defined specifically for the "**aws_instance**" resource type.

The Terraform documentation for providers like AWS, Microsoft Azure, Google Cloud Platform, Kubernetes and so on has the list of resource types and arguments for the development of code for creating the infrastructure.

Terraform variables

Input variables are parameters for Terraform module. Terraform's variable allows us to create customizable modules without changing the source code and allows modules to be shared between different configurations.

We can also set the values of the variable in root nodes using CLI, and environment variables and child modules can also access them. However, the variables from child modules should pass values in the module block for other modules to use them.

Just like traditional programming languages, Terraform modules are like function definitions and may have the following:

- Input variables as function arguments
- Output values as function return values
- Local values as a function's temporary local variables

Note: In Terraform, input variables are referred to as just "variables" or "Terraform variables". Terraform also has two more kinds of variables: environment variables and expression variables.

Reason for using Terraform variables

Consider the following Terraform file without using a variable:

```
provider "aws" {
  region = "eu-west-1"
}
resource "aws_instance" "example_client" {
  ami           = "ami-0aef57767f5404a3c"
  instance_type = "t2.micro"
}
resource "aws_instance" "example_server" {
  ami           = "ami-0aef57767f5404a3c"
  instance_type = "t2.micro"
}
```

The preceding Terraform **main.tf** file consists of a declaration of provider as '**aws**' and two resources '**aws_instance**' to create AWS EC2 instances for client and server each with the provided configurations. In this example, we have multiple declarations of **ami** and **instance_type**. Also, the value of the AWS **region** may change later.

From this example, we already know some of the reasons for using Terraform input variable in our Terraform infrastructure as code. They are as follows:

- Everything in one file is not great.

- Variables can help you hide secrets; you would not want the AWS credentials in your GIT repository.

- Use variables for elements that might change—AMIs are different per region.

- Variables make it easier to reuse Terraform files.

- Use a variable to make your Terraform file more configurable and to avoid manual mistakes while updating infrastructure configuration.

Introducing Input Variable

You may sometimes have to define the values to some variables multiple times in your configuration, such as **ami** in the Terraform .tf file; these variables are the User Data configuration. Defining these values multiple times violates the **Don't Repeat Yourself** (DRY) principle: every piece of knowledge must have a single, unambiguous, authoritative representation within a system. If you have AWS ami copy pasted in two places in the **main.tf** file, updating it in one place is easier than to make the same change in multiple places in your infrastructure code.

Terraform allows you to define input variables to make your Terraform code more configurable.

Declaring Input Variable

Each input variable accepted by a module must be declared using a **variable** block, as shown in the following syntax:

```
variable "NAME" {

  [CONFIG ...]

}
```

Let's declare all our AWS-related variables in the following **vars.tf** file. We can start by declaring what's usually known as the **AWS_REGION**, **AWS_ACCESS_KEY**, **AWS_ACCESS_KEY**, and **AMIS** variables:

```
variable "AWS_ACCESS_KEY" {
    description = "AWS Access Key"
}
variable "AWS_SECRET_KEY" {
    description = "AWS Secret Key"
}
variable "AWS_REGION" {
  default = "eu-west-1"
  description = "AWS Region"
}
variable "AMIS" {
  type = map(string)
  description = "Region specific AWS Machine Images (AMI) "
  default = {
    us-east-1 = "ami-0a798643589ffd450"
    us-west-2 = "ami-0bc75469433986212"
  }
}
```

The labels after the **variable** keyword in the above **vars.tf** file—**AWS_REGION**, **AWS_ACCESS_KEY**, **AWS_ACCESS_KEY**, and **AMIS**—are the unique names for the variables among all variables in the same module. This name is used to assign a value to the variable from outside and also to access the variable's value within the module.

These names of the variables can be any valid identifier (except source, version, providers, count, for_each, lifecycle, depends_on, and locals, which are reserved for meta-arguments).

Note: Argument names, block type names, and the names of most Terraform-specific constructs like resources, input variables, etc. are all identifiers.

Identifiers can contain letters, digits, underscores (_), and hyphens (-). The first character of an identifier must not be a digit to avoid ambiguity with literal numbers.

For complete identifier rules, Terraform implements the Unicode identifier syntax, which is extended to include the ASCII hyphen character -.

We can see some of the arguments in the variable declaration, like default, description, and type in **vars.tf**. The following is the list of optional arguments that Terraform CLI defines that can be used in the variable declaration:

- **default**: One can set the default value to such a variable where we do not often change the value but are required at multiple places (in our case, **AWS_REGION** and AMIS map defaults). This makes the variable optional as we already have some value set.

- **type**: This argument specifies what types of input values can be accepted for the variable.

- **description**: This argument is for the input variable's documentation.

- **validation**: This is a block to define validation rules, and it is usually added to type constraints.

- **sensitive**: This argument limits Terraform UI output when the configuration is using the variable.

Before looking at the implementation of variables, let's understand these augments and how we can use these arguments in our Terraform implementation.

Input variable arguments

Terraform CLI has some optional arguments for input variable; the following are the arguments that can be defined with Terraform variables:

Default

Variable declaration can include a **default** argument (like we have in **AWS_REGION** default value as **eu-west-1** in above **vars.tf**). The **default** argument requires a literal value, which means it cannot reference other objects/variables declared in the configuration. If the **default** argument is present in the variable declaration block, that variable is considered to be **optional**, and the **default** value will be used if you do not set the value while calling the module or running Terraform.

Type

The **type** argument in variable declaration allows you to restrict the type of value that will be accepted as the value for a variable. If you do not specify the type argument, then any type of value is accepted by the variable.

Specifying the type in variables is optional, but it is recommended to specify it. It can be a helpful reminder for users, and it also allows Terraform to return the wrong type error message, which is very helpful to avoid type-related mistakes.

Type constraints are created from both **type** keywords and type constructors (that allow you to specify complex types like collections).

Type keywords are as follows:

- **string**: Strings are mostly represented by a double-quoted sequence, like "**eu-west-1**" in **vars.tf** in the **AWS_REGION** variable. The string is the most complex type of literal expression in Terraform. A "**heredoc**" syntax is also available for more complex strings in the Terraform documentation.

- **number**: Numbers are series/sequences of digits that may or may not have a decimal point, for example, 15 or 6.28787.

- **bool**: Bools are Boolean symbols true and false.

- **Null**: The null value is represented by just type value as null.

Type constructors are as follows:

- **list(type)**: Lists are represented by a pair of square brackets. They contain a comma-separated sequence of values, like [10, 15, 2]. List values can be added on multiple lines for readability, but they should always have commas in between. A comma after the last value is optional. A list is always ordered; it'll always return 10,15,2 and not 2,15,10.

- **set(type)**: Set is similar to a list, but it does not keep the order in which you put it. Set only contains unique values; for example, a list that has [5, 1, 1, 2] becomes [1,2,5] in a set (Terraform will sort it when you output it).

- **map(type)**: Maps are represented by curly braces that contain a series of **<KEY> = <VALUE>** pairs; for example, we have a map for **AMIS** in **vars.tf**:

```
{
    us-east-1 = "ami-0a798643589ffd450"

    us-west-2 = "ami-0bc75469433986212"

    eu-west-1 = "ami-0aef57767f5404a3c"
}
```

These key/value pairs should be separated by a comma or line break. In the map, each element should be of the same type. The map can also have arbitrary expressions as values. Additionally, the keys in a map should be strings; keys can be left unquoted if they are identifiers, which is valid, but they must be quoted in other cases.

- **object({<attr name> = <type>, ... })**: Objects are also represented in curly braces, just like maps. However, in objects, each element can have a different type. Here's an example:

```
{
    name = "Ram"

    age  = 28
}
```

- **tuple([<type>, ...])**: Tuples are represented just like a list with square brackets; for example, ["a", 15, true]. The only difference is that each element can have a different type.

The most common types of constructors used in Terraform code are list and map; the other types are used rarely in exceptional cases. The important ones to remember are the simple variable types **string**, **number**, **bool**, **list** and **map**.

The **any** keyword may be used to indicate that any type of value is acceptable by the variable. If both **type** and **default** arguments are specified in a variable declaration, the type of the given default value must be the same as the specified type.

Elements of **list**, **tuple**, **map**, and **object** values can be accessed using square-bracket index notation, just like other programming languages; for example, **local.list[3]** or **var.list[3]**. Using our **vars.tf** example from earlier, we can access a specific AMI by feeding the AMIS map with the region variable.. **var.AMIS[var.AWS_REGION]**.The expression within the square brackets must be a string for map and object values or a whole number for list and tuple values.

Map/object attributes with names that have valid identifiers can be also accessed using the dot-separated attribute notation, like **var.AMIS.eu-west-1**. For the map, we recommend using only the square-bracket index notation (**var.map["key"]**) in cases where a map contains arbitrary user-specified keys.

Description

Description argument is optional in variable declaration. Input variables are part of the module's user interface, so it is recommended to briefly describe the purpose of each variable using the **description** argument, like we declared the description argument in all variables in **vars.tf** in topic '**Declaring Input Variable**'. Example from this file is the "**AMIS**" variable whose description is "**Region specific AWS Machine Images (AMI)** ". The description should also explain what type of value is expected from the user.

Validation

In addition to **Type**, the author can specify custom validation rules using a validation argument nested within a variable declaration, like in the following example:

```
variable "AMIS" {
```

```
    type = string

    description = "AWS Machine Images (AMI) for different Regions"

    default = "ami-0aef57767f5404a3c"

    validation {
        condition    = length(var.AMIS) > 4 && substr(var.
AMIS, 0, 4) == "ami-"

        error_message = "The image_
id value must be a valid AMI id, starting with \"ami-\"."

    }

}
```

The **condition** argument is an expression that uses the value of the variable (like **var.AMIS** in the example) to return true if the value is valid or false if it is invalid. In validation, the expression can refer only to the variable to which that the condition applies. If condition output is invalid, Terraform will display an error message in **error_message**. The error message string should be a sentence explaining the constraint that failed using a sentence structure as shown in the previous examples.

Sensitive

Declaring a variable as **sensitive** does not allow Terraform to display its value in the plan or apply output. Sensitive variable values are recorded in the state, so they are visible to anyone who accesses the state data. The **sensitive** argument only prevents the value of that variable from being displayed in logs or output.

We can define a variable as sensitive by declaring a sensitive argument to true in the variable declaration block:

```
    sensitive = true
```

This was all about different arguments in the **Variable** block. Now, let's look at how to use these variables that we declared in **vars.tf**.

Verify **vars.tf** carefully; you will see that the default value for **AWS_ACCESS_KEY** and **AWS_SECERT_KEY** are not set yet. So, if you do not pass these values from any Terraform specific files, it will ask you to give these values through the command line when you execute the '**terraform apply**' command.

Let's try to execute the '**terraform apply**' command to see what happens:

```
C:\Users\Ankita\Terraform\Chapter-2\Variables>terraform apply
var.AWS_ACCESS_KEY
AWS Access Key
Enter a value:
```

This will ask for a value for your variable named **AWS_ACCESS_KEY**, and then it will ask for **AWS_SECERT_KEY**. You can continue providing values through command-line, but for better use, Terraform provides a way to define the values to this variable in a file that is called by the '**terraform.tfvars**' extension. Let's understand *variable definitions* in Terraform.

Assigning values to Terraform input variables

Variables declared in the root module of your Terraform configuration can be set in a number of ways:

- In command-line option **-var**

- In variable definitions (**.tfvars**) files

- As environment variables

- In a Terraform Cloud workspace

Let's look at examples for each of these, but we will be using only **.tfvars** files in our implementations later.

Command-line option –var

To specify individual variables on the command line, use the **-var** option when running the Terraform plan and the '**terraform apply**' commands:

```
terraform apply -var="AWS_ACCESS_KEY=<your AWS ACCESS KEY>"
```
```
terraform apply -var="AWS_ACCESS_KEY=<your AWS ACCESS KEY>" -var="AWS_
SECRET_KEY=<your AWS SECRET KEY>"
```

The **-var** option can be used any number of times in a single command.

Variable definitions (.tfvars) files

When we want to set many variables, it is convenient to specify their values in a single variable definitions file (ending in **.tfvars** or **.tfvars.json**). Then, we can specify the same file on the command line as an option **-var-file**, as in the following **apply** command:

```
terraform apply -var-file="example.tfvars"
```

This file uses the same syntax as Terraform language files, but it only consists of variable name assignments.

To avoid manually specifying the file in the '**terraform apply**' command, Terraform automatically loads several variable definitions files if they are present.

Here are the two ways to achieve automatic loading for variables:

- Files named exactly **terraform.tfvars** or **terraform.tfvars.json**.

  In our example, we will use the **terraform.tfvars** file, as shown in the following code:

  ```
  AWS_ACCESS_KEY = "<your AWS_ACCESS_KEY >"

  AWS_SECRET_KEY = "<your AWS_SECRET_KEY >"
  ```

  Do not check this **terraform.tfvars** file into the source control repository as it contains your secrets. It is recommended to use an example file instead (that is: **terraform.tfvars.example**) to declare your commonly defined values and check in to a source code repository. Then, just remove **.example** from the file and use the **terraform.tfvars** file for the creation of Terraform configuration when you want to add a user-defined value to this file. You can also add the **terraform.tfvars** file to ignore the configuration of your source control repository. It's recommended to use a dedicated Terraform user for AWS, not the root account.

- Any files with names ending in **.auto.tfvars** or **.auto.tfvars.json**.

  Files whose names end with **.json** are parsed as JSON objects, with the root object properties corresponding to variable names:

  ```
  {
      "AWS_REGION": "eu-west-1",
      "AMIS": {
          "us-east-1" : "ami-0a798643589ffd450",
          "us-west-2" : "ami-0bc75469433986212",
          "eu-west-1" : "ami-0aef57767f5404a3c"
      }
  }
  ```

As environment variables

Terraform also, by default, searches environment variables named **TF_VAR_** followed by the name of a declared variable. So, if you do not assign any value to a variable in the default argument, the command line, and or the .tfvars file, Terraform will also look for an environment variable for the variable value.

This is very useful when we are running Terraform in automation, or when we're running a series of Terraform commands one after the other with the same variables, for example, at a bash prompt on a Unix system:

```
export TF_VAR_AWS_REGION=eu-west-1
```

On operating systems where environment variable names are case-sensitive, Terraform matches the variable name exactly as given in the configuration, so the required environment variable name usually has a mix of upper and lower case letters, as in the preceding example.

In a Terraform Cloud workspace

Terraform Cloud passes workspace variables to Terraform just like using the `.tfvars` file.

Variable definition precedence

Terraform loads variables in the order given here, with every future source taking precedence over earlier ones:

1. Environment variables.

2. The **terraform.tfvars** file, if present.

3. The **terraform.tfvars.json** file, if present.

4. Any ***.auto.tfvars** or ***.auto.tfvars.json** files are processed in the lexical order of their filenames.

5. Any **-var** and **-var-file** options on the command line are processed in the order they are provided in. (This includes variables set by a Terraform Cloud workspace.)

Now that we have declared the variables, let's use them in providers and resources and learn how to reference them from normal Terraform files.

Accessing input variables

You can use the following syntax to get the value of the input variable in normal Terraform files:

```
var.AWS_SECRET_KEY
```

The following **provider.tf** file is the cloud provider declaration in our example; we will refer to AWS cloud provider in this chapter. You can look at the use of syntax to tie the value for variables in Terraform code.

```
# provider.tf
provider "aws" {
  region = var.AWS_REGION
  access_key = var.AWS_ACCESS_KEY
  secret_key = var.AWS_SECRET_KEY
}
```

In the preceding code, we accessed three variables from our **vars.tf** file: file **AWS_ACCESS_KEY**, **AWS_SECERT_KEY**, and **AWS_REGION**. Now, we should not be prompted to enter a value for file **AWS_ACCESS_KEY** and **AWS_SECERT_KEY** on execution, as was the case earlier. Let's execute the '**terraform apply**' command.

```
C:\Users\Ankita\Terraform\Chapter-2\Variables>terraform apply
Apply complete! Resources: 0 added, 0 changed, 0 destroyed.
```

Now, it says apply complete, but no resource has been created as we have not declared any Terraform resources section. Let's create a new **main.tf** file with Terraform resource "**aws_instance**", as follows:

```
resource "aws_instance" "example_client" {
  ami           = var.amis[var.aws_region]
  instance_type = "t2.micro"
  tags = {
    Name        = "Terraform_test_ec2"
  }
}
```

The above "**resource**" in **main.tf** file will create an AWS instance server with the name **Terraform_test_ec2**. This server will be on **instance_type** as t2 and will be created from **ami** from **AMIS** map with key as a region. Now, we have all the configuration required for creating an AWS instance in **var.tf**, **terraform.tfvars**, **provider.tf**, and **main.tf**. Now, let's execute '**terraform apply**' and see the output we get on the creation of AWS instance.

So, running the '**terraform apply**' command to create the AWS instance will first perform '**terraform plan**' for you, and then it will ask you for verification to create the resources you mentioned in Terraform code. The following console log is the plan created from the preceding Terraform code:

```
C:\Users\Ankita\Terraform\Chapter-2\Variables>terraform apply
```

An execution plan has been generated and is shown below.

Resource actions are indicated with the following symbols:

```
    + create

Terraform will perform the following actions:

  # aws_instance.example_client will be created
  + resource "aws_instance" "example_client" {
      + ami                    = "ami-0aef57767f5404a3c"
      + instance_type          = "t2.micro"
      + ipv6_address_count     = (known after apply)
.      + source_dest_check      = true
      + subnet_id              = (known after apply)
      + tags                   = {
          + "Name" = "Terraform_test_ec2"
        }
      + tenancy                = (known after apply)
      + vpc_security_group_ids = (known after apply)

      + ebs_block_device {
          + delete_on_termination = (known after apply)
          + device_name           = (known after apply)

            .

          + volume_type           = (known after apply)
        }

      + enclave_options {
          + enabled = (known after apply)
        }

      + ephemeral_block_device {
          + device_name  = (known after apply)
          + no_device    = (known after apply)
          + virtual_name = (known after apply)
        }

      + metadata_options {
```

```
        + http_endpoint              = (known after apply)
        + http_put_response_hop_limit = (known after apply)
        + http_tokens                = (known after apply)
    }

  + network_interface {
      + delete_on_termination = (known after apply)
      + device_index          = (known after apply)
      + network_interface_id   = (known after apply)
    }

  + root_block_device {
      + delete_on_termination = (known after apply)

        .

      + volume_type           = (known after apply)
    }
  }
}

Plan: 1 to add, 0 to change, 0 to destroy.

Do you want to perform these actions?
  Terraform will perform the actions described above.
  Only <yes> will be accepted to approve.

Enter a value:
```

Once you enter **yes** to the command line input, AWS instance will be created with the following output:

```
Enter a value: yes

aws_instance.example_client: Creating...
aws_instance.example_client: Still creating... [10s elapsed]
aws_instance.example_client: Still creating... [20s elapsed]
aws_instance.example_client: Still creating... [30s elapsed]
aws_instance.example_client: Creation complete after 33s [id=i-0a2xxxx]

Apply complete! Resources: 1 added, 0 changed, 0 destroyed.
```

Now, let's verify that this instance is created at AWS Console. Log in to AWS Console with AWS credentials. Now, go to **Service | Compute | EC2 | Instances**; you will see the newly created AWS EC2 instance, as shown in the following screenshot:

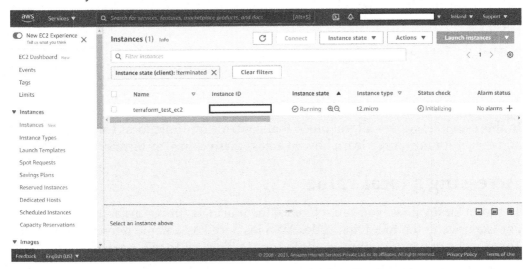

Figure 2.4: *AWS EC2 instance creation from Terraform*

In this figure, you can see that the AWS EC2 instance is successfully created and tagged with the same tag name configuration mentioned in your **main.tf** file—"**terraform_test_ec2**"—and with "**instance_type**" as **t2.micro**. This is how you can make your Terraform code more configurable with the help of Terraform input variables.

Now that we have seen input variables, let's understand how to declare local values and make the Terraform code more configurable as needed.

Terraform local values

Local values are like a function's temporary local variables. An expression's name is assigned by local value, so we can use it multiple times within the same module.

Local values help avoid repeating the same values or expressions several times in a module configuration. The key advantage of local values is the ability to easily change the value in a single place. However, the overuse of local values can also make a configuration difficult to read by other maintainers as it hides the actual values used in configurations. So, we should use local values only in moderation, i.e., only in cases where a value or result is used in multiple places and that value may change in future.

Declaring a local value

A single locals block can be used to declare a set of related local values together, as shown in the following example:

```
locals {
  name = "test_local"
  owner       = "DevOps Team"
}
```

In this example, we see a local block that contains multiple local values, like name and owner for now. Let's learn how to access these values in Terraform code.

Accessing a local value

To access local values, you can reference them using expressions as `local.<NAME>`. For example, in the following code, AWS instance has a name referenced from the `local` value of the preceding example `locals` block as `local.name` in tags.

```
resource "aws_instance" "example" {
  ami             = var.AMIS[var.AWS_REGION]
  instance_type = "t2.micro"
  tags = {
    Name        = local.name
  }
}
locals {
  name = "test_local"
  owner       = "DevOps Team"
}
```

Now that we know how to declare and effectively use variables, output, and local values, let's jump into understanding Terraform functions.

Terraform functions

Terraform includes many built-in functions that we can use within expressions to manipulate values. The syntax for function calls is a function name followed by a comma-separated list of arguments or a string in quotation marks in round parentheses, as shown in the following examples:

```
max(1,12,21)
```

```
min(0,22,12)
```

```
upper("hello")
```

There is no support for user-defined functions in Terraform, so only the Terraform built-in functions are available for use.

To experiment with the behavior of Terraform's built-in functions in the Terraform console, run the Terraform console command as shown in the following logs:

```
C:\Users\Ankita\Terraform\Chapter-2\Functions>terraform console
```

```
> max(1,12,21)
```

```
21
```

```
> min(0,22,12)
```

```
0
```

```
> upper("hello")
```

```
HELLO
```

Now that we have seen how to use these built-in functions from Terraform code and function, let's look at the types of built-in Terraform functions available. Here is the list of common built-in Terraform functions:

- Numeric functions

- String functions

- Collection functions

- Encoding functions

- Filesystem functions

- Date and time functions

- Hash and Crypto functions

- IP network functions

- Type conversion functions

These functions internally have many options to manipulate the **data/values** in Terraform. We will not see all these functions in detail as there is a huge list; you can refer to the documentation at **https://www.terraform.io/docs/language/functions/ index.html** for reference.

Terraform resource graph

Terraform first creates a *dependency graph* of the **Directed Acyclic Graph (DAG)** type from the Terraform configurations you provide in `.tf` files. It then walks through this graph to generate plans, refresh the state, and more. We will look at the details of what parts are included in this graph, what node types these are, and how the edges are determined for this graph.

> **Note: You don't need to know the details of the resource graph or how Terraform compiles and walks through it if you don't want to. It's just useful to know that Terraform uses this to help interpret your IaC and the order of dependencies.**

Terraform applies the graph theory to *Infrastructure as Code* you created using Terraform configurations. Just like graph theory, Terraform resource graph has nodes (resources and providers), edges, and directions to walk through what's created and when, as shown in the following image:

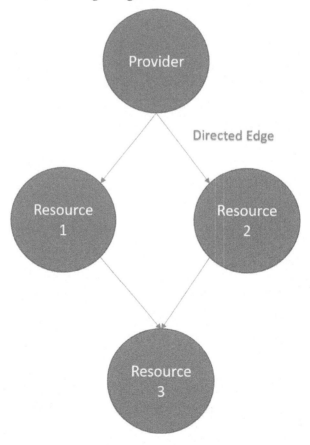

Figure 2.5: *Basic graph concept of Terraform*

We can see nodes, edges, and the direction of edges in the preceding image. Let's understand the graph nodes and various types of nodes in Terraform graph.

Terraform graph nodes

There are only three types of nodes in the Terraform resource graph:

- **Resource node**: Represents a single resource in your infrastructure as code. The change in the resource's configuration, diff, state, and such is attached to this particular node.

- **Provider node**: Represents the fully configured provider block, like AWS provider with AWS credentials configured.

- **Resource meta node**: Represents a group of resources just to make the graph look more pretty. This node is only present when any of the resources have a **count** parameter value greater than 1.

Let's take a look at the graph for the sample code we created in the **Variables** section and run the "**terraform graph**" command. In the following logs, you can see all of these nodes present.

Now, let's understand how this graph is created:

```
C:\Users\Ankita\Terraform\Chapter-2\Variables>terraform graph

digraph {
        compound = "true"
        newrank = "true"
        subgraph "root" {
                "[root] aws_instance.example (expand)" [label = "aws_
instance.example", shape = "box"]
                "[root] output.public_ip" [label = "output.public_
ip", shape = "note"]
                "[root] provider[\"registry.terraform.io/hashicorp/
aws\"]" [label = "provider[\"registry.terraform.io/hashicorp/
aws\"]", shape = "diamond"]
                "[root] var.AMIS" [label = "var.AMIS", shape = "note"]
                "[root] var.AWS_ACCESS_KEY" [label = "var.AWS_ACCESS_
KEY", shape = "note"]
                "[root] var.AWS_REGION" [label = "var.AWS_
REGION", shape = "note"]
                "[root] var.AWS_SECRET_KEY" [label = "var.AWS_SECRET_
KEY", shape = "note"]
```

```
                 "[root] aws_instance.example (expand)" -> "[root] local.
name (expand)"

                 "[root] aws_instance.
example (expand)" -> "[root] provider[\"registry.terraform.io/hashicorp/
aws\"]"

                 "[root] aws_instance.example (expand)" -> "[root] var.
AMIS"

                 "[root] meta.count-
boundary (EachMode fixup)" -> "[root] local.owner (expand)"

                 "[root] meta.count-
boundary (EachMode fixup)" -> "[root] output.public_ip"

                 "[root] output.public_ip" -> "[root] aws_instance.
example (expand)"

                 "[root] provider[\"registry.terraform.io/hashicorp/
aws\"] (close)" -> "[root] aws_instance.example (expand)"

                 "[root] provider[\"registry.terraform.io/hashicorp/
aws\"]" -> "[root] var.AWS_ACCESS_KEY"

                 "[root] provider[\"registry.terraform.io/hashicorp/
aws\"]" -> "[root] var.AWS_REGION"

                 "[root] provider[\"registry.terraform.io/hashicorp/
aws\"]" -> "[root] var.AWS_SECRET_KEY"

                 "[root] root" -> "[root] meta.count-
boundary (EachMode fixup)"

                 "[root] root" -> "[root] provider[\"registry.terraform.
io/hashicorp/aws\"] (close)"

        }

}
```

Terraform graph building

The following steps are involved in building the graph:

1. Resource nodes are added based on the configuration in the **.tf** files. The meta-data of diff(plan) or state is attached to each resource node if present.

2. Resources are mapped to specific provisioners, if defined.

3. Edges between resource nodes are created using edependencies (i.e. depends_on).

4. If a state is present, "**orphan**" resources are added to the graph.

5. Resources are mapped to specific providers. Provider configuration nodes created for specific providers and edges are created for all resources depending on the respective providers.

6. To determine dependencies, interpolations are parsed in resource and provider configurations. Resource and provider attributes are treated as dependencies from the resource or provider node.

7. Create a root node that points to all resources and the reason to create root node is to have a single root to the dependency graph.

8. If there is a diff between the current configuration and the state, the graph is split in two: one for the resources to be destroyed and the other to create new resources if any. This is because the order for destroying resources is different from the one for the creation of resources.

9. Verify that the graph is acyclic and has a single root.

Now, let's see how to go through this graph.

Traverse the graph

A standard depth-first traversal is performed while walking through the graph. As soon as all of its dependencies are traversed the resource node is also traversed in parallel.

We can set a **–parallelism** flag on the Terraform plan, apply, and destroy commands to prevent too many parallel operations, which can overload the resources of the machine running Terraform. By default, 10 nodes will be processed concurrently from a graph. Setting **–parallelism** is an advanced operation and is not recommended for normal usage of Terraform. Terraform will do its best to manage the system resources when determining dependencies and the order in which to create the infrastructure. However, it can be overridden if required.

Terraform output

Terraform module has return values that are referred to as output values, and it has multiple uses, which are listed as follows:

- Terraform outputs can be used to expose a subset of child module resource attributes to a parent module.

- Terraform apply prints the output from module in the CLI log output.

- When using a remote state, root module outputs can be accessed by other configurations via a **terraform_remote_state** data source.

Resource instances that are managed by Terraform, exports attributes whose values can be used in other configuration or to display values or ids assigned to resources.

The following code shows an example of declaring output values in the variable file:

```
output "public_ip" {
value = aws_instance.example_client.public_ip
}
```

In the preceding example, you can see that we can get the value of **public_ip** of example AWS EC2 instance that we created from **aws_instance.example_client.public_ip** in Terraform code in the same module using the **resource_type.<resource_name>.<resource_attribute_name>** syntax. In our example, **resource_type** is **aws_instance**, **resource_name** is an example, and **resource_attribute_name** is **public_ip**. When you execute '**terraform apply**', you can see the output of **public_ip** at the end of the resource created, and it will be as shown in the following logs:

```
Apply complete! Resources: 1 added, 0 changed, 0 destroyed.
Outputs:
public_ip = "172.33.16.222"
```

Now, we know how to declare output value from any module.

This output can be used by other modules as well, and just like in other programming languages, functions of one module return some value to be accessible to other modules. To access the outputs of any child modules, we need to use expressions as a module: **<MODULE NAME>.<OUTPUT NAME>**. For example, if a child module named **example_client** declares an output named **public_ip_addr**, you can access that value as an expression **module.example_client.public_ip_addr**.

You get these outputs printed in logs when you run '**terraform apply**', but to access these output values after the creation of infrastructure using '**terraform apply**', you can use the following command:

terraform **output <OUTPUT NAME>**

Let's try to execute this command for output **public_ip** of the example ec2 server we created:

```
C:\Users\Ankita\Terraform\Chapter-2\Variables>terraform output public_ip
"172.33.16.222"
```

In the '**terraform output**' command, you will get the same return value as was shown in the logs of '**terraform apply**'.

Terraform keeps attributes of all the resources you create, for example, the above `aws_instance` resource has the **public_ip** attribute and more. These attributes can be queried and outputted, and they are useful to output valuable information or feed information to external software.

When you have your output variables defined, they will be printed in the logs of the '**terraform apply**' command, but you can also use them in files to feed them to infrastructure provisioning code. Let's see how to use output values from Terraform code to a file.

Exporting Terraform output in JSON

We have already seen what Terraform outputs are, and we know that the "**terraform apply**" command will print out these outputs in the console. Terraform output allows you to have output values for the execution of Terraform configuration. These outputs can then be retrieved by a program and can be used by another operation; for example, ansible execution or CICD operations.

In this section, we will learn how to retrieve these values in a JSON file so that they can be used by other programs. In the previous section, we saw the declaration of output in this code:

```
output "public_ip" {

value = aws_instance.example_client.public_ip

}
```

We also looked at its log on the '**terraform apply**' command:

```
C:\Users\Ankita\Terraform\Chapter-2\Variables>terraform apply

----MORE logs-----

Apply complete! Resources: 1 added, 0 changed, 0 destroyed.

Outputs:

public_ip = "172.33.16.222"
```

Now, let's get this output in the JSON format on console with the "**terraform output -json**" command. When you execute this command on your command line, you will get the output in the JSON format, as in this log:

```
C:\Users\Ankita\Terraform\Variables>terraform output -json

{

  "public_ip": {

    "sensitive": false,
```

```
    "type": "string",
    "value": "172.33.16.222"
  }
}
```

The previous output not only tells you the value of your output variable but also lets you know the type and sensitive flag. Then, you can use the following command to generate **output.json** in your workspace:

```
terraform output -json >> output.json
```

This command will get you the output in as JSON file, and then you can use this file in other programs/operations. You can use any tools/plugins(like jq) to further parse the JSON data in the format you want in your program.

Here's an example:

```
terraform output -json | jq .public_ip.value
"172.33.16.222"
```

This is how we can retrieve the values from '**terraform output**' in the JSON structure and use them as per our requirement.

Terraform states - Desired and current states

Terraform stores the state about your remote infrastructure and its configuration. This state is used in your Terraform configuration to map real world infrastructure resources, it tracks metadata and also improve performance for remote infrastructures.

The state is stored in a JSON structured file named "**terraform.tfstate**" by default in your local workspace. Terraform also maintains a backup file for Terraform state; this is called "**terraform.tfstate.backup**". While executing the variables section of this chapter, you may have noticed these files in your local workspace updating when you execute the **terraform apply** command.

The following is the sample Terraform state file called **terraform.tfstate** in JSON format for the creation of EC2 instance:

```
{
  "version": 4,
  "terraform_version": "1.1.6",
  "serial": 1,
  "lineage": "37af008b-4fc5-8430-3e47-fd6c53aaddcd",
```

```
"outputs": {},
"resources": [
  {
    "mode": "managed",
    "type": "aws_instance",
    "name": "example_client",
    "provider": "provider[\"registry.terraform.io/hashicorp/aws\"]",
    "instances": [
      {
        "schema_version": 1,
        "attributes": {
          "ami": "ami-0aef57767f5404a3c",
          "arn": "arn:aws:ec2:eu-west-1:222902352367:instance/i-
0ee4af210febb5ee8",
          "associate_public_ip_address": true,
          "availability_zone": "eu-west-1c",
          "cpu_core_count": 1,
          "cpu_threads_per_core": 1,
          "disable_api_termination": false,
          "ebs_optimized": false,
          "get_password_data": false,
          "hibernation": false,
          "id": "i-0ee4hfee7bb5ee8",
          "instance_state": "running",
          "instance_type": "t2.micro",
          "metadata_options": [
            {
              "http_endpoint": "enabled",
              "http_put_response_hop_limit": 1,
              "http_tokens": "optional"
            }
          ],
          "primary_network_interface_id": "eni-0d58ef0b0f226bb02",
```

```
        "private_dns": "ip-172-31-23-103.eu-west-1.compute.internal",
        "private_ip": "172.31.23.103",
        "public_dns": "ec2-18-200-196-240.eu-west-1.compute.
amazonaws.com",
        "public_ip": "18.200.196.240",
        "root_block_device": [
          {
            "delete_on_termination": true,
            "device_name": "/dev/sda1",
            "encrypted": false,
            "iops": 100,
            "throughput": 0,
            "volume_id": "vol-0634dfe91d76f355f",
            "volume_size": 8,
            "volume_type": "gp2"
          }
        ],
        "source_dest_check": true,
        "subnet_id": "subnet-149a835c",
        "vpc_security_group_ids": [
          "sg-868511dc"
        ]
      }
    }
  ]
}
]
}
```

Using this sample state file in JSON format, Terraform knows that **aws_instance. example_client** represents an AWS EC2 instance in AWS account having ID **i-0ee4hfee7bb5ee8**. Every time you run the '**terraform apply**' command, it fetches the current state of this EC2 Instance from AWS and then compares it to the desired state as per your Terraform configurations to know what changes Terraform needs to apply. You can see many details in this sample file; these details can be useful to find the information you require about the EC2 instance you created without going to AWS.

A new `terraform.tfstate` is created every time during the execution of '`terraform apply`', and backup is written to the backup file. This is how Terraform keeps track of the state of your remote infrastructure. If the remote state has changed and you execute '`terraform apply`' again, Terraform will first make changes to match the remote state. For example, if you terminate an instance manually in AWS, which is managed by Terraform, it will be created again after '`terraform apply`' to match the local state held in Terraform.

The state file can also be maintained remotely to enable us to work in a team environment. You can use version control system like Git to store this state at a remote location to work with a team, but it can cause conflicts when two or more people work in the same infrastructure simultaneously as we cannot lock the state files in the version control system. However, there are other options to deal with these state files better, like S3, consul, and Terraform enterprise.

Terraform plan command uses local state to create plans and make changes to your remote infrastructure. Before performing any operation, Terraform refreshes the state with the current infrastructure.

The main purpose of Terraform state is to maintain and store bindings between the resources in your Terraform configuration and objects in a remote infrastructure. Terraform records the identity of a remote object when it creates a resource from your Terraform configuration against a particular resource instance, and then it updates or deletes that particular object in response to changes in future Terraform configuration.

> **Tip: The terraform.tfstate is easily readable by opening the file in any text editor (prefer IDE for better readability) as it is in JSON format. It can even be changed manually (if you have made manual changes to your remote infrastructure, or you can create a new file by looking at configuration from remote infrastructure if you delete this file).**

Current state and desired state

You may have noticed the terms current state and desired state in the previous sections; let's understand what they are.

Current state

The current state is the state of Terraform that is stored in the `terraform.tfstate` file and not the current state of your remote infrastructure created by Terraform. After the creation of infrastructure, manual changes made to any configuration outside of terraform configuration will not be taken into the current state. So, next time during Terraform execution, Terraform will revert all your manual changes in infrastructure and make the infrastructure the same as that in the current state.

Desired state

When you make a change in your Terraform code to create or update the resources in your remote infrastructure, that is the new desired state. Desired state is new state expected from your Terraform configurations, and it is compared with the current state every time to create a plan to update your infrastructure accordingly on **'terraform apply'**. Once the plan is ready, **'terraform apply'** will only apply the changes that are required to update the remote infrastructure to match the desired state. Once the desire state is matched and the infrastructure is updated, the desired state becomes the new current state, and the **terraform.tfstate** file has the new current state stored in it. Old current state is backed up in the **terraform.tfstate.backup** file to rollback in case of any issue.

Benefits of using state files

From the above-mentioned brief about Terraform states, we can understand the following benefits of state files:

- Real-world resource mapping.

- Collaboration among teams to automate infrastructure.

- Tracks the metadata of resources, such as the AWS account ID from where resources are created, the IP address of EC2 instance, dependency with other resources, etc.

- Cache resource attributes.

Remote storage for Terraform state

In a team, it is common to share a set of files among multiple team members and to use common source code repository such as Git to store these files and work in distributed manner. However, to store Terraform state in source code repository is not a recommended way to store state files in code repository.

Here are the reasons for not using SCM as storage for Terraform state files:

1. Two members working simultaneously without locking the state can break the infrastructure as a source code repository does not provide locking mechanism.

2. Two or more members working simultaneously can get conflicts in merging state file, which can cause loosing configuration while solving this conflict in state file.

3. Possibility of manual errors due to reasons like forgetting to pull changes from source code repository before running '`terraform apply`' and pushing this state will cause loss of previous configuration by another team member. This type of manual error will cause accidental rollbacks or duplicate deployments.

4. Exposing secrets in source code: Terraform stores all the details of your infrastructure in JSON format, which includes secrets in plain text format. Terraform, as of now, doesn't provide a way to hide this secret, so it is bad idea to include sensitive data in the source code repository.

So, to avoid issues like the above-mentioned, the best way is to use remote state storage, which has built-in support by Terraform. Terraform supports Amazon S3, HashiCorp Consul, Azure storage and the high-end Terraform subscriptions (Terraform Pro and Terraform Enterprise) to use as remote storage for state.

We will use the '`terraform remote config`' command to configure Terraform remote store to get and store Terraform state data every time we run '`terraform apply`'.

We will configure Amazon **Simple Storage Service (S3)** as the remote store for working specifically with AWS. We can use S3 remote store for working with other providers as well.

We recommend using S3 for the following reasons:

1. It's a managed service by **Amazon Web Service (AWS)**, so you don't need to manage infrastructure to use this service.

2. It is inexpensive as it allows 5GB of storage in free tier for the first 12 months of your AWS subscription. Terraform usage easily fits into the free tier usage allowances.

3. It is highly durable and reliable, which means your data will be always available without any loss.

4. It supports encryption, which reduces worries about storing sensitive data in state files. So, at least your data is stored in encrypted form in a remote location.

5. It supports versioning so that you can always roll back to an older version if something goes wrong.

6. It supports locking, so no conflicts will be caused and no manual error will occur due to working in s team when you work on infrastructure.

Configuring Amazon S3 as remote store

The following steps are to create and configure Amazon S3 as a remote store:

1. Add AWS **provider** to Terraform config as follows:

```
provider "aws" {

  region = "eu-west-1"

}
```

2. Save and execute the '**terraform init**' command in terminal; it should get output log as follows:

```
C:\Users\Ankita\Terraform\Chapter-2\Remote_State>terraform init
Initializing the backend...
Initializing provider plugins...
Finding latest version of hashicorp/aws...
Installing hashicorp/aws v3.36.0...
Installed hashicorp/aws v3.36.0 (signed by HashiCorp)
Terraform has created a lock file .terraform.lock.hcl to record
the provider selections it made above. Include this file in your
version control repository so that Terraform can guarantee to
make the same selections by default when you run "terraform init"
in the future.


Terraform has been successfully initialized!
You may now begin working with Terraform. Try running
"terraform plan" to see any changes that are required for your
infrastructure. All Terraform commands should now work.
If you ever set or change modules or backend configuration for
Terraform, rerun this command to reinitialize your working
directory. If you forget, other commands will detect it and
remind you to do so if necessary.
```

3. Create Amazon S3 bucket. The following is the Terraform configuration file **s3_remotestore.tf** to create S3:

```
resource "aws_s3_bucket" "bucket" {
  bucket = "terraformstateremotestore"
```

```
versioning {
  enabled = true
}
lifecycle {
  prevent_destroy = true
}
}
```

This code sets three parameters:

- **Bucket**: This is the name of the S3 bucket that you want to create. This name must be globally unique.

- **Versioning**: This block parameter is used to enable versioning on Amazon S3 bucket by setting the enable value as true. This will create a new version of files, in our case, a Terraform state file on every update from the 'terraform apply' command.

- **prevent_destroy**: This parameter can be set to any resource configuration in Terraform; this is not S3 specific. When **prevent_ destroy** is set to true on a Terraform resource, trying to delete that resource (e.g., '**terraform destroy**') will cause an exit with an error. This will stop us from accidentally deleting this remote store.

4. Run the '**terraform plan**' command to get output log as follows:

```
C:\Users\Ankita\Terraform\Chapter-2\Remote_State>terraform plan

An execution plan has been generated and is shown below.
Resource actions are indicated with the following symbols:
  + create

Terraform will perform the following actions:

  # aws_s3_bucket.bucket will be created
  + resource "aws_s3_bucket" "bucket" {
      + acceleration_status          = (known after apply)
      + acl                          = "private"
      + arn                          = (known after apply)
      + bucket                       = "terraformstateremotestore"
      + bucket_domain_name           = (known after apply)
      + bucket_regional_domain_name  = (known after apply)
```

```
        + force_destroy              = false
        + hosted_zone_id             = (known after apply)
        + id                         = (known after apply)
Plan: 1 to add, 0 to change, 0 to destroy.

------------------------------------------------------------------

Note: You didn't specify an "-out" parameter to save this plan,
so Terraform can't guarantee that exactly these actions will be
performed if "terraform apply" is subsequently run.
```

5. Run 'terraform apply' if everything is fine; it should provide output as follows:

```
C:\Users\Ankita\Terraform\Chapter-2\Remote_State>terraform apply

An execution plan has been generated and is shown below.
Resource actions are indicated with the following symbols:
  + create

Terraform will perform the following actions:
  # aws_s3_bucket.bucket will be created
  + resource "aws_s3_bucket" "bucket" {
      + acceleration_status            = (known after apply)
      + acl                            = "private"
      + arn                            = (known after apply)
      + bucket                         = "terraformstateremotestore"
      + bucket_domain_name             = (known after apply)
      + bucket_regional_domain_name    = (known after apply)
      + force_destroy                  = false
      + hosted_zone_id                 = (known after apply)
      + id                             = (known after apply)
      + region                         = (known after apply)
      + request_payer                  = (known after apply)
      + website_domain                 = (known after apply)
      + website_endpoint               = (known after apply)
      + versioning {
          + enabled     = true
```

```
        + mfa_delete = false
      }
   }

Plan: 1 to add, 0 to change, 0 to destroy.

Do you want to perform these actions?
  Terraform will perform the actions described above.
  Only 'yes' will be accepted to approve.

  Enter a value: yes

aws_s3_bucket.bucket: Creating...
aws_s3_bucket.bucket: Creation complete after 5s
[id=terraformstateremotestore]

Apply complete! Resources: 1 added, 0 changed, 0 destroyed.
```

If you get **Apply Complete!** as the output, then you have successfully created the S3 bucket using terraform.

6. Now, verify that your Amazon S3 bucket is created by looking into the Amazon portal. Login at **https://us-east-1.signin.aws.amazon.com/** and go to **Services | Storage | S3**; you should be able to see the bucket in AWS Region (in example eu-west-1) you created with the name **terraformstateremotestore**, as shown in the following screenshot:

Figure 2.6: *Amazon S3 bucket for S3*

7. To add bucket policy, click on **terraformstateremotestore | Permissions | ** on this page, scroll down to **Bucket Policy**, click on **Edit**, and add the policy as follows:

```
{
    "Version": "2012-10-17",
    "Statement": [
        {
            "Effect": "Allow",
            "Principal": {
                "AWS": ["arn:aws:iam::<AWS Account ID>:user/<USER
NAME>","arn:aws:iam::<AWS Account ID>:user/<USERNAME2>","arn:aws:
iam::<AWS Account ID>:user/<USERNAME3>"]
            },
            "Action": "s3:ListBucket",
            "Resource": "arn:aws:s3:::terraformstateremotestore"
        },
        {
            "Effect": "Allow",
            "Principal": {
                "AWS": ["arn:aws:iam::<AWS Account ID>:user/<USER
NAME>","arn:aws:iam::<AWS Account ID>:user/<USERNAME2>","arn:aws:
iam::<AWS Account ID>:user/<USERNAME3>"]
            },
            "Action": [
                "s3:GetObject",
                "s3:PutObject"
            ],
            "Resource": "arn:aws:s3:::terraformstateremotestore/*"
        }
    ]
}
```

In the above policy, you can update the principle AWS array with Amazon Resource Names (ARN) of list of users from your AWS Account you want to grant access to this S3 bucket and then click on the **Save changes** button in the bottom right.

8. Now, we are ready to use this S3 bucket in Terraform as our remote store for Terraform state. Let's configure the Terraform backend (that is, remote store connection to Terraform) for S3 bucket by adding the following code to the **terraform.tf** file:

```
terraform {
  backend "s3" {
    bucket = "terraformstateremotestore"
    key = "terraform.tfstate"
    region = "eu-west-1"
    encrypt = true
    access_key = <your AWS ACCESS KEY>
    secret_key = <Your AWS SECRET KEY>
  }
}
```

Here, we declared terraform backend as s3 and provided the value of bucket name to parameters passed in above block, value of key is the **path/terraform.tfstate** the path to terraform file in the bucket.

Parameter encrypt is set to true to encrypt the state file that we store in S3 bucket to hide sensitive data and prevent it from getting leaked.

9. Now, we need to run the '**terraform init**' command again to initialize the Terraform workspace to use S3 bucket to store the **terraform.tfstate** file that we want to share with different team members. The output of this command should look like this:

```
C:\Users\Ankita\Terraform\Chapter-2\Remote_State>terraform init

Initializing the backend...

Do you want to copy existing state to the new backend? Pre-ex-
isting state was found while migrating the previous "lo-
cal" backend to the newly configured "s3" backend. No ex-
isting state was found in the newly configured "s3" back-
end. Do you want to copy this state to the new "s3" backend? En-
ter "yes" to copy and "no" to start with an empty state.


  Enter a value: yes


Successfully configured the backend "s3"! Terraform will automati-
cally use this backend unless the backend configuration changes.
```

```
Initializing provider plugins...

- Reusing previous version of hashicorp/aws from the dependen-
cy lock file

- Installing hashicorp/aws v3.36.0...

- Installed hashicorp/aws v3.36.0 (signed by HashiCorp)


Terraform has been successfully initialized!
```

If Terraform successfully updates the remote backend, you will see a message saying '**Successfully configured the backend S3!**', as we see in the previous logs in green color.

10. When '**terraform init**' is successful, we can see the object in the S3 bucket, as in the following image:

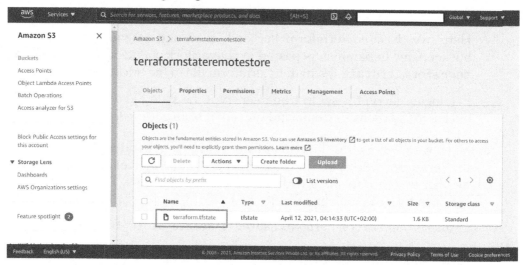

Figure 2.7: terraform.tfstate in S3 bucket

We have successfully configured Terraform state in Amazon S3 bucket named **teraformstateremotestore**. You can now try to add multiple changes and run '**terraform apply**' to see how the version is getting maintained in this S3 bucket for **terraform.tfstate**.

Go to **Amazon S3 Bucket | terraform.tfstate | Versions** to see the list of the versions of the state file, as shown in the following image, which we can use to roll back:

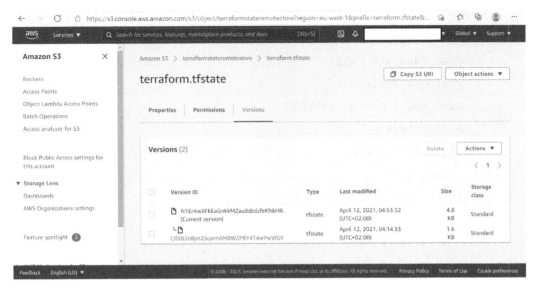

Figure 2.8: Terraform.tfstate versions in S3 Bucket

In this image, you can easily recognize the latest version of the current state through the current version text in round brackets in the version ID.

We have successfully configured storage using S3 for Terraform state file to work in team. However, to make the best use of this store, we need to add locking mechanism to this storage with the use of Dynamo DB, which also supports consistency checks.

Configuring DynamoDB with Amazon S3 for locking Terraform states

Terraform supports locking the Terraform state to prevent simultaneous runs against the same state. Locking helps us ensure that only one member of the team runs Terraform configuration at a time. It prevents conflicts, state file corruption, and data loss due to multiple concurrent runs on the same state file.

DynamoDB can be used for locking remote storage backend S3 to store state files. The DynamoDB table has a key on "**LockID**", such as **bucketName/path**, so we won't have any problem in getting locks and running Terraform safely until we have a unique combination of this key and **LockID**. Terraform offers this support out of the box within its 'backend' resource with S3.

Follow these steps to create and configure Dynamo DB and S3 for Terraform state locking:

1. Create Dynamo DB table in AWS using the **dynamoDB.tf** file with the following Terraform code:

```
resource "aws_dynamodb_table" "terraform_state_lock" {
  name           = "terraform-state-lock"
  read_capacity = 5
  write_capacity = 5
  hash_key       = "LockID"
  attribute {
    name = "LockID"
    type = "S"
  }
  lifecycle {
    prevent_destroy = true
  }


}
```

2. Run Terraform apply, which produces the following logs:

```
C:\Users\Ankita\Terraform\Chapter-2\Remote_State>terraform apply
aws_s3_bucket.
bucket: Refreshing state... [id=terraformstateremotestore]
aws_instance.example_client: Refreshing state... [id=i-05cxxxx]

An execution plan ..  generated and is shown below.
Resource actions are indicated with the following symbols:
  + create

Terraform will perform the following actions:

  # aws_dynamodb_table.terraform_state_lock will be created
  + resource "aws_dynamodb_table" "terraform_state_lock" {
      + arn            = (known after apply)
  .

  .


      + attribute {
          + name = "LockID"
```

```
        + type = "S"
      }

    + point_in_time_recovery {
        + enabled = (known after apply)
      }

    + server_side_encryption {
        + enabled     = (known after apply)
        + kms_key_arn = (known after apply)
      }
  }

Plan: 1 to add, 0 to change, 0 to destroy.

Do you want to perform these actions?
  Terraform will perform the actions described above.
  Only <yes> will be accepted to approve.

  Enter a value: yes

aws_dynamodb_table.terraform_state_lock: Creating...
aws_dynamodb_table.terraform_state_
lock: Creation complete after 9s [id=terraform-state-lock]

Apply complete! Resources: 1 added, 0 changed, 0 destroyed.
```

3. Now, we can go and check whether the DynamoDB table is created in the AWS Portal. To do this, log in to the AWS console and navigate to **Services** | **Databases** | **DynamoDB** | **Tables**. You will now be able to see the DynamoDB

table just created with the name "**terraform-state-lock**", as illustrated in the following figure:

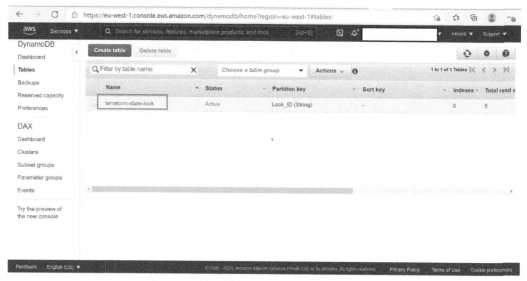

Figure 2.9: Dynamo DB table for locking Terraform state

In this image, you can see the partition key as "**LockID**", which is the string type that we provided in the **dynamoDB.tf** file in step one.

4. Now, we need to add the policy to update this table using Terraform script with particular users, like we added for the S3 bucket. To do so, add the following policy to the IAM users/group of your team in AWS:

```
{
    "Version": "2012-10-17",
    "Statement": [
        {
            "Effect": "Allow",
            "Action": [
                "dynamodb:PutItem",
                "dynamodb:DeleteItem",
                "dynamodb:GetItem"
            ],
            "Resource": "arn:aws:dynamodb:eu-west-1:<ACCOUNT
ID>:table/terraform-state-lock"
        }
```

```
    ]
}
```

5. Update the **terraform.tf** file with the following code. This code is the same as in the previous topic, where we just configured Amazon S3 as the backend to Terraform config. Now, to use dynamoDB table to lock the **terraform.tfstate** file in S3, we need to add just one line to the backend config: **dynamodb_table = "terraform-state-lock"**.

```
terraform {
  backend "s3" {
    bucket = "terraformstateremotestore"
    key = "terraform.tfstate"
    region = "eu-west-1"
    encrypt = true
    access_key = <your AWS ACCESS KEY>
    secret_key = <Your AWS SECRET KEY>
    dynamodb_table = "terraform-state-lock"
  }
}
```

6. We just updated terraform.tf, not the other resource-specific configuration files. To apply these changes, we need to run '**terraform init**' and '**terraform apply**' again. In the following log, you will now notice a line – "**aws_dynamodb_table.terraform_state_lock: Refreshing state... [id=terraform-state-lock]**" – on line 4, which checks and locks the **terraform.state** file that we store in the S3 bucket. To manually disable the lock, you can use the **-lock=false** flag with the '**terraform apply**' and destroy command. We have a few resources already under TF control, but we can see the **tfstate** file and locking operation at work:

```
C:\Users\Ankita\Terraform\Chapter-2\Remote_State>terraform apply

aws_s3_bucket.
bucket: Refreshing state... [id=terraformstateremotestore]

aws_instance.example_client1: Refreshing state... [id=i-02fxxxx]

aws_dynamodb_table.terraform_state_
lock: Refreshing state... [id=terraform-state-lock]


An execution plan … generated and is shown below.

Resource actions are indicated with the following symbols:
```

```
Terraform will perform the following actions:

Plan: 0 to add, 0 to change, 0 to destroy.

Do you want to perform these actions?
    Terraform will perform the actions described above.
    Only ‹yes› will be accepted to approve.

    Enter a value: yes
Apply complete! Resources: 0 added, 0 changed, 0 destroyed.
```

7. We can also verify this lock and get the digest from AWS console from the DynamoDB table, as shown in the following figure. You should have **LockID** created for your S3 bucket and Terraform file (refer to *figure 2.9*).

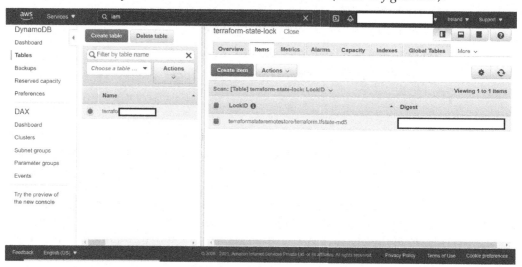

***Figure 2.10**: LockID created in DynamoDB*

This is how locking is performed on a state file stored in the Amazon S3 bucket. We will also learn how to manage state in Azure Storage in *Chapter 5 Automating Infrastructure Deployments in Azure Using Terraform*.

Terraform expressions

We use expressions to refer to or compute the values within a Terraform configuration. Literal values like '**string**' or 2 are simple Terraform expressions, and Terraform also allows complex expressions: arithmetic, conditional, referencing values, and more.

There are some limits on where we can use expressions, like which type of expression constructs are allowed, or whether a literal value of a particular type is required sometimes.

We can play with various Terraform expressions from the Terraform console by running the '`terraform console`' command.

The features of Terraform's expression are as follows:

- **Types and values**: Every Terraform expression has a value, and these have a defined type. This types tells where these values can be used and what kind of transformations can be applied to it. We have already seen the types in detail in the variable section. The expression that directly represents a constant value is called a **literal expression**.

- **Strings and templates**: Strings are the most commonly used and complex form of literal expression in Terraform. Quoted syntax is supported by terraform and a "**heredoc**" syntax for strings. The backslash character in quoted strings serves as an escape sequence. Both of these string syntaxes support template sequences that may start with ${ and %{ for interpolation and manipulation.

- **References to values**: There are many types of named values in Terraform, and each of these named values are expressions. The main types of named values are:

  o   Resources referred to as **<RESOURCE TYPE>.<NAME>**

  o   Input variables referred to as **var.<NAME>**

  o   Local values referred to as **local.<NAME>**

  o   Child module outputs referred to as **module.<MODULE NAME>**

  o   Data sources referred to as **data.<DATA TYPE>.<NAME>**

  o   Filesystem and workspace info referred to as **path.module** , **path. root** and **path.cwd**

  o   Block-local values referred to as **count.index**, each.key / **each.value** and self

- **Operators**: Operators in Terraform consist of arithmetic, comparison, and logical operators. An operator is an expression type that transforms or combines one or more expressions. Operators combine two values to produce a third value or transform a single value to a single result. The order of evaluation of these operators in an expression is as follows:

  o   !, - (multiplication by -1)

  o   *, /, %

o $+$, - (subtraction)

o $\geq$, >=, <, <=

o $==$, !=

o &&

o ||

- **Function calls**: Many of Terraform's built-in functions can also be used as expressions to combine and transform values. We have already seen Terraform functions that have syntax as **<FUNCTION NAME>(<ARGUMENT 1>, <ARGUMENT 2>)**.

- **Conditional expressions**: Conditional expressions have syntax **<CONDITION> ? <TRUE VAL> : <FALSE VAL>**, which uses the value (true or false) of a boolean expression to choose one value.

- **For Expressions**: In Terraform, 'for expressions' is like syntax **[for s in var.list : upper(s)]**; this expression can transform a complex type value to another complex type value.

- **Splat expressions**: This expressions syntax is **var.list[*].id**; this expression extracts simple collections from more complicated expressions.

- **Dynamic Blocks** is a way to create n number of repeatable nested blocks within a resource or other construct.

- **Type constraints**: It is a syntax for referring to a type. Input variables expect this syntax in their type argument. The details of type constraints are covered in the topic of Type in input variable arguments earlier in this chapter.

- **Version constraints**: These are expressions that are special strings and define a set of allowed software versions. Terraform uses version constraints in several places, like modules, provider requirements, and in the **required_ version** setting in the Terraform block. We can use operators to show the range of versions in version constraints.

Provisioning multiple resources

A large infrastructure needs horizontal scalability, which means there should be n number of duplicate resources. This horizontal scalability reduces the load on single resource (like fixed pool of compute instances) but divides the load on n number of resources. By default, the Terraform "**resource**" block configures only one real infrastructure object. In such cases, the "**count**" or "**for_each**" meta arguments of Terraform come into the picture. Let's see how to declare this count argument in the resource block.

Count

If a resource block has a **count** argument with its value as a whole number, Terraform creates that many instances on the execution of the configuration. Each instance created from this count has a distinct infrastructure object associated with it, and each of this instance is separately created, destroyed, or updated when the Terraform configuration is applied. This argument can be used with each type of resource block.

Syntax:

```
resource "aws_instance" "example" {

  count = 2

  ami           = "ami-0aef57767f5404a3c"

  instance_type = "t2.micro"

}
```

As per the above **resource**, two AWS EC2 instances should be created as the value of the count argument is **2**.

Count.index

To modify each of these instances, Terraform provides an expression to access a specific instance, that is, **count.index**. So, we can use the **count.index** expression in our Terraform configuration in all the blocks where the count argument is declared. The index numbers always start with 0.

Let's look at the following recipe to create multiple resource using **count** and **count.index**:

1. Add the following code to the **main.tf** file; the count in this code is 2, and there is an **${count.index}** expression inside a string function format in the **main.tf** file:

```
resource "aws_instance" "example" {

  count = 2

  ami           = "ami-0aef57767f5404a3c"

  instance_type = "t2.micro"

  tags = {

      Name = format("%s%s",local.name,"-${count.index}")

  }

}
```

```
locals {
  name = "example_instance"
}
```

This example will create two EC2 instances with the names "**example_instance-0**" and "**example_instance-1**".

2. Execute the '**terraform apply**' command to check this configuration; it will give the following output:

```
PS C:\Users\Ankita\Terraform\Count> terraform apply
An execution plan has been generated and is shown below.
Resource actions are indicated with the following symbols:
  + create


Terraform will perform the following actions:

  # aws_instance.example[0] will be created
  + resource "aws_instance" "example" {
      + ami                    = "ami-0aef57767f5404a3c"
      + get_password_data      = false
      + instance_type          = "t2.micro"
      + source_dest_check      = true)
      + tags                   = {
          + "Name" = "example_instance-0"
        }
    }

  # aws_instance.example[1] will be created
  + resource "aws_instance" "example" {
      + ami                    = "ami-0aef57767f5404a3c"
      + get_password_data      = false
      + instance_type          = "t2.micro"
      + source_dest_check      = true
      + tags                   = {
          + "Name" = "example_instance-1"
```

```
            }
        }
```

Plan: 2 to add, 0 to change, 0 to destroy.

Do you want to perform these actions?

   Terraform will perform the actions described above.

   Only ‹yes› will be accepted to approve.

   Enter a value: yes

aws_instance.example[0]: Creating...

aws_instance.example[1]: Creating...

aws_instance.example[1]: Creation complete after 34s [id=i-027xxxxx]

aws_instance.example[0]: Creation complete after 34s [id=i-0c6xxxxx]

Apply complete! Resources: 2 added, 0 changed, 0 destroyed.

Here, you must have noticed that tags with the names having**count.index** at the end will be created, as we expected from the Terraform configuration for resource.

3. Let's check the AWS EC2 console to see this in effect in the following screenshot:

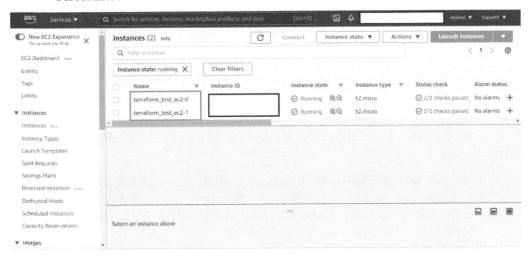

Figure 2.11: *EC2 resource created with count and tagged with name having count.index*

We have successfully created these instances using the **count** argument and **count.index** to name them; now the other point is to refer to these instances once they are created.

> **Tip: You can use a variable to pass the value to the count argument in the resource block to make the count value configurable. If you have the count variable declared, then you can update/scale down just by passing the variable value to the terraform plan command in command-line. Example: terraform plan –var instance_count=4 , where the variable name is instance_count.**

When **count** is used while creating resources, instances can be identified using the index number, like we do in array, starting with 0.

- When we want to refer to the resource block, we use **<RESOURCE_TYPE>.<NAME>** or module.**<NAME>** (in our example, it is **aws_instance.example**).

- We can refer to a resource with an individual instance in the resource block having count (N) as **<RESOURCE_TYPE>.<NAME>[<INDEX>]** or **module.<NAME>[<INDEX>]**.

This is how we work with horizontal scaling using count argument in the resource block for creating multiple resources.

There is a limitation of using **count** arguments that if you want to scale down, then this will always remove the last instance. We cannot delete a specific instance from the middle of count, but this issue can be overcome using the **for_each** argument, which we will cover in the next section.

For_each

The **Count** argument will only take the whole number as value; this cannot work in scenarios where we want to create multiple resources mapping the values in **map** or a **string**. So, **for_each** looping can be used when the value is either a **map** or a **set** of strings. Terraform resource block having **for_each** will create one instance for each value in **map** or **set**. **For_each** allows us to create n number of resources of the same type but with different properties.

Let's look at the step-by-step configuration to create n number of AWS EC2 instances having a map.

1. We can use the **vars.tf** file from earlier and declare the **webservers** variables to pass the map value for creating two **webservers**: **webserver1** with name **"WebAPI-Server"**, and **webserver2** with name **"WebApp-Server"**, as shown in the following code:

```
variable "webservers" {
    type = map(map(string))
```

```
    description = "AWS EC2 webserver instance with names WebAPI-
Server and WebApp-Server "
    default = {
        "webserver1" = {
            "name" = "WebAPI-Server"
        }
        "webserver2" = {
            "name" = "WebApp-Server"
        }
    }
}
```

We use the map in this code, and its type is again map of strings, so the type of variable webservers is **map(map(string))**. We defined the default value in this variable block itself, but you can add these values to **terraform. auto.tfvars.json** to make the code more customizable.

2. Remember that we created a **main.tf** file when we set up an EC2 instance and then looped through a Count to create additional EC2 servers. Now, update **main.tf**, which has the resource block with type **aws_instance**, comment out old code and add the **aws_instance** resource block, as shown in the following code block. This resource block is taking input from variable to **for_each** argument to create AWS EC2 instance from the values declared in map in the above-mentioned **vars.tf** configuration. Add the following code to this **main.tf** file:

```
resource "aws_instance" "webserver" {

for_each = var.webservers

ami          = "ami-0aef57767f5404a3c"

instance_type = "t2.micro"

tags = {

Name = each.value["name"]

}

}
```

Here, you have to pass **var.webservers** as the value to **for_ each** so that it refers to the map we set to variable value. Now that we have a map inside the map, we refer to the value of the **name** key as **each.value["name"]**. In Terraform, the current value for map in **for_each** is referred to as **each.value**, and the **key** (i.e., the name) in current map is referred to as **each.value[<KEY>]**.

3. Now, execute the '**terraform init**' command.

4. Execute the '**terraform plan**' command.

5. Execute the '**terraform apply**' command in your workspace if you find that the plan is correct and you want to create the resource. You should get the following log:

```
PS C:\Users\Ankita\Terraform\For_each> terraform apply

An execution plan has been generated and is shown below.
Resource actions are indicated with the following symbols:
  + create

Terraform will perform the following actions:

  # aws_instance.webserver["webserver1"] will be created
  + resource "aws_instance" "webserver" {
      + ami                     = "ami-0aef57767f5404a3c"
      + get_password_data       = false
      + instance_type           = "t2.micro"
      + source_dest_check       = true
      + tags                    = {
          + "Name" = "WebAPI-Server"
        }
    }

  # aws_instance.webserver["webserver2"] will be created
  + resource "aws_instance" "webserver" {
      + ami                     = "ami-0aef57767f5404a3c"
      + get_password_data       = false
      + instance_type           = "t2.micro"
      + source_dest_check       = true
      + tags                    = {
          + "Name" = "WebApp-Server"
        }
    }


Plan: 2 to add, 0 to change, 0 to destroy.
```

```
Do you want to perform these actions?

  Terraform will perform the actions described above.

  Only <yes> will be accepted to approve.


  Enter a value: yes

aws_instance.webserver["webserver1"]: Creating...

aws_instance.webserver["webserver2"]: Creating...

aws_instance.
webserver["webserver2"]: Creation complete after 34s [id=i-
047xxxx]

aws_instance.
webserver["webserver1"]: Creation complete after 34s [id=i-
0e4xxxx]

Apply complete! Resources: 2 added, 0 changed, 0 destroyed.
```

Here, you must have noticed that the tag name value of the two webserver are as mentioned in the map default values(**WebAPI-Server** and **WebApp-Server**).

6. Now, let's verify them in the AWS EC2 console. These servers were created as we expected them to have different names, as shown in the following screenshot:

Figure 2.12: Multiple EC2 instance creation using the for_each argument

This is how we can create multiple similar resources with different values of properties using the **for_each** argument in the resource block.

Referring to each object in the for_each block

In resource blocks where **for_each** is used, an each object is automatically available in Terraform expressions. This means you can use this each object to modify the configuration of each instance in resource block. Each object of **for_each** has two attributes:

- **each.key**: Map key or set member that corresponds to the current instance in the for each map/set.

- **each.value**: Map value that corresponds to the current instance. In the case of a set, this is the same as **each.key**.

Referring to **for_each** is similar to referring to count, only here we don't have index, we have key. So, referring to a resource block remains the same, but referring to an individual instance changes, which is **<RESOURCE_TYPE>.<NAME>[<KEY>]** or **module.<NAME>[<KEY>]**.

Both count and **for_each** have their own limitations, but they serve the purpose of provisioning multiple resources without writing duplicate code.

Debugging the Terraform execution

We have already learned how to execute Terraform commands and seen their logs many times in our execution of Terraform configuration in Terraform variables, Terraform outputs, and Terraform states.

We have used the **"init"**, **"plan"**, and **"apply"** commands without the debug mode enabled; now, let's see how to enable the debug mode and how we can see the debug logs with all the details.

- Terraform init

- Terraform plan

- Terraform apply

To print debug logs, Terraform recognizes the **TF_LOG** environment variable to be set in your system. Follow these steps to get the debug logs from Terraform command:

1. To see **TF_LOG** in your Windows machine and to use cmd, set the environment variable value as shown in the following screenshot:

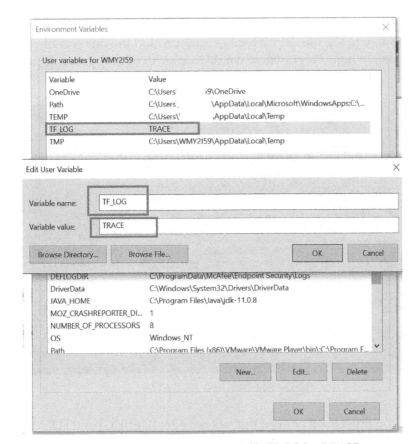

Figure 2.13: *Environment variable TF_LOG = TRACE*

OR

Use the following command if you are using powershell (for windows user); your environment variable **TF_LOG** will be set.

```
$env:TF_LOG = "TRACE"
```

Mac and Linux users can do this using the export command from terminal, as follows:

```
export TF_LOG="TRACE"
```

2. Once this variable is set, run any command from **init**, **plan**, or **apply**; you will be able to see the debug logs getting printed in your console logs. Refer as follows where "**terraform init**" is executed, and you will get DEBUG logs.

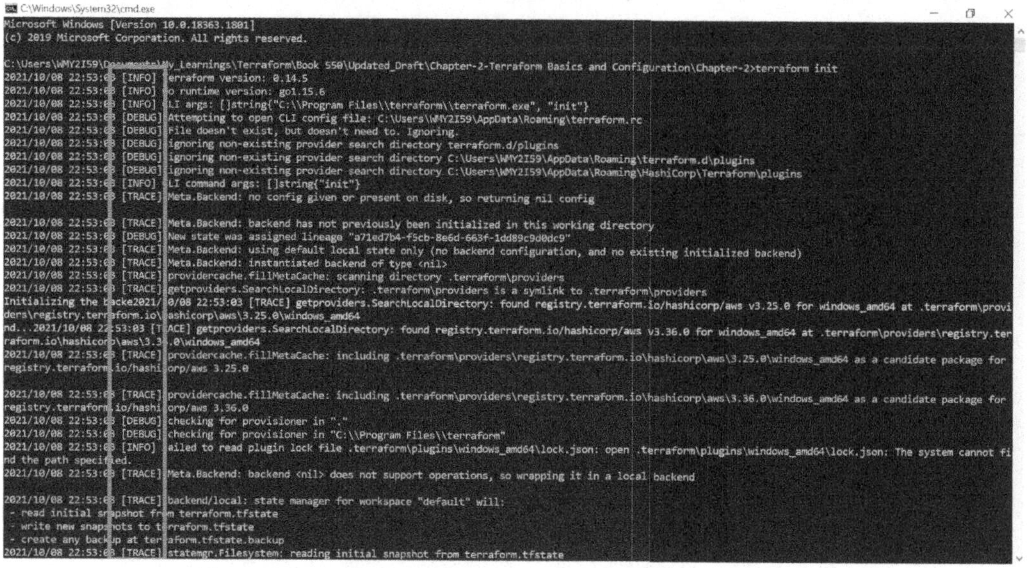

Figure 2.14: Terraform DEBUG log

Here, you must have noticed that we now get [DEBUG] and [TRACE] logs in the console where we execute the "**terraform init**" command. To disable these logs, we just need to keep the value of **TF_LOG** as empty. For example, in powershell, the command will be **$env: TF_LOG = ""**.

This is how you can get the entire stacktrace in your debug logs.

Logs are difficult to read in console, so it's better to write them to a log file. If you want to save these logs in some log file, this can be also done via an environment variable **TF_LOG_PATH**. You need to provide the path to the log file where you want to write these logs, as shown in the following example for Mac and Linux users:

```
export TF_LOG_PATH="terraform.txt"
```

By now, you must have understood Terraform basics and how Terraform should be configured and used in team.

Conclusion

In this chapter, we covered Terraform workflow and looked at Terraform basic concepts and configurations required to work with Terraform to build an automated infrastructure. The basic topics that we have covered will be used in the upcoming chapters as the basic structure of the recipes. This chapters explained the basic concepts that Terraform provides, Terraform resources, Terraform variables, Terraform functions, Working with Terraform Output and expressions, and Terraform state management using the Amazon S3 bucket and DynamoDB for locking these states. We also explored the creation of multiple resources with no duplicate code and learned how to get stacktrace debug information while executing Terraform.

In the next chapter, we will understand Terraform provisioners and the implementation of local-exec and remote-exec provisioners.

CHAPTER 3
Terraform Provisioners

Terraform provisioners helps execute scripts/shell commands install or configure packages on a machine (local or remote). Provisioner runs only once at the launch of resource. All actions cannot always be modeled in Terraform's declarative model. We can use provisioners to model specific actions on the local machine or on a remote machine available in cloud environment in order to prepare resources for service. Terraform supports provisioners for as some behaviors can't be directly represented in Terraform's declarative model. Provisioners are a last resort.

In this chapter, we will discuss different types of provisioners and how Packer can be utilized. You will have to complete some exercises on your own. We would like you to explore things, fail and recover fast, and gain confidence about your own capabilities in building **Infrastructure as Code** using Terraform.

Structure

We will discuss the following topics in this chapter:

- Using provisioners in Terraform
- Implementing remote-exec provisioners
- Implementing local-exec provisioners
- Creation-time and Destroy-time provisioners

Objectives

After studying this chapter, you will learn about different provisioners. You should be able to use local-exec, remote-exec and other provisioners with some useful notes. You will also learn how to utilize Packer.

Using provisioners in Terraform

There will be always some scenarios or behaviors, which cannot be directly implemented by Terraform's declarative model, such behaviors can be handled by the concept called provisioners in Terraform. However, provisioners add complexity and uncertainty in Terraform implementation.

Terraform provisioners helps execute scripts/shell commands and install or configure packages on machine (local or remote).

Provisioner runs only once at the launch of resource. It is possible that not all actions can be modeled in Terraform's declarative model. This is where provisioners help; they are similar to **user_data** and **custom_data** available in Amazon EC2 instances and Microsoft Azure Virtual Machines, respectively.

It is similar to what we can achieve by providing commands while launching EC2 instances.

Figure 3.1: User data in Amazon Ec2 instances

Generic provisioners like file, local-exec, and remote-exec are available, and so are vendor provisioners like chef, puppet, salt-masterless, and so on. Terraform provisioners are plugins available as part of Terraform Core.

Note: Even if your specific use-case is not described in the following sections, we recommend attempting to solve it using other techniques first, and use provisioners only if there is no other option.

Reference: Official Terraform Documentation https://www.terraform.io/docs/language/resources/provisioners/syntax.html

Implementing local-exec provisioners

The **local-exec** provisioner executes a local script where we are executing Terraform commands. This command or script is not executed on the resource we are creating using Terraform code.

The following are the three arguments available in the **local-exec** block.

Argument	Description
`Command`	Command to execute with relative path or as an absolute path to the current working directory. Environment variables or Terraform variables are accessible.
`working_dir`	It is a directory where command will be executed.
`Interpreter`	Interpreter to execute the command.

`Environment`	Key value pairs that represent the environment.
	
	environment = {
	
	    secConfigStatus = "Completed"
	
	    deploymentEnvironments = 3
	
	    deleteFlag = "true"
	
	}

Table 3.1: Arguments available in local-exec block

We'll work on a scenario where we've built our own AMI image and want to output the details of the Instance ID, Public DNS hostname, and AMI Instance ID to a local file for later use for keeping track of EC2 instances created using a specific AMI or for audit purpose as well where internal audits requires at times to give details regarding instances.

Here's what we'll be doing:

- Use packer to create an AMI in AWS.

- Create a log file that stores data about instance ID, AMI ID, and public DNS of instances created using Terraform script.

- Use the latest AMI created using packer every time you execute Terraform script (Packer is not required for **local_exec**; it is just an additional demonstration of Terraform functionality with custom data. Packer helps demonstrate the User Data block with the AWS TF Provider to feed in data when building a resource.)

Let's use Visual Studio Code to create Terraform script:

1. Create a file named **example-local-exec.tf**.

2. We intend to create a virtual machine; hence, we use resource block to create AWS instance and set the **ami** and **instance_type** attributes. Let's add provisioner block in VS Code.

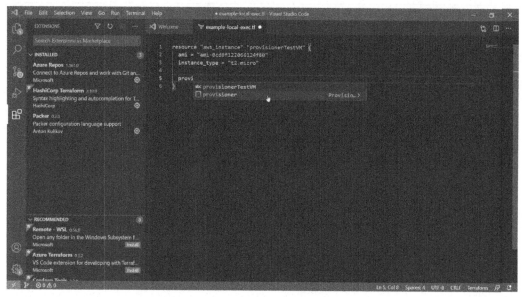

Figure 3.2: Provisioner block

3. Before working with provisioners, let's change the color theme in Visual Studio Code. Go to **File** | **Preferences** | **Color Theme**, as shown here:

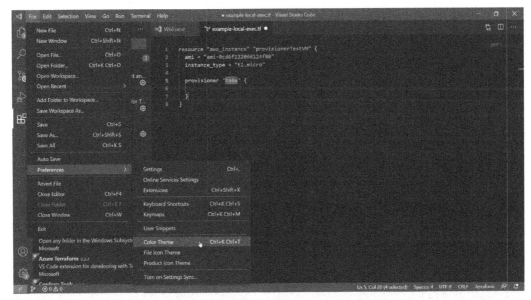

Figure 3.3: *Color Theme in Visual Studio Code*

Note: Provisioners should only be used as a last resort; configuration Management tools such as Chef/Puppet/Ansible can be utilized instead. Similar functionalities can be achieved using Packer or Cloud Native features such as user_data in AWS.

4. Select an appropriate light color theme:

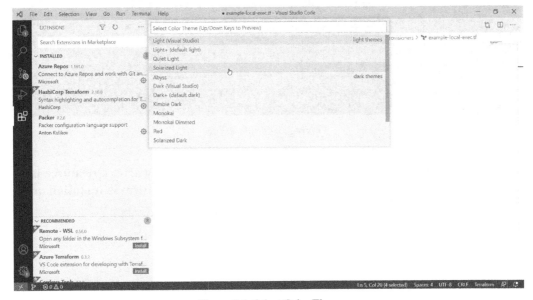

Figure 3.4: *Select Color Theme*

5. Our script looks as follows:

```
#Provides an EC2 instance resource.
resource "aws_instance" "provisionerTestVM" {
  ami = "ami-0c6615d1e95c98aca"
  instance_type = "t2.micro"
}
```

6. Initialize provide plugin using the **terraform init** command. Then, execute the **terraform init** command in command prompt, as illustrated here:

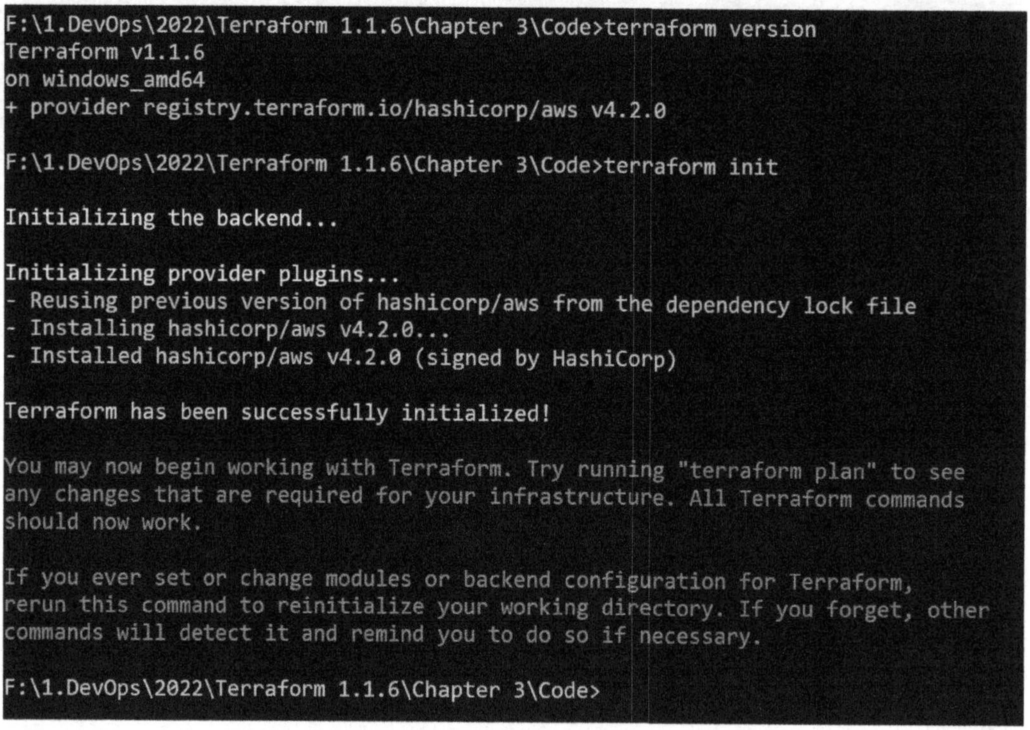

```
F:\1.DevOps\2022\Terraform 1.1.6\Chapter 3\Code>terraform version
Terraform v1.1.6
on windows_amd64
+ provider registry.terraform.io/hashicorp/aws v4.2.0

F:\1.DevOps\2022\Terraform 1.1.6\Chapter 3\Code>terraform init

Initializing the backend...

Initializing provider plugins...
- Reusing previous version of hashicorp/aws from the dependency lock file
- Installing hashicorp/aws v4.2.0...
- Installed hashicorp/aws v4.2.0 (signed by HashiCorp)

Terraform has been successfully initialized!

You may now begin working with Terraform. Try running "terraform plan" to see
any changes that are required for your infrastructure. All Terraform commands
should now work.

If you ever set or change modules or backend configuration for Terraform,
rerun this command to reinitialize your working directory. If you forget, other
commands will detect it and remind you to do so if necessary.

F:\1.DevOps\2022\Terraform 1.1.6\Chapter 3\Code>
```

Figure 3.5: Terraform Init

Note: The local-exec provisioner executes command locally after a resource is created. This invokes a process on the system where Terraform is installed and configured, not on the resource created using Terraform.

7. Execute **terraform validate** to verify the existing script. In case of errors, fix the errors in terraform script first.

Figure 3.6: Terraform validate

8. We need to set region argument in provider block. For this, add provider block in terraform script (if you run terraform plan, it will also ask you to provide a region as an argument via the console).

```
provider "aws" {
  region = "ap-south-1"
}


#Provides an EC2 instance resource.
resource "aws_instance" "provisionerTestVM" {
  ami = "ami-0c6615d1e95c98aca"
  instance_type = "t2.micro"
}
```

Execute **terraform validate** again.

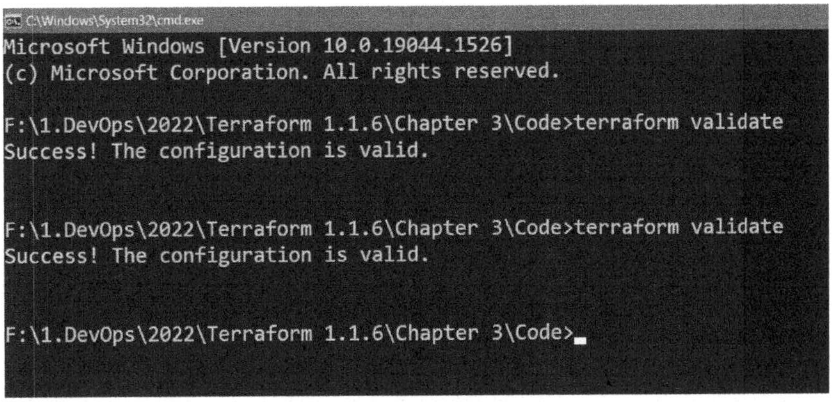

Figure 3.7: AWS region added

9. Execute the **terraform plan** command to verify the execution plan:
```
F:\1.DevOps\2022\Terraform 1.1.6\Chapter 3\Code>terraform plan
```

```
An execution plan has been generated and is shown below.
Resource actions are indicated with the following symbols:
  + create

Terraform will perform the following actions:

  # aws_instance.provisionerTestVM will be created
  + resource "aws_instance" "provisionerTestVM" {
      + ami                          = " ami-0c6615d1e95c98aca"
      + arn                          = (known after apply)
            .

            .

      + tenancy                      = (known after apply)
      + vpc_security_group_ids       = (known after apply)


      + ebs_block_device {
          + delete_on_termination = (known after apply)
                .

                .

          + volume_type           = (known after apply)
        }

      + enclave_options {
          + enabled = (known after apply)
        }

      + ephemeral_block_device {
          + device_name  = (known after apply)
          + no_device    = (known after apply)
          + virtual_name = (known after apply)
        }

      + metadata_options {
```

```
            + http_endpoint                = (known after apply)
            + http_put_response_hop_limit  = (known after apply)
            + http_tokens                  = (known after apply)
          }

        + network_interface {
            + delete_on_termination = (known after apply)
            + device_index          = (known after apply)
            + network_interface_id  = (known after apply)
          }

        + root_block_device {
            + delete_on_termination = (known after apply)
                  .

                  .

            + volume_type           = (known after apply)
          }
      }

Plan: 1 to add, 0 to change, 0 to destroy.

------------------------------------------------------------------

Note: You didn't specify an "-out" parameter to save this plan,
so Terraform can't guarantee that exactly these actions will be
performed if "terraform apply" is subsequently run.
```

There are no provisioner details available as they will create after AWS Instance is created.

10. Let's add provisioner block in resource:

    Refer to *Chapter 2, Terraform Basics and Configuration,* to look up a valid AMI ID for the region, or use an AMI ID based on your preferred region as per AWS Management Console.

```
provider "aws" {
  region = "ap-south-1"
}


#Provides an EC2 instance resource.
```

```
resource "aws_instance" "provisionerTestVM" {

     ami = "ami-0c6615d1e95c98aca"

     instance_type = "t2.micro"

     provisioner "local-exec" {

          command = "echo Instance Type=${self.instance_type},
Instance ID=${self.id}, Public DNS=${self.public_dns}, AMI
ID=${self.ami} >> allinstancedetails"

     }

}
```

Use **Instance Type=${self.instance_type}, Instance ID=${self.id}, Public DNS=${self.public_dns}, AMI ID=${self.ami}** to store details in a file available in the system from which Terraform scripts are being executed.

Note: How can you run provisioners that aren't directly associated with a specific resource? We can bind them with a null_resource. Use the Trigger argument to decide when the provisioners should run.

11. Execute the **terraform apply** command to create an instance in AWS:

```
F:\1.DevOps\2022\Terraform 1.1.6\Chapter 3\Code>terraform apply

Terraform used the selected providers to generate the following
execution plan. Resource actions are indicated with the following
symbols:

  + create

Terraform will perform the following actions:

  # aws_instance.provisionerTestVM will be created
  + resource "aws_instance" "provisionerTestVM" {
      + ami                                 = "ami-
0c6615d1e95c98aca"

      + arn                                 = (known after
apply)

      + associate_public_ip_address         = (known after
apply)

  .


  .


  .
```

```
Plan: 1 to add, 0 to change, 0 to destroy.
```

```
Do you want to perform these actions?
  Terraform will perform the actions described above.
  Only 'yes' will be accepted to approve.

  Enter a value: yes
```

```
aws_instance.provisionerTestVM: Creating...

aws_instance.provisionerTestVM: Still creating... [10s elapsed]

aws_instance.provisionerTestVM: Still creating... [20s elapsed]

aws_instance.provisionerTestVM: Still creating... [30s elapsed]

aws_instance.provisionerTestVM: Provisioning with 'local-exec'...

aws_instance.provisionerTestVM (local-exec): Executing:
["cmd" "/C" "echo Instance Type=t2.micro, Instance ID=i-
0174620a88e0c0058, Public DNS=ec2-13-126-110-148.ap-south-1.
compute.amazonaws.com, AMI ID=ami-0c6615d1e95c98aca >>
allinstancedetails"]

aws_instance.provisionerTestVM: Creation complete after 31s
[id=i-0174620a88e0c0058]
```

```
Apply complete! Resources: 1 added, 0 changed, 0 destroyed.
```

If you get a firewall warning as shown in the following screenshot, allow access:

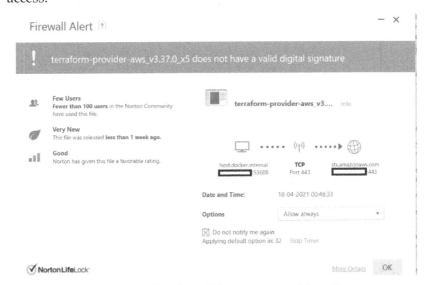

Figure 3.8: Terraform AWS connection and firewall

Depending on your local system security software, you may get asked to let the console / Terraform access the network to create the resources.

12. Verify the **myinstanceid** file, which is available in the same directory as the terraform script:

```
Instance Type=t2.micro, Instance ID=i-0174620a88e0c0058, Public
DNS=ec2-13-126-110-148.ap-south-1.compute.amazonaws.com,        AMI
ID=ami-0c6615d1e95c98aca
```

13. Install packer using chocolatey by referring to **https://community.chocolatey.org/packages/packer/1.2.2**:

```
PS C:\WINDOWS\system32> choco install packer

Chocolatey v0.10.15

Installing the following packages:

packer

By installing you accept licenses for the packages.

Progress: Downloading packer 1.7.10... 100%


packer v1.7.10 [Approved]

packer package files install completed. Performing other installation
steps.

The package packer wants to run 'chocolateyInstall.ps1'.

Note: If you don't run this script, the installation will fail.

Note: To confirm automatically next time, use '-y' or consider:

choco feature enable -n allowGlobalConfirmation

Do you want to run the script?([Y]es/[A]ll - yes to all/[N]o/[P]
rint): yes


Removing old packer plugins

Downloading packer 64 bit

 from 'https://releases.hashicorp.com/packer/1.7.10/packer_1.7.10_
windows_amd64.zip'

Progress: 100% - Completed download of C:\Users\Mitesh\AppData\
Local\Temp\chocolatey\packer\1.7.10\packer_1.7.10_windows_amd64.
zip (30.8 MB).

Download of packer_1.7.10_windows_amd64.zip (30.8 MB) completed.
```

Hashes match.

Extracting   C:\Users\Mitesh\AppData\Local\Temp\chocolatey\
packer\1.7.10\packer_1.7.10_windows_amd64.zip to C:\ProgramData\
chocolatey\lib\packer\tools...

C:\ProgramData\chocolatey\lib\packer\tools

ShimGen has successfully created a shim for packer.exe

The install of packer was successful.

   Software installed to 'C:\ProgramData\chocolatey\lib\packer\
tools'

Chocolatey installed 1/1 packages.

See the log for details (C:\ProgramData\chocolatey\logs\chocolatey.
log).

You can, of course, use your preferred package manager utilities (like homebrew for Mac and different packages for the different Linux distributions - visit https://learn.hashicorp.com/tutorials/packer/get-started-install-cli#installing-packer for more details).

14. The following is a script to create an AMI in Amazon EC2 using Packer:

```
{
    "variables": {
      "aws_access_key": "",
      "aws_secret_key": ""
    },
    "builders": [
      {
        "type": "amazon-ebs",
        "access_key": "{{user `aws_access_key`}}",
        "secret_key": "{{user `aws_secret_key`}}",
        "region": "ap-south-1",
        "source_ami": "ami-0851b76e8b1bce90b",
        "instance_type": "t2.micro",
        "ssh_username": "ubuntu",
        "ami_name": "packer-cf-ami-{{timestamp}}"
```

```
        }
    ],
    "provisioners": [


    ]
}
```

Save the file as **firstawsami-packer.json**.

15. Execute following packer command to create AMI:

    ```
    packer build -var "aws_access_key=XXXXXXXXXXXXXXXXXXXXX" -var "aws_
    secret_key=XXXXXXXXXXXXXXXXXXXX" firstawsami-packer.json.
    ```

16. Verify the output of the packer command execution. Note the AMI ID:

    ```
    amazon-ebs: output will be in this color.

    ==> amazon-ebs: Prevalidating any provided VPC information
    ==> amazon-ebs: Prevalidating AMI Name: packer-cf-ami-1645472290
        amazon-ebs: Found Image ID: ami-0851b76e8b1bce90b
    ==> amazon-ebs: Creating temporary keypair: packer_6213ea22-d155-
    9179-5cdb-be7b67aa6365
    ==> amazon-ebs: Creating temporary security group for this instance:
    packer_6213ea23-ad39-14a3-f6ba-d88dc671959f
    ==> amazon-ebs: Authorizing access to port 22 from [0.0.0.0/0] in
    the temporary security groups...
    ==> amazon-ebs: Launching a source AWS instance...
    ==> amazon-ebs: Adding tags to source instance
        amazon-ebs: Adding tag: "Name": "Packer Builder"
        amazon-ebs: Instance ID: i-05dc53e10b96c4772
    ==> amazon-ebs: Waiting for instance (i-05dc53e10b96c4772) to
    become ready...
    ==> amazon-ebs: Using SSH communicator to connect: 13.232.83.20
    ==> amazon-ebs: Waiting for SSH to become available...
    ==> amazon-ebs: Connected to SSH!
    ==> amazon-ebs: Stopping the source instance...
    ```

```
    amazon-ebs: Stopping instance
==> amazon-ebs: Waiting for the instance to stop...
==> amazon-ebs: Creating AMI packer-cf-ami-1645472290 from instance
i-05dc53e10b96c4772
    amazon-ebs: AMI: ami-09264f5d9a8d66002
==> amazon-ebs: Waiting for AMI to become ready...
==> amazon-ebs: Skipping Enable AMI deprecation...
==> amazon-ebs: Terminating the source AWS instance...
==> amazon-ebs: Cleaning up any extra volumes...
==> amazon-ebs: No volumes to clean up, skipping
==> amazon-ebs: Deleting temporary security group...
==> amazon-ebs: Deleting temporary keypair...
Build 'amazon-ebs' finished after 3 minutes 30 seconds.

==> Wait completed after 3 minutes 30 seconds

==> Builds finished. The artifacts of successful builds are:
--> amazon-ebs: AMIs were created:
ap-south-1: ami-09264f5d9a8d66002
```

Note: Refer to *Chapter 2, Terraform Basics and Configuration*, to look up a valid AMI ID for the region or use AMI ID based on your preferred region as per AWS Management Console.

17. Let's configure terraform script in a way that AMI is considered based on the latest creation time.

    Expressions in provisioner blocks can use the special "**self**" object. It represents the provisioner's parent resource and all its attributes.

    For example, use **self.public_ip** to refer **public_ip** of an **aws_instance**:

```
provider "aws" {
  region = "ap-south-1"
}

#Get latest AMI ID based on Filter - Here AMI created using Packer
data "aws_ami" "packeramis" {
```

```
    owners        = ["10xxxxxxxxxx"] #change the owner ID as per your
account

    most_recent = true

    filter {
      name    = "name"
      values = ["packer-cf*"]
    }


}

#Provides an EC2 instance resource.
resource "aws_instance" "provisionerTestVM" {
        ami = data.aws_ami.packeramis.id
        instance_type = "t2.micro"

        provisioner "local-exec" {
                command  =  "echo   Instance   Type=${self.instance_
type}, Instance ID=${self.id}, Public DNS=${self.public_dns}, AMI
ID=${self.ami} >> allinstancedetails"
        }
}
```

Using data block, Terraform can read from a data source "**aws_ami**" and export the result under the local name "**packeramis**." The name is used to refer to this resource from the same Terraform module; the data source and name must be unique identifiers for a given resource. Additionally, provide Owner ID from the AWS portal based on your account.

Tip: You can find "Owner" ID by accessing the AMIs section in the AWS web-based console for the region we set it up in.

1. Execute following packer command to create AMI:

    ```
    packer build -var "aws_access_key=XXXXXXXXXXXXXXXXXXXXX" -var "aws_
    secret_key=XXXXXXXXXXXXXXXXXXXX" firstawsami-packer.json
    ```

    Executing this command will again create another AMI with a different AMI ID (`ami-0f19cf13c5279d1d0`):

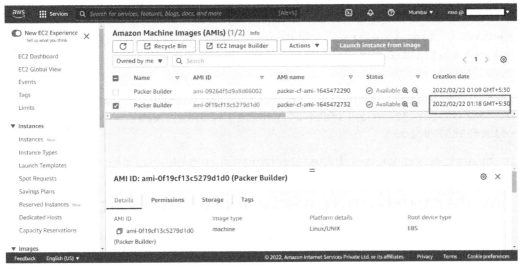

Figure 3.9: Packer AMIs

Note: Destroy-time provisioner executes commands only during a destroy operation. However, it will not run if the resource that contains Destroy-time provisioner is "tainted."

2. Execute **terraform apply** to determine which AMI ID is utilized by terraform script. Verify the AMI ID:

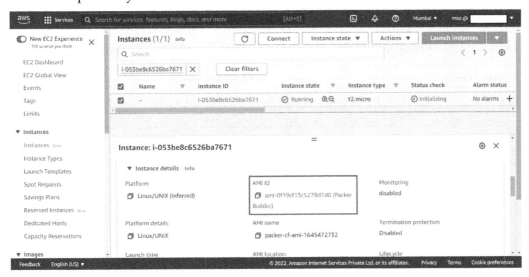

Figure 3.10: AWS Instance

Verify the local file:

```
Instance   Type=t2.micro,   Instance   ID=i-0174620a88e0c0058,   Public
DNS=ec2-13-126-110-148.ap-south-1.compute.amazonaws.com,   AMI   ID=ami-
0c6615d1e95c98aca

Instance   Type=t2.micro,   Instance   ID=i-053be8c6526ba7671,   Public
DNS=ec2-13-126-32-40.ap-south-1.compute.amazonaws.com,   AMI   ID=ami-
0f19cf13c5279d1d0
```

In the next section, we will discuss implementing remote-exec provisioners.

Implementing remote-exec provisioners

The remote-exec provisioner provides you with the facility to execute a script on the resource created by Terraform script. The following things can be achieved:

- Connecting with remote resource using SSH/Winrm
- Executing a list of commands
- Executing Scripts

User data or configuration management tool is still a preferred choice to execute operations on a remote resource.

Note: Provisioners should only be used as a last resort. There are better alternatives for most common situations.

Here are the three arguments available in the **Remote-exec** block:

Argument	Description
Inline	List of command strings that are executed in the order that they are given.
Script	Absolute or relative path to a local script that will be copied to the remote resource (i.e., Amazon EC2 instance) and then executed.
Scripts	Absolute or relative paths to a local script that will be copied to the remote resource (i.e., Amazon EC2 instance) and then executed in the order that they are given.

Table3.2: Arguments available in remote-exec block

Let's consider a scenario where we would like to install Nginx using the **remote-exec** block.

Now, we will create a **vars.tf** file to declare variables that we will utilize in the main Terraform script. We will declare instance type, region, and other variables:

The following code block will create the following resources in AWS:

- Virtual private cloud
- Public subnet
- Security group
    - Inbound and outbound rules
- EC2 instance

Go to Network & Security and click on Key Pairs in EC2 dashboard. Create key pair and save the PEM file. We will use the PEM (**terraform.pem**) file to connect to EC2 instance.

We want to install Nginx using **remote-exec**; hence, let's add the following block to perform the **remote-exec** execution. Add installation commands to the provisioner block and connection details such as user and key to the Connection block:

```
# Configure region in provider block using variable
provider "aws" {
  region = var.apac_region
}


# Query all avilable Availability Zone; we will use specific availability
zone using index
data "aws_availability_zones" "available" {}


# VPC Creation using cidr block available in vars.tf
resource "aws_vpc" "provisionerVPC" {
  cidr_block           = var.vpc_cidr
  enable_dns_hostnames = true
  enable_dns_support   = true


  tags = {
    Name = "dev-terraform-vpc"
  }
}


# Public Subnet public cidr block available in vars.tf and
provisionerVPC
resource "aws_subnet" "public_subnet" {
```

```
  cidr_block               = var.public_cidr
  vpc_id                   = aws_vpc.provisionerVPC.id
  map_public_ip_on_launch = true
  availability_zone        = data.aws_availability_zones.available.
names[1]

  tags = {
    Name = "dev-public-subnet"
  }
}
#To access EC2 instance inside a Virtual Private Cloud (VPC) we need
an Internet Gateway and a routing table connecting the subnet to the
Internet Gateway
# Creating Internet Gateway

resource "aws_internet_gateway" "gw" {
  vpc_id = aws_vpc.provisionerVPC.id

  tags = {
    Name = "dev-gw"
  }
}

# Public Route Table
resource "aws_route_table" "public_route" {
  vpc_id = aws_vpc.provisionerVPC.id

  route {
    cidr_block = var.cidr_blocks
    gateway_id = aws_internet_gateway.gw.id
  }

  tags = {
    Name = "dev-public-route"
  }
}
# Associate Public Subnet with Public Route Table
```

```
resource "aws_route_table_association" "public_subnet_assoc" {
  count          = 1
  route_table_id = aws_route_table.public_route.id
  subnet_id      = aws_subnet.public_subnet.id
  depends_on     = [aws_route_table.public_route, aws_subnet.public_
subnet]
}

# Security Group Creation for provisionerVPC
resource "aws_security_group" "dev_terraform_sg_allow_ssh_http" {
  name  = "dev-sg"
  vpc_id = aws_vpc.provisionerVPC.id
}

# Ingress Security Port 22 (Inbound)
resource "aws_security_group_rule" "ssh_ingress_access" {
  from_port         = 22
  protocol          = "tcp"
  security_group_id = aws_security_group.dev_terraform_sg_allow_ssh_http .id
  to_port           = 22
  type              = "ingress"
  cidr_blocks       = [var.cidr_blocks]
}

# Ingress Security Port 80 (Inbound)
resource "aws_security_group_rule" "http_ingress_access" {
  from_port         = 80
  protocol          = "tcp"
  security_group_id = aws_security_group.dev_terraform_sg_allow_ssh_http .id
  to_port           = 80
  type              = "ingress"
  cidr_blocks       = [var.cidr_blocks]
}

# All egress/outbound Access
resource "aws_security_group_rule" "all_egress_access" {
```

```
    from_port           = 0
    protocol            = "-1"
    security_group_id = aws_security_group.dev_terraform_sg_allow_ssh_http .id
    to_port             = 0
    type                = "egress"
    cidr_blocks         = [var.cidr_blocks]
}

# Instance Configuration
resource "aws_instance" "provisioner-remoteVM" {
    ami                     = "ami-0c6615d1e95c98aca"
    instance_type           = var.instance_type
    key_name                = "terraform"
    vpc_security_group_ids = [aws_security_group.dev_terraform_sg_allow_
ssh_http.id]
    subnet_id = aws_subnet.public_subnet.id
    tags = {
      Name = "remote-instance"
    }
    provisioner "remote-exec" {
        inline = [
          "sudo yum update -y",
          "sudo amazon-linux-extras install -y nginx1",
          "sudo service nginx start"
        ]
    }
    connection {
      type     = "ssh"
      host = aws_instance.provisioner-remoteVM.public_ip
      user     = "ec2-user"
      password = ""
      private_key = file("${path.module}/terraform.pem")
    }
}
```

The **remote-exec** provisioner needs to connect with the resources to execute commands. SSH can be used to connect with the resources. Connections are as per resource or as per provisioner; Create use private key to connect with the resources / instance in this case.

Note: When Creation-time provisioner execution is not successful, Terraform marks the resource as a "tainted" resource that will be planned for destruction and recreation at the time of the next terraform apply execution.

Execute terraform validate to verify the script.

Once the validation is successful, execute terraform apply.

Let's highlight specific logs that provide details of the Terraform script execution:

```
aws_vpc.provisionerVPC: Creating...

aws_vpc.provisionerVPC: Still creating... [10s elapsed]

aws_vpc.provisionerVPC: Creation complete after 12s [id=vpc-
0f2d53b5535a2c404]

aws_internet_gateway.gw: Creating...

aws_security_group.dev_terraform_sg_allow_ssh_http: Creating...

aws_subnet.public_subnet: Creating...

    .

    .

    .

aws_instance.provisioner-remoteVM: Still creating... [40s elapsed]

aws_instance.provisioner-remoteVM: Provisioning with 'remote-exec'...

aws_instance.provisioner-remoteVM (remote-exec): Connecting to remote
host via SSH...

aws_instance.provisioner-remoteVM (remote-exec):   Host: 3.110.158.91

aws_instance.provisioner-remoteVM (remote-exec):   User: ec2-user

aws_instance.provisioner-remoteVM (remote-exec):   Password: false

aws_instance.provisioner-remoteVM (remote-exec):   Private key: true

aws_instance.provisioner-remoteVM (remote-exec):   Certificate: false

aws_instance.provisioner-remoteVM (remote-exec):   SSH Agent: false

aws_instance.provisioner-remoteVM (remote-exec):   Checking Host Key:
false

aws_instance.provisioner-remoteVM (remote-exec):   Target Platform: unix

aws_instance.provisioner-remoteVM (remote-exec): Connected!
```

```
aws_instance.provisioner-remoteVM (remote-exec): Loaded plugins: extras_
suggestions,

aws_instance.provisioner-remoteVM (remote-exec):                    :
langpacks, priorities,

aws_instance.provisioner-remoteVM (remote-exec):                        : update-
motd

    .

    .

    .

aws_instance.provisioner-remoteVM (remote-exec): --> Running transaction
check

aws_instance.provisioner-remoteVM (remote-exec): ---> Package aws-cfn-
bootstrap.noarch 0:2.0-9.amzn2 will be updated

    .

    .

    .

aws_instance.provisioner-remoteVM (remote-exec): Dependencies Resolved

aws_instance.provisioner-remoteVM (remote-exec): ========================
==================

aws_instance.provisioner-remoteVM (remote-exec):  Package        Arch
Version

aws_instance.provisioner-remoteVM (remote-exec):
Repository  Size

aws_instance.provisioner-remoteVM (remote-exec): ========================
==================

aws_instance.provisioner-remoteVM (remote-exec): Updating:

aws_instance.provisioner-remoteVM (remote-exec):  aws-cfn-bootstrap

aws_instance.provisioner-remoteVM (remote-exec):                    noarch
2.0-10.amzn2

    .

    .

    .

aws_instance.provisioner-remoteVM (remote-exec): (14/14): vim-commo |
7.3 MB   00:00

aws_instance.provisioner-remoteVM (remote-exec): ----------------------
------------------
```

```
aws_instance.provisioner-remoteVM (remote-exec): Total        35 MB/s |
14 MB   00:00
.
.
.
aws_instance.provisioner-remoteVM (remote-exec): Installing nginx
aws_instance.provisioner-remoteVM (remote-exec): Loaded plugins: extras_
suggestions,
aws_instance.provisioner-remoteVM (remote-exec):                 :
langpacks, priorities,
aws_instance.provisioner-remoteVM (remote-exec):                    : update-
motd
.
.
.
aws_instance.provisioner-remoteVM (remote-exec): --> Running transaction
check
aws_instance.provisioner-remoteVM (remote-exec): ---> Package nginx.
x86_64 1:1.20.0-2.amzn2.0.4 will be installed
.
.
.
aws_instance.provisioner-remoteVM (remote-exec): Installed:
aws_instance.provisioner-remoteVM (remote-exec):   nginx.x86_64
1:1.20.0-2.amzn2.0.4
.
.
.
aws_instance.provisioner-remoteVM (remote-exec): Redirecting to /bin/
systemctl start nginx.service
aws_instance.provisioner-remoteVM: Creation complete after 1m10s [id=i-
03d68a8450b0ea67a]


Apply complete! Resources: 10 added, 0 changed, 0 destroyed.
```

Let's verify the EC2 instance **"remote-instance"**:

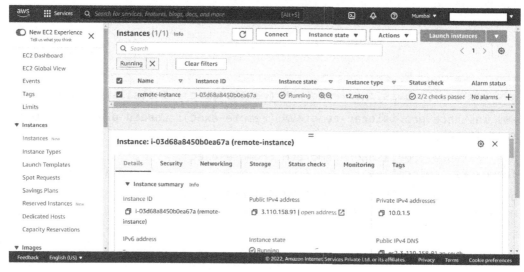

Figure 3.11: *AWS instance created using Terraform*

Note: Connection blocks can be defined within a resource or a provisioner. A connection block within a resource is applicable to all provisioners of that resource, and a connection block within a provisioner block is applicable to that specific provisioner. A provisioner level connection block will override a resource-level connection.

Click on the VPC link to verify VPC **"dev-terraform-vpc"** details in the following image.

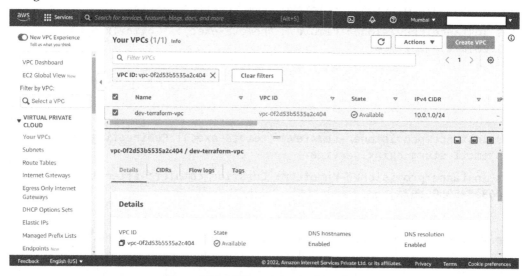

Figure 3.12: *VPC created using Terraform*

Verify the Security Group **"dev-sg"**.

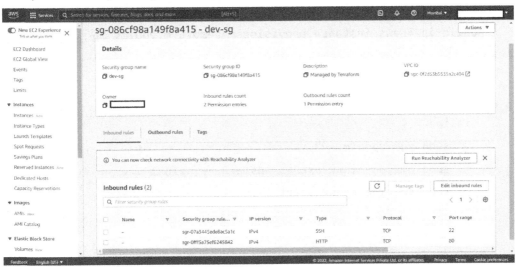

Figure 3.13: Security Group created using Terraform

Verify that Nginx is installed and working.

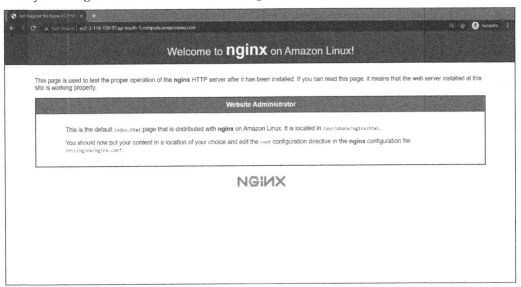

Figure 3.14: Nginx installed on AWS Instance

Additionally, we can use **"null_resource"** to help us configure provisioners that are independent of any resource. In this case, we need to define triggers that help us execute a set of provisioners. Try to use the following code as a reference and perform **null_resource** configuration:

```
resource "null_resource" "prov_null_resource" {
  triggers = {
    public_ip = aws_instance.provisioner-remoteVM.public_ip
  }

  provisioner "remote-exec" {
      inline = [
        "sudo yum update -y",
        "sudo amazon-linux-extras install -y nginx1",
        "sudo service nginx start"
      ]
  }
  connection {
    type     = "ssh"
    host = aws_instance.provisioner-remoteVM.public_ip
    user     = "ec2-user"
    password = ""
    private_key = file("${path.module}/terraform.pem")
  }
}
```

This can be achieved using the packer tool as well.

Try to use packer AMI in Terraform as an exercise. The steps are listed on pages 10-12 of this chapter. Use the following script to create an AMI in AWS, and use Amazon Linux AMI as **source_ami**:

```
{
    "variables": {
      "aws_access_key": "",
      "aws_secret_key": ""
    },
    "builders": [
      {
        "type": "amazon-ebs",
        "access_key": "{{user `aws_access_key`}}",
```

```
        "secret_key": "{{user `aws_secret_key`}}",
        "region": "ap-south-1",
        "source_ami": "ami-0c6615d1e95c98aca",
        "instance_type": "t2.micro",
        "ssh_username": "ec2-user",
        "ami_name": "packer-cf-ami-{{timestamp}}"
    }
  ],
  "provisioners": [
      {
        "type": "shell",
        "inline": [
          "sudo yum update -y",
            "sudo amazon-linux-extras install -y nginx1",
            "sudo service nginx start"
        ]
      }
    ]
}
```

We can specify multiple provisioners within a resource. They are executed in the order of their definition in the Terraform configuration file:

```
# EC2 Instance Configuration
resource "aws_instance" "provisioner-remoteVM" {
  ami                   = "ami-0c6615d1e95c98aca"
  instance_type         = var.instance_type
  key_name              = "terraform"
  vpc_security_group_ids = [aws_security_group.dev_terraform_sg_allow_
ssh_http.id]
  subnet_id = aws_subnet.public_subnet.id
      tags = {
            Name = "remote-instance"
      }
      provisioner "remote-exec" {
        inline = [
```

```
                "sudo yum update -y",

                "sudo amazon-linux-extras install -y nginx1",

                "sudo service nginx start"

            ]

        }

        provisioner "local-exec" {

                command = "echo Instance Type=${self.instance_type},
Instance ID=${self.id}, Public DNS=${self.public_dns}, AMI ID=${self.
ami} >> allinstancedetails"

        }

        connection {

                type      = "ssh"

                host = aws_instance.provisioner-remoteVM.public_ip

                user      = "ec2-user"

                password = ""

                private_key = file("${path.module}/terraform.pem")

        }

}
```

Note: The remote-exec provisioner supports ssh and winrm type connections to
execute a script on a remote resource after creating it.

In the next section, we will look at implementing file provisioners.

Creation-time and destroy-time provisioners

Let's understand the difference between creation-time and destroy-time
provisioners.

Creation-time provisioners:

Let's learn about creation-time provisioners:

- Usually, Terraform provisioners are executed when their parent resources
  are created

- Creation-time provisioners run only during the creation time of resource

- Creation-time provisioners do not run during any other lifecycle
- Their objective is to perform bootstrapping of a resource
- If provisioner creation fails, the resource is marked as tainted

The following is an example of creation-time provisioners:

```
resource "aws_instance" "provisionerTestVM" {
  ami = data.aws_ami.packeramis.id
  instance_type = "t2.micro"

  provisioner "local-exec" {
      command = "echo Instance ID=${self.id}, Public DNS=${self.public_
dns}, AMI ID=${self.ami} >> myinstanceid"
  }
}
```

Destroy-time provisioners:

Now, let's learn about destroy-time provisioners:

- If **when = "destroy"** is available, the provisioner will be executed when the parent resource is destroyed
- If they fail, Terraform will throw an error and rerun the provisioners on the execution of the next terraform apply
- A destroy-time provisioner will not run if parent resource is tainted

Here's an example of :

```
resource "aws_instance" "provisionerTestVM" {
  ami = data.aws_ami.packeramis.id
  instance_type = "t2.micro"

  provisioner "local-exec" {
      when    = "destroy"
    command = "echo Instance ID=${self.id}, Public DNS=${self.public_
dns}, AMI ID=${self.ami} >> myinstanceid"
  }
}
```

Note: If provisioners fail, Terraform apply will also fail. We can use the on_ failure setting to ignore the error and continue with the other operations or raise an error and stop applying with continue or fail values.

```
# EC2 Instance Configuration
resource "aws_instance" "provisioner-remoteVM" {
    .

    .

  provisioner "remote-exec" {
      inline = [
        "sudo yum update -y",
        "sudo amazon-linux-extras install -y Nginx1",
        "sudo service Nginx start"
      ]
      on_failure = continue
  }
  connection {
    .

    .

  }
}
```

Conclusion

In this chapter, we learned that provisioner helps in performing multiple operations on the system where Terraform is running or on a resource created using Terraform. We understood how packer is useful in similar situations. Multiple types of provisioners are available, and it is important to use them wisely as Terraform itself says that provisioners should be used as a last resort.

In the next chapter, we will use Terraform to manage and maintain resources in AWS Cloud.

Points to remember

- Provisioner runs only once at the launch of resource. It is possible that not all actions can be modeled in Terraform's declarative model.
- The local-exec provisioner executes a local script where we are executing Terraform commands. This command or script is not executed on the resource we are creating using Terraform code.

- The remote-exec provisioner provides you with the facility to execute a script on the resource created by Terraform script.

- Destroy-time provisioner executes commands only during a destroy operation. However, it will not run if the resource that contains Destroy-time provisioner is "tainted.

Multiple choice questions

1. **How can you run provisioners that aren't directly associated with a specific resource?**

   a. Bind provisioners with a local_resource and use the Trigger argument to decide when the provisioners should run.

   b. Bind provisioners with a local_remote and use the Trigger argument to decide when the provisioners should run.

   c. Bind provisioners with a null_resource and use the Trigger argument to decide when the provisioners should run.

   d. Bind provisioners with a scheduler.

2. **State True or False: "Provisioner runs only once at the launch of resource."**

   a. True

   b. False

3. **State True or False: "The local-exec provisioner executes command locally after a resource is created."**

   a. True

   b. False

Answers

1. c
2. a
3. a

Questions

1. What are remote-exec provisioners and how they are useful?

2. What are local-exec provisioners and how they are useful?

CHAPTER 4
Automating Infrastructure Deployments in the AWS Using Terraform

In the production environment, we need resources configured in such a way that high availability, disaster recovery, and business continuity is achieved with the highest quality and cost-effectiveness. We need to have auto-scaling and load balancer configured to achieve high availability, and we will configure auto-scaling groups and elastic load balance in this chapter after creating **virtual private cloud**. We will use Jenkins Pipelines later in the book; hence, we will take the Jenkins application to demonstrate EC2 instance creation with Jenkins and to show how to manage JENKINS_HOME in the **Amazon Elastic File System**.

Structure

We will discuss the following topics in this chapter:

- Configuring AWS credentials in Terraform files
- Adding key-pair to an instance
- Creating VPC in AWS
- Creating a security group in AWS
- Creating a packer AMI for Jenkins
- Creating an EC2 instance in AWS

- Creating an EC2 instance using the latest packer AMI

- Creating IAM Role

- Creating an autoscaling group in AWS

- Creating an elastic load balancer in AWS

- Implementing S3 Buckets and Bucket Policies

Objectives

After studying this unit, you should be able to create AMIs using the packer tool. Additionally, you will have used Jenkins application and Nginx webserver to demonstrate VPC, EFS, autoscaling, and load balancer creation and management using Terraform in AWS Cloud.

Creating Jenkins instance using Terraform

We want to create a Jenkins instance available in the AWS environment using Terraform. To accomplish it, we will have to create the following components as well:

- Configure provider

- Availability zones

- Virtual private cloud
  - Public subnet
  - Private subnet
  - Internet gateway
  - Public route table
  - Associate public subnet with public route table
  - Security group
    - Ingress security port 22 (Inbound)
    - Ingress security port 80 (Inbound)
    - Egress security (Outbound)

- Configuration of public key to access instance

- Get latest AMI ID based on filter - Here AMI created using Packer

- Create an Instance using the latest Packer AMI and apply User Data

The "terraform fmt" command automatically updates configurations in the current working directory for readability and consistency. Terraform will print out the names of the files it modified on the console, and no file names will be printed if there is no modification. Use the "terraform validate" command to verify configuration syntactically.

Let's start with creating the **vars.tf** file that will contain different variables used during terraform script execution.

Variables in Terraform files

Define the "**AWS_ACCESS_KEY**" and "**AWS_SECRET_KEY**" variables with default values:

```
# vars.tf
# Input Variables https://www.terraform.io/language/values/variables
variable "aws_access_key" {


}
variable "aws_secret_key" {


}
```

If values are not given, then it will prompt you to add them at the time of executing the **terraform apply** command.

Similarly, configure other variables based on the requirements, such as **instance_type**, **vpc_cidr**, **public_cidr**, **private_cidr**, and so on. We will refer to variables in different files for creating AWS components.

```
variable "apac_region" {
        default = "ap-south-1"
}
variable "cidr_blocks" {
        default = "0.0.0.0/0"
}
#Network Mask - 255.255.255.0 Addresses Available - 256
variable "vpc_cidr" {
        default = "10.0.1.0/24"
}
```

```
variable "public_cidr" {
     default = "10.0.1.0/28"
}
variable "private_cidr" {
     default = "10.0.1.16/28"
}
variable "instance_type" {
     default = "t2.micro"
}
```

Configuring AWS credentials in Terraform files

Create a provider block for AWS and refer to the variables **AWS_ACCESS_KEY** and **AWS_ SECRET _KEY** created in the **vars.tf** file in the preceding section. For more details refer Sensitive section in Chapter 2 Terraform Basics and Configuration.

```
#Providers are a logical abstraction of an upstream API. They help to
understand API interactions and exposing provider resources such AWS,
Google, Azure - https://registry.terraform.io/browse/providers.

provider "aws" {
    region = var.apac_region
}
```

In the next section, we will create VPC in AWS using Terraform script with the name **devVPC.tf**.

Creating VPC in AWS

Now, we will create VPC, subnets, security group, and other components in AWS, as shown in the following figure:

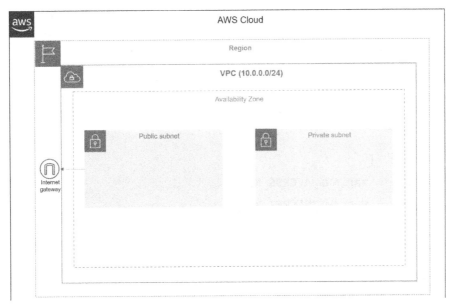

Figure 4.1: *Big Picture - Amazon VPC*

VPC **classless inter-domain routing (CIDR)** will be 10.0.0.0/24 in our case, while **public_cidr** will be 10.0.1.0/28 and **private_cidr** will be 10.0.1.16/28. The following is a description of /28 networks with a network address, host range, and broadcast address.

All 16 of the possible /28 Networks for 10.0.1.*:

Network Address	Usable Host Range	Broadcast Address
10.0.1.0	10.0.1.1 - 10.0.1.14	10.0.1.15
10.0.1.16	10.0.1.17 - 10.0.1.30	10.0.1.31
10.0.1.32	10.0.1.33 - 10.0.1.46	10.0.1.47
10.0.1.48	10.0.1.49 - 10.0.1.62	10.0.1.63
10.0.1.64	10.0.1.65 - 10.0.1.78	10.0.1.79
10.0.1.80	10.0.1.81 - 10.0.1.94	10.0.1.95
10.0.1.96	10.0.1.97 - 10.0.1.110	10.0.1.111
10.0.1.112	10.0.1.113 - 10.0.1.126	10.0.1.127
10.0.1.128	10.0.1.129 - 10.0.1.142	10.0.1.143
10.0.1.144	10.0.1.145 - 10.0.1.158	10.0.1.159
10.0.1.160	10.0.1.161 - 10.0.1.174	10.0.1.175
10.0.1.176	10.0.1.177 - 10.0.1.190	10.0.1.191
10.0.1.192	10.0.1.193 - 10.0.1.206	10.0.1.207
10.0.1.208	10.0.1.209 - 10.0.1.222	10.0.1.223
10.0.1.224	10.0.1.225 - 10.0.1.238	10.0.1.239
10.0.1.240	10.0.1.241 - 10.0.1.254	10.0.1.255

Table 4.1: *Network addresses and ranges*

The following block is a part of the **devVPC.tf** file. It creates VPC, public and private subnet, internet gateway, public route table, and association between public subnet with public route table.

```
# devVPC.tf
# Providers are a logical abstraction of an upstream API. They help to
understand API interactions and exposing provider resources such AWS,
Google, Azure

provider "aws" {
  #access_key = var.AWS_ACCESS_KEY
  #secret_key = var.AWS_SECRET_KEY
  region = var.apac_region
}

# Query all available Availability Zone; we will use specific
availability zone using index - The Availability Zones data source
provides access to the list of AWS Availability Zones which can be
accessed by an AWS account specific to region configured in the provider.
data "aws_availability_zones" "available" {}

# Provides a VPC resource
resource "aws_vpc" "devVPC" {
  cidr_block          = var.vpc_cidr
  enable_dns_hostnames = true
  enable_dns_support   = true

  tags = {
    Name = "dev_terraform_vpc"
  }
}

# Public Subnet - Provides an VPC subnet resource
resource "aws_subnet" "public_subnet" {
  cidr_block              = var.public_cidr
  vpc_id                  = aws_vpc.devVPC.id
  map_public_ip_on_launch = true
  availability_zone        = data.aws_availability_zones.available.
names[1]

  tags = {
```

```
      Name = "dev_terraform_vpc_public_subnet"
  }
}

# Private Subnet - Provides an VPC subnet resource
resource "aws_subnet" "private_subnet" {
  cidr_block            = var.private_cidr
  vpc_id                = aws_vpc.devVPC.id
  map_public_ip_on_launch = false
  availability_zone     = data.aws_availability_zones.available.
names[1]

  tags = {
    Name = "dev_terraform_vpc_private_subnet"
  }
}

#To access EC2 instance inside a Virtual Private Cloud (VPC) we need
an Internet Gateway and a routing table connecting the subnet to the
Internet Gateway
# Creating Internet Gateway
# Provides a resource to create a VPC Internet Gateway
resource "aws_internet_gateway" "igw" {
  vpc_id = aws_vpc.devVPC.id

  tags = {
    Name = "dev_terraform_vpc_igw"
  }
}
# Provides a resource to create a VPC routing table
resource "aws_route_table" "public_route" {
  vpc_id = aws_vpc.devVPC.id

  route {
    cidr_block = var.cidr_blocks
    gateway_id = aws_internet_gateway.igw.id
  }

  tags = {
```

```
        Name = "dev_terraform_vpc_public_route"
    }
}

# Provides a resource to create an association between a Public Route
Table and a Public Subnet
resource "aws_route_table_association" "public_subnet_association" {
    route_table_id = aws_route_table.public_route.id
    subnet_id       = aws_subnet.public_subnet.id
    depends_on      = [aws_route_table.public_route, aws_subnet.public_
subnet]
}
```

In above code, we have **"aws_vpc"**, **"aws_subnet"**, **"aws_internet_gateway"**, **"aws_route_table"** and **"aws_route_table_association"** resource blocks which will create a below resources in AWS:

1. VPC named **"dev_terraform_vpc"**

2. Private subnet named **"dev_terraform_vpc_private_subnet"**

3. Public subnet named **"dev_terraform_vpc_public_subnet"**

4. Internet gateway named **"dev_terraform_vpc_igw"**

5. Route table named **"dev_terraform_vpc_public_route"**

> **Note: Refer to the following resources for more details on resources created in the previous terraform script:**
>
> - Resource: **aws_vpc** https://registry.terraform.io/providers/hashicorp/aws/latest/docs/resources/vpc
>
> - Resource: **aws_internet_gateway** https://registry.terraform.io/providers/hashicorp/aws/latest/docs/resources/internet_gateway
>
> - Resource: **aws_subnet** https://registry.terraform.io/providers/hashicorp/aws/latest/docs/resources/subnet
>
> - Resource: **aws_route_table** https://registry.terraform.io/providers/hashicorp/aws/latest/docs/resources/route_table
>
> - Resource: **aws_route_table_association** https://registry.terraform.io/providers/hashicorp/aws/latest/docs/resources/route_table_association

In the next section, we will create a security group in the same file.

Creating a Security Group in AWS

In this section, we will create security group; ingress security rule for port 22, 80, and 8080; (jenkins) and egress security rule.

Following script have the **"aws_security_group_rule"** resource block to create **"dev_terraform_sg_allow_ssh_http"** security group. The script also have **"aws_security_group_rule"** resource blocks to cree security rules for inbound access to port 22, 80 and 8080 with type **"ingress"**, and outbound access with type as **"egress"**. Add the following script to devVPC.tf file:

```
# Provides a security group resource - https://registry.terraform.io/
providers/hashicorp/aws/latest/docs/resources/security_group

resource "aws_security_group" "sg_allow_ssh_http" {

  vpc_id = aws_vpc.devVPC.id

  name = "dev_terraform_vpc_allow_ssh_http"

  tags = {

    Name = "dev_terraform_sg_allow_ssh_http"

  }

}


# Ingress Security Port 22 (Inbound) - Provides a security group rule
resource (https://registry.terraform.io/providers/hashicorp/aws/latest/
docs/resources/security_group_rule)

resource "aws_security_group_rule" "ssh_ingress_access" {

  from_port         = 22

  protocol          = "tcp"

  security_group_id = aws_security_group.sg_allow_ssh_http.id

  to_port           = 22

  type              = "ingress"

  cidr_blocks       = [var.cidr_blocks]

}


# Ingress Security Port 80 (Inbound)

resource "aws_security_group_rule" "http_ingress_access" {

  from_port         = 80
```

```
    protocol          = "tcp"
    security_group_id = aws_security_group.sg_allow_ssh_http.id
    to_port           = 80
    type              = "ingress"
    cidr_blocks       = [var.cidr_blocks]
}

# Ingress Security Port 8080 (Inbound)
resource "aws_security_group_rule" "http8080_ingress_access" {
    from_port         = 8080
    protocol          = "tcp"
    security_group_id = aws_security_group.sg_allow_ssh_http.id
    to_port           = 8080
    type              = "ingress"
    cidr_blocks       = [var.cidr_blocks]
}

# Egress Security (Outbound)
resource "aws_security_group_rule" "egress_access" {
    from_port         = 0
    protocol          = "-1"
    security_group_id = aws_security_group.sg_allow_ssh_http.id
    to_port           = 0
    type              = "egress"
    cidr_blocks       = [var.cidr_blocks]
}
```

Note: Refer to the following for more details about the resources created in the preceding terraform script:

- Resource: aws_security_group https://registry.terraform.io/providers/ hashicorp/aws/latest/docs/resources/security_group

- Resource: aws_security_group_rule https://registry.terraform.io/ providers/hashicorp/aws/latest/docs/resources/security_group_rule

Now, the entire script – **devVPC.tf** along with **vars.tf** – enables us to create a VPC environment in AWS. Before we execute it with Terraform Plan, the next task is to create Packer AMI that has Jenkins available in it.

Creating a Packer AMI for Jenkins

The following is a script to create an AMI in Amazon EC2 using Packer. AMI will have Java and Jenkins installed in it. Create the **jenkinsami-packer.json** file:

```
# jenkinsami-packer.json
{
    "variables": {
      "aws_access_key": "",
      "aws_secret_key": ""
    },
    "builders": [
      {
        "type": "amazon-ebs",
        "access_key": "{{user `aws_access_key`}}",
        "secret_key": "{{user `aws_secret_key`}}",
        "region": "ap-south-1",
        "source_ami": "ami-0c6615d1e95c98aca",
        "instance_type": "t2.micro",
        "ssh_username": "ec2-user",
        "ami_name": "packer-jenkins-ami-{{timestamp}}"
      }
    ],
    "provisioners": [
      {
        "type": "shell",
        "inline": [
                    "sudo yum update -y",
                    "sudo yum remove java -y",
                    "sudo yum install java-1.8.0-openjdk-devel -y",
                    "sudo wget -O /etc/yum.repos.d/jenkins.repo
http://pkg.jenkins-ci.org/redhat/jenkins.repo",
                    "sudo rpm --import https://pkg.jenkins.io/redhat/
jenkins.io.key",
                    "sudo yum install jenkins -y"
```

```
            ]
        }
    ]
}
```

Note: If the preceding command throws an error, try this commands:

"sudo amazon-linux-extras install epel -y",

"sudo yum update -y",

"sudo wget -O /etc/yum.repos.d/jenkins.repo https://pkg.jenkins.io/red-hat-stable/jenkins.repo",

"sudo rpm --import https://pkg.jenkins.io/redhat-stable/jenkins.io.key",

"sudo yum install jenkins java-1.8.0-openjdk-devel -y"

Let's look at the given steps to create AMI using packer:

1. Execute **packer build -var "aws_access_key=XXXXXXXXXXXXXXXXXXXX"** **-var "aws_secret_key=XXXXXXXXXXXXXXXXXXXX" jenkinsami-packer.json**.

2. Verify the output of packer command execution, and note the AMI ID:

   ```
   amazon-ebs: output will be in this color.

   ==> amazon-ebs: Prevalidating any provided VPC information
   ==> amazon-ebs: Prevalidating AMI Name: packer-jenkins-
   ami-1645559549
       amazon-ebs: Found Image ID: ami-0c6615d1e95c98aca
   ==> amazon-ebs: Creating temporary keypair: packer_62153efe-c67b-
   f924-12b5-efbc976baaba
   ==> amazon-ebs: Creating temporary security group for this
   instance: packer_62153efe-7b0b-9e67-42e3-e62614538968
   ==> amazon-ebs: Authorizing access to port 22 from [0.0.0.0/0] in
   the temporary security groups...
   ==> amazon-ebs: Launching a source AWS instance...
   ==> amazon-ebs: Adding tags to source instance
       amazon-ebs: Adding tag: "Name": "Packer Builder"
       amazon-ebs: Instance ID: i-0d85fc64f6b5dec8c
   ==> amazon-ebs: Waiting for instance (i-0d85fc64f6b5dec8c) to
   become ready...
   ```

```
==> amazon-ebs: Using SSH communicator to connect: 3.110.31.161
==> amazon-ebs: Waiting for SSH to become available...
==> amazon-ebs: Connected to SSH!
    .

    .

    .

    amazon-ebs: --> Running transaction check
    amazon-ebs: ---> Package java-1.8.0-openjdk-devel.x86_64
1:1.8.0.312.b07-1.amzn2.0.2 will be installed
    amazon-ebs: --> Processing Dependency: java-1.8.0-
openjdk(x86-64) = 1:1.8.0.312.b07-1.amzn2.0.2 for .
        .

        .

        .

    amazon-ebs: --> Finished Dependency Resolution
    amazon-ebs:
    amazon-ebs: Dependencies Resolved
    amazon-ebs:
    amazon-ebs: ================================================
==============================
    amazon-ebs: Package                  Arch    Version
Repository  Size
    amazon-ebs: ================================================
==============================
    amazon-ebs: Installing:
    amazon-ebs:  java-1.8.0-openjdk-devel
    .

    .

    .

    amazon-ebs: Installed:
    amazon-ebs:    java-1.8.0-openjdk-devel.x86_64 1:1.8.0.312.
b07-1.amzn2.0.2
    amazon-ebs:
    amazon-ebs: Dependency Installed:
    amazon-ebs:    alsa-lib.x86_64 0:1.1.4.1-2.amzn2
```

.

.

.

```
        amazon-ebs:    xorg-x11-fonts-Type1.noarch 0:7.5-9.amzn2

        amazon-ebs:

        amazon-ebs: Complete!

==> amazon-ebs: --2022-02-22 19:53:37--  http://pkg.jenkins-ci.
org/redhat/jenkins.repo

==> amazon-ebs: Resolving pkg.jenkins-ci.org (pkg.jenkins-ci.
org)... 52.202.51.185

==> amazon-ebs: Connecting to pkg.jenkins-ci.org (pkg.jenkins-ci.
org)|52.202.51.185|:80... connected.

==> amazon-ebs: HTTP request sent, awaiting response... 200 OK

==> amazon-ebs: Length: 71

==> amazon-ebs: Saving to: '/etc/yum.repos.d/jenkins.repo'

==> amazon-ebs:

==> amazon-ebs:        0K
100% 9.83M=0s

==> amazon-ebs:

==> amazon-ebs: 2022-02-22 19:53:38 (9.83 MB/s) - '/etc/yum.
repos.d/jenkins.repo' saved [71/71]

==> amazon-ebs:

    amazon-ebs: Loaded plugins: extras_suggestions, langpacks,
priorities, update-motd

==> amazon-ebs: Existing lock /var/run/yum.pid: another copy is
running as pid 3533.

==> amazon-ebs: Another app is currently holding the yum lock;
waiting for it to exit...

==> amazon-ebs:    The other application is: yum

==> amazon-ebs:        Memory : 157 M RSS (376 MB VSZ)

==> amazon-ebs:        Started: Tue Feb 22 19:53:36 2022 - 00:04 ago

==> amazon-ebs:        State  : Running, pid: 3533

    amazon-ebs: Resolving Dependencies

    amazon-ebs: --> Running transaction check

    amazon-ebs: ---> Package jenkins.noarch 0:2.336-1.1 will be
installed
```

```
    amazon-ebs: --> Finished Dependency Resolution

    amazon-ebs:

    amazon-ebs: Dependencies Resolved

    amazon-ebs:

    amazon-ebs: =================================================
=============================

    amazon-ebs: Package              Arch           Version
Repository      Size

    amazon-ebs: =================================================
=============================

    amazon-ebs: Installing:

    amazon-ebs: jenkins              noarch         2.336-1.1
jenkins         90 M

    amazon-ebs:

    amazon-ebs: Transaction Summary

    amazon-ebs: =================================================
=============================

    amazon-ebs: Install  1 Package

    amazon-ebs:

    amazon-ebs: Total download size: 90 M

    amazon-ebs: Installed size: 90 M

    amazon-ebs: Downloading packages:

    amazon-ebs: Running transaction check

    amazon-ebs: Running transaction test

    amazon-ebs: Transaction test succeeded

    amazon-ebs: Running transaction

    amazon-ebs:   Installing : jenkins-2.336-1.1.noarch
1/1

    amazon-ebs:   Verifying  : jenkins-2.336-1.1.noarch
1/1

    amazon-ebs:

    amazon-ebs: Installed:

    amazon-ebs:   jenkins.noarch 0:2.336-1.1

    amazon-ebs:

    amazon-ebs: Complete!
```

```
==> amazon-ebs: Stopping the source instance...

    amazon-ebs: Stopping instance

==> amazon-ebs: Waiting for the instance to stop...

==> amazon-ebs: Creating AMI packer-jenkins-ami-1645559549 from
instance i-0d85fc64f6b5dec8c

    amazon-ebs: AMI: ami-03a8315958a648860

==> amazon-ebs: Waiting for AMI to become ready...

==> amazon-ebs: Skipping Enable AMI deprecation...

==> amazon-ebs: Terminating the source AWS instance...

==> amazon-ebs: Cleaning up any extra volumes...

==> amazon-ebs: No volumes to clean up, skipping

==> amazon-ebs: Deleting temporary security group...

==> amazon-ebs: Deleting temporary keypair...

Build 'amazon-ebs' finished after 4 minutes 21 seconds.

==> Wait completed after 4 minutes 21 seconds

==> Builds finished. The artifacts of successful builds are:

--> amazon-ebs: AMIs were created:

ap-south-1: ami-03a8315958a648860
```

3. Go to **Network & Security** and click on **Key Pairs** in EC2 dashboard. **Create key pair** and save the PEM file. We will use the PEM (terraform. pem) file to connect to EC2 instance.

Note: Create a key-pair using a third-party tool and import the public key to Amazon EC2 https://docs.aws.amazon.com/AWSEC2/latest/UserGuide/ec2-key-pairs.html#how-to-generate-your-own-key-and-import-it-to-aws.

Let's put it all together in the next section.

Creating an EC2 instance using the latest Packer AMI

The following is the high-level diagram of what we will achieve using Terraform script in the AWS environment:

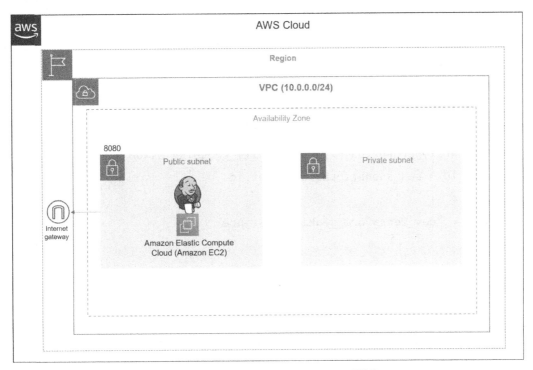

Figure 4.2: *Jenkins instance in Amazon VPC*

Let's look at the steps for creating an EC2 instance using the latest Packer AMI:

Configure Terraform script in a way that the AMI is considered based on the latest creation time using **most_recent = true** in **"aws_ami"** data block. We will create **"dev_terraform_jenkins_instance"** AWS instance using the AMI reference in **"aws_instance"** resource block. Add following terraform script to **devVPC.tf** file:

```
#Get latest AMI ID based on Filter - Here AMI created using Packer
data "aws_ami" "packeramis" {
  owners      = ["10xxxxxxxxxx"] #change the owner ID as per your
account
  most_recent = true

  filter {
    name   = "name"
    values = ["packer-jenkins*"]
  }

}
```

```
#Create an Instance using latest Packer AMI
resource "aws_instance" "jenkins-instance" {
  ami                     = data.aws_ami.packeramis.id
  instance_type           = var.instance_type
  key_name                = "terraform"
  vpc_security_group_ids = [aws_security_group.sg_allow_ssh_http.id]
  subnet_id = aws_subnet.public_subnet.id
  tags = {
    Name = "dev_terraform_jenkins_instance"
  }
}
```

1. We have a complete script now, as follows:

```
#Providers are a logical abstraction of an upstream API. They
help to understand API interactions and exposing provider
resources such AWS, Google, Azure - https://registry.terraform.
io/browse/providers.

provider "aws" {
  #access_key = var.AWS_ACCESS_KEY
  #secret_key = var.AWS_SECRET_KEY
  region = var.apac_region
}

# Query all avilable Availability Zone; we will use specific
availability zone using index - The Availability Zones data
source provides access to the list of AWS Availability Zones
which can be accessed by an AWS account specific to region
configured in the provider.

data "aws_availability_zones" "available" {}

# Provides a VPC resource - https://registry.terraform.io/
providers/hashicorp/aws/latest/docs/resources/vpc

resource "aws_vpc" "devVPC" {
  cidr_block              = var.vpc_cidr
  enable_dns_hostnames = true
  enable_dns_support    = true
```

```
   tags = {
     Name = "dev_terraform_vpc"
   }
}

# Public Subnet - Provides an VPC subnet resource - https://
registry.terraform.io/providers/hashicorp/aws/latest/docs/
resources/subnet.
resource "aws_subnet" "public_subnet" {
  cidr_block              = var.public_cidr
  vpc_id                  = aws_vpc.devVPC.id
  map_public_ip_on_launch = true
  availability_zone       = data.aws_availability_zones.
available.names[1]

   tags = {
     Name = "dev_terraform_vpc_public_subnet"
   }
}

# Private Subnet - Provides an VPC subnet resource - https://
registry.terraform.io/providers/hashicorp/aws/latest/docs/
resources/subnet.
resource "aws_subnet" "private_subnet" {
  cidr_block              = var.private_cidr
  vpc_id                  = aws_vpc.devVPC.id
  map_public_ip_on_launch = false
  availability_zone       = data.aws_availability_zones.
available.names[1]

   tags = {
     Name = "dev_terraform_vpc_private_subnet"
   }
}

#To access EC2 instance inside a Virtual Private Cloud (VPC)
we need an Internet Gateway and a routing table connecting the
subnet to the Internet Gateway
# Creating Internet Gateway
```

```
# Provides a resource to create a VPC Internet Gateway - https://
registry.terraform.io/providers/hashicorp/aws/latest/docs/
resources/internet_gateway.
resource "aws_internet_gateway" "igw" {
  vpc_id = aws_vpc.devVPC.id


  tags = {
    Name = "dev_terraform_vpc_igw"
  }
}
# Provides a resource to create a VPC routing table - https://
registry.terraform.io/providers/hashicorp/aws/latest/docs/
resources/route_table
resource "aws_route_table" "public_route" {
  vpc_id = aws_vpc.devVPC.id

  route {
    cidr_block = var.cidr_blocks
    gateway_id = aws_internet_gateway.igw.id
  }


  tags = {
    Name = "dev_terraform_vpc_public_route"
  }
}

# Provides a resource to create an association between a Public
Route Table and a Public Subnet - https://registry.terraform.
io/providers/hashicorp/aws/latest/docs/resources/route_table_
association
resource "aws_route_table_association" "public_subnet_
association" {
  route_table_id = aws_route_table.public_route.id
  subnet_id      = aws_subnet.public_subnet.id
  depends_on     = [aws_route_table.public_route, aws_subnet.
public_subnet]
}
```

```
# Provides a security group resource - https://registry.
terraform.io/providers/hashicorp/aws/latest/docs/resources/
security_group
resource "aws_security_group" "sg_allow_ssh_http" {
  vpc_id = aws_vpc.devVPC.id
  name = "dev_terraform_vpc_allow_ssh_http"


  tags = {
    Name = "dev_terraform_sg_allow_ssh_http"
  }
}

# Ingress Security Port 22 (Inbound) - Provides a security group
rule resource (https://registry.terraform.io/providers/hashicorp/
aws/latest/docs/resources/security_group_rule)
resource "aws_security_group_rule" "ssh_ingress_access" {
  from_port         = 22
  protocol          = "tcp"
  security_group_id = aws_security_group.sg_allow_ssh_http.id
  to_port           = 22
  type              = "ingress"
  cidr_blocks       = [var.cidr_blocks]
}

# Ingress Security Port 80 (Inbound)
resource "aws_security_group_rule" "http_ingress_access" {
  from_port         = 80
  protocol          = "tcp"
  security_group_id = aws_security_group.sg_allow_ssh_http.id
  to_port           = 80
  type              = "ingress"
  cidr_blocks       = [var.cidr_blocks]
}

# Ingress Security Port 8080 (Inbound)
resource "aws_security_group_rule" "http8080_ingress_access" {
```

```
      from_port        = 8080
      protocol         = "tcp"
      security_group_id = aws_security_group.sg_allow_ssh_http.id
      to_port          = 8080
      type             = "ingress"
      cidr_blocks      = [var.cidr_blocks]
}

# Egress Security (Outbound)
resource "aws_security_group_rule" "egress_access" {
   from_port         = 0
   protocol          = "-1"
   security_group_id = aws_security_group.sg_allow_ssh_http.id
   to_port           = 0
   type              = "egress"
   cidr_blocks       = [var.cidr_blocks]
}

#Get latest AMI ID based on Filter - Here AMI created using
Packer
data "aws_ami" "packeramis" {
   owners      = ["10xxxxxxxxxx "] #change the owner ID as per
your account
   most_recent = true


   filter {
     name    = "name"
     values = ["packer-jenkins*"]
   }


}

#Create an Instance using latest Packer AMI and apply User Data
- This allows instances to be created, updated, and deleted -
https://registry.terraform.io/providers/hashicorp/aws/latest/
docs/resources/instance
resource "aws_instance" "jenkins-instance" {
```

```
    ami                     = data.aws_ami.packeramis.id

    instance_type           = var.instance_type

    key_name                = "terraform"

    vpc_security_group_ids = [aws_security_group.sg_allow_ssh_http.
  id]

    subnet_id = aws_subnet.public_subnet.id

    tags = {

      Name = "dev_terraform_jenkins_instance"

    }

  }
```

2. Observe the **outputs** section: it provides us details about the identifiers of specific resources because we created the **output.tf** file:

```
output "vpc_id" {

  value = aws_vpc.devVPC.id

}
output "aws_internet_gateway" {

  value = aws_internet_gateway.igw.id

}
output "public_subnet" {

  value = aws_subnet.public_subnet.id

}
output "security_group" {

  value = aws_security_group.sg_allow_ssh_http.id

}
output "packer_ami" {

  value = data.aws_ami.packeramis.id

}
output "aws_instance" {

  value = aws_instance.jenkins-instance.id

}
#For more attributes: https://registry.terraform.io/providers/
hashicorp/aws/latest/docs/resources/instance#attributes-reference

output "public_ip" {
```

```
      value = aws_instance.jenkins-instance.public_ip
}
output "public_dns" {
      value = aws_instance.jenkins-instance.public_dns
}
```

3. Let's initialize the backend and provider plugin using the **terraform init** command:

```
F:\1.DevOps\2022\Terraform 1.1.6\Chapter 4\Code>terraform version
Terraform v1.1.6
on windows_amd64
+ provider registry.terraform.io/hashicorp/aws v4.2.0

F:\1.DevOps\2022\Terraform 1.1.6\Chapter 4\Code>terraform init

Initializing the backend...

Initializing provider plugins...
- Reusing previous version of hashicorp/aws from the dependency
lock file
- Installing hashicorp/aws v4.2.0...
- Installed hashicorp/aws v4.2.0 (signed by HashiCorp)

Terraform has been successfully initialized!

You may now begin working with Terraform. Try running "terraform
plan" to see
any changes that are required for your infrastructure. All
Terraform commands
should now work.

If you ever set or change modules or backend configuration for
Terraform,
rerun this command to reinitialize your working directory. If you
forget, other
commands will detect it and remind you to do so if necessary.
```

Note: The "terraform init" command finds the configuration for references to providers and tries to load the required plugins. It finds modules used in the configuration and retrieve them. It also scans the root configuration directory and initializes the selected backend.

5. Once Terraform has been successfully initialized, we will validate the script using the **terraform validate** command.

```
terraform validate

Success! The configuration is valid.
```

6. Execute **terraform plan -out tf.plan** to compare the current configuration to the prior state and note the differences:

```
Plan: 12 to add, 0 to change, 0 to destroy.

Changes to Outputs:
    + aws_instance          = (known after apply)
    + aws_internet_gateway = (known after apply)
    + packer_ami            = "ami-03a8315958a648860"
    + public_dns            = (known after apply)
    + public_ip             = (known after apply)
    + public_subnet         = (known after apply)
    + security_group        = (known after apply)
    + vpc_id                = (known after apply)
```

```
Saved the plan to: tf.plan

To perform exactly these actions, run the following command to apply:
    terraform apply "tf.plan"
```

Note: Use the "terraform show" command to get human-readable output from a state or plan file:

```
terraform plan -out=tf.plan

terraform show -json tf.plan
```

7. Let's execute **terraform apply tf.plan** and verify Jenkins instance creation:

```
F:\1.DevOps\2022\Terraform 1.1.6\Chapter 4\Code>terraform apply
tf.plan
aws_vpc.devVPC: Creating...
aws_vpc.devVPC: Still creating... [10s elapsed]
aws_vpc.devVPC: Creation complete after 11s [id=vpc-
0dfed409e2dc5dcbe]
aws_internet_gateway.igw: Creating...
aws_subnet.public_subnet: Creating...
.


.


.


aws_instance.jenkins-instance: Still creating... [10s elapsed]
aws_instance.jenkins-instance: Still creating... [20s elapsed]
aws_instance.jenkins-instance: Creation complete after 21s [id=i-
0d064b5f5471f3d18]


Apply complete! Resources: 12 added, 0 changed, 0 destroyed.


Outputs:


aws_instance = "i-0d064b5f5471f3d18"
aws_internet_gateway = "igw-035a33f87495eecf8"
packer_ami = "ami-03a8315958a648860"
public_dns = "ec2-13-234-30-144.ap-south-1.compute.amazonaws.com"
public_ip = "13.234.30.144"
public_subnet = "subnet-0e66c8c1968c6d5d3"
security_group = "sg-03825c4fa1d9afded"
vpc_id = "vpc-0dfed409e2dc5dcbe"
```

8. Let's verify the instance using the **ssh** command:

```
ssh -i "terraform.pem" ec2-user@ec2-13-234-30-144.ap-south-1.
compute.amazonaws.com


The authenticity of host 'ec2-13-234-30-144.ap-south-1.compute.
amazonaws.com (13.234.30.144)' can't be established.
```

```
ECDSA key fingerprint is
SHA256:wRX9rwr2RpUsedp3d+hki6M16V8p4IQbQzYHihIDNAY.
```

Are you sure you want to continue connecting (yes/no/ [fingerprint])? yes

Warning: Permanently added 'ec2-13-234-30-144.ap-south-1.compute. amazonaws.com,13.234.30.144' (ECDSA) to the list of known hosts.

```
       __|  __|_  )
       _|  (     /   Amazon Linux 2 AMI
      ___|\___|___|
```

https://aws.amazon.com/amazon-linux-2/

8 package(s) needed for security, out of 14 available

Run "sudo yum update" to apply all updates.

9. Verify Jenkins status:

```
[ec2-user@ip-10-0-1-8 ~]$ sudo -s

[root@ip-10-0-1-8 ec2-user]# service jenkins status
● jenkins.service - Jenkins Continuous Integration Server
   Loaded: loaded (/usr/lib/systemd/system/jenkins.service;
disabled; vendor preset: disabled)
   Active: inactive (dead)

[root@ip-10-0-1-8 ec2-user]# service jenkins start
Starting jenkins (via systemctl):
                                                       [  OK
]
[root@ip-10-0-1-8 ec2-user]#
[root@ip-10-0-1-8 ec2-user]# service jenkins status
● jenkins.service - Jenkins Continuous Integration Server
   Loaded: loaded (/usr/lib/systemd/system/jenkins.service;
disabled; vendor preset: disabled)
   Active: active (running) since Tue 2022-02-22 20:59:02 UTC;
39s ago
 Main PID: 5625 (java)
   CGroup: /system.slice/jenkins.service
           └─5625 /usr/bin/java -Djava.awt.headless=true
```

```
-jar /usr/share/java/jenkins.war --webroot=%C/jenkins/war
--httpPort=8080
```

.

.

.

```
Feb 22 20:59:04 ip-10-0-1-8.ap-south-1.compute.internal
jenkins[5625]: 2022-02-22 20:59:04.335+0000 [id=43]          INFO
h.m.DownloadService$Do...taller

Feb 22 20:59:04 ip-10-0-1-8.ap-south-1.compute.internal
jenkins[5625]: 2022-02-22 20:59:04.335+0000 [id=43]          INFO
hudson.util.Retrier#st...mpt #1

Feb 22 20:59:04 ip-10-0-1-8.ap-south-1.compute.internal
jenkins[5625]: 2022-02-22 20:59:04.339+0000 [id=43]          INFO
hudson.model.AsyncPeri...954 ms

Hint: Some lines were ellipsized, use -l to show in full.

[root@ip-10-0-1-8 ec2-user]#
```

10. Let's visit the public DNS provided in terraform output section with 8080 port: ec2-18-134-180-8.eu-west-2.compute.amazonaws.com:8080:

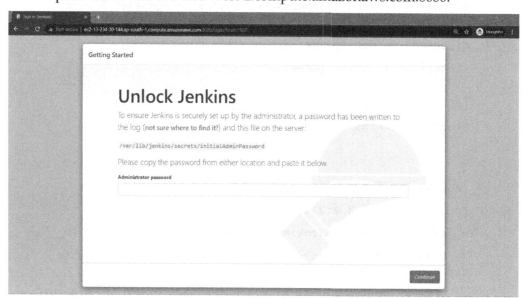

Figure 4.3: Unlock Jenkins

How can you get the password? Connect with the instance using ssh and execute **sudo cat /var/lib/jenkins/secrets/initialAdminPassword**:

```
[root@ip-10-0-1-8 ec2-user]# cat /var/lib/jenkins/secrets/
initialAdminPassword
cb9c4ea996d742878d9e6605aa097cd5
```

11. Copy the password, paste it into the browser, and click on **Continue**. Click on **Installed suggested plugins**, as shown here:

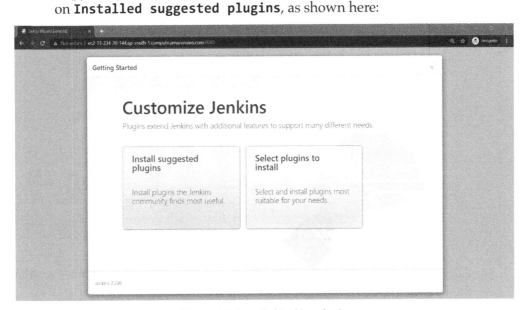

Figure 4.4: Installed Jenkins plugins

12. Wait until the plugin installation completes.

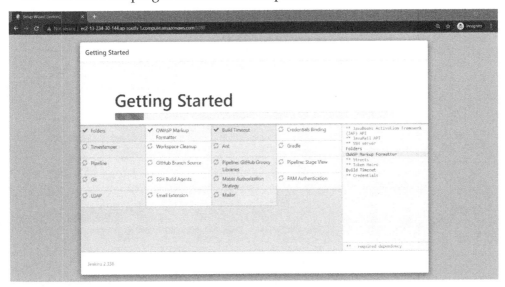

Figure 4.5: Plugin installation

13. Provide admin details and click on **Save and Continue**.

Figure 4.6: Admin user in Jenkins

14. Click on **Save and Finish** on the instance configuration page after verifying the Jenkins URL.

Figure 4.7: Jenkins instance configuration

15. Our Jenkins setup is complete now, and we can start using it. We have successfully created VPC, Subnets, Internet Gateway, Route Table Entry, Security Group, Inbound and Outbound rules, Packer AMI, and Filtered Packer AMI, and we have used them in AWS instance creation using Terraform.

16. Jenkins instance is ready.

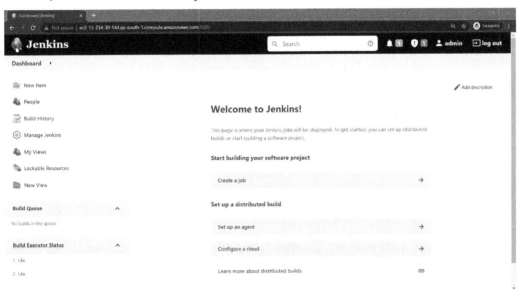

Figure 4.8: *Jenkins home page*

For those who are familiar with Jenkins FreeStyle jobs—just to test that its functionally is working correctly before we move on—as an exercise, create a Freestyle Job and add an ssh step in the build section . Write the **ifconfig** command and execute build.

17. Verify the **Console Output**.

Figure 4.9: *Jenkins Freestyle Job execution*

18. Connect with Jenkins instance using the shell command and execute the **ifconfig** command.

```
$ ssh -i "terraform.pem" ec2-user@ec2-13-234-30-144.ap-south-1.
compute.amazonaws.com
Last login: Tue Feb 22 20:56:40 2022 from 111.119.197.119
```

```
https://aws.amazon.com/amazon-linux-2/
8 package(s) needed for security, out of 14 available
Run "sudo yum update" to apply all updates.
[ec2-user@ip-10-0-1-8 ~]$ ifconfig
eth0: flags=4163<UP,BROADCAST,RUNNING,MULTICAST>  mtu 9001
        inet 10.0.1.8  netmask 255.255.255.240  broadcast
10.0.1.15
        inet6 fe80::86a:d0ff:fea9:5fa0  prefixlen 64  scopeid
0x20<link>
```

```
        ether 0a:6a:d0:a9:5f:a0  txqueuelen 1000   (Ethernet)
        RX packets 66321  bytes 94019428 (89.6 MiB)
        RX errors 0  dropped 0  overruns 0  frame 0
        TX packets 28357  bytes 7714612 (7.3 MiB)
        TX errors 0  dropped 0 overruns 0  carrier 0  collisions
0

lo: flags=73<UP,LOOPBACK,RUNNING>  mtu 65536
        inet 127.0.0.1  netmask 255.0.0.0
        inet6 ::1  prefixlen 128  scopeid 0x10<host>
        loop  txqueuelen 1000  (Local Loopback)
        RX packets 0  bytes 0 (0.0 B)
        RX errors 0  dropped 0  overruns 0  frame 0
        TX packets 0  bytes 0 (0.0 B)
        TX errors 0  dropped 0 overruns 0  carrier 0  collisions
0
```

You will get similar output as both commands are executed on the same instance. Jenkins agent is the same machine where Jenkins is installed. Explore Jenkins agent details as an exercise and understand the difference between master and Jenkins Agent.

Userdata in AWS

Let's consider a scenario where the Jenkins instance created using Terraform has crashed or terminated for some reason.

We can execute terraform apply; then, our Jenkins instance will be available, but all our configuration and jobs/pipelines will be lost as the **JENKINS_HOME** directory will be lost as well.

How do we ensure that you can persist state with the **JENKINS_HOME** directory?

We can use the **Elastic File System** (**EFS**) to store the **JENKINS_HOME** directory and mount it in the EC2 instance every time the instance is created.

We can use following script to build a packer AMI:

```
{
    "variables": {
        "aws_access_key": "",
```

```
        "aws_secret_key": ""
    },
    "builders": [
      {
        "type": "amazon-ebs",
        "access_key": "{{user `aws_access_key`}}",
        "secret_key": "{{user `aws_secret_key`}}",
        "region": "ap-south-1",
        "source_ami": "ami-0c6615d1e95c98aca",
        "instance_type": "t2.micro",
        "ssh_username": "ec2-user",
        "ami_name": "packer-jenkins-ami-{{timestamp}}"
      }
    ],
    "provisioners": [
        {
          "type": "shell",
          "inline": [
                    "sudo yum update -y",
                    "sudo yum remove java -y",
                    "sudo yum install java-1.8.0-openjdk-devel -y",
                    "echo pwd",
                    "sudo wget https://get.jenkins.io/war-
stable/2.319.3/jenkins.war",
                    "sudo chmod 755 jenkins.war"
          ]
        }
    ]
}
```

Execute **packer build -var** "aws_access_key=XXXXXXXXXXXXXXXXXXXX" **-var** "aws_secret_key=XXXXXXXXXXXXXXXXXXXX" Jenkins-generic-ami-packer.json

The following is the Terraform script that creates security group for EFS. Note the name of security group that we will refer to in the upcoming script:

```
# Ingress Security Port 2049 (Inbound)
resource "aws_security_group" "sg_jenkins_efs" {
  name_prefix = "sg_jenkins_efs"
  vpc_id      = aws_vpc.devVPC.id

  ingress {
    from_port = 2049
    to_port   = 2049
    protocol  = "tcp"

    cidr_blocks = [var.cidr_blocks]
  }
}
```

Let's create EFS by clicking on the **Create file system** button on the Elastic File System service page in AWS Console.

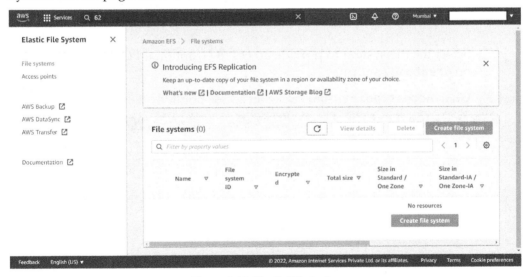

Figure 4.10: *Elastic File System*

> **Note: Terraform no longer manages a specific resource if you remove it from the terraform state file. It doesn't make any difference to the existing resource, but it won't be managed by Terraform further.**

Let's create a file system.

1. Select VPC created using Terraform script.

2. Select **Regional** under **Availability and Durability** and click on **Create**.

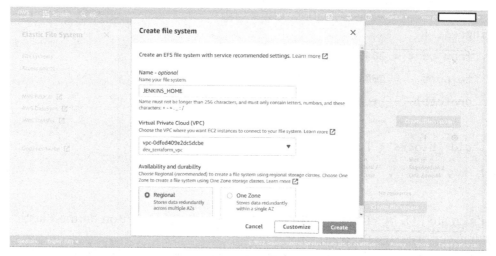

Figure 4.11: Create file system

Select the file system to provide access to (+ optional POSIX settings). Click on **Create** to confirm.

3. Go to **Access points** and create an access point.

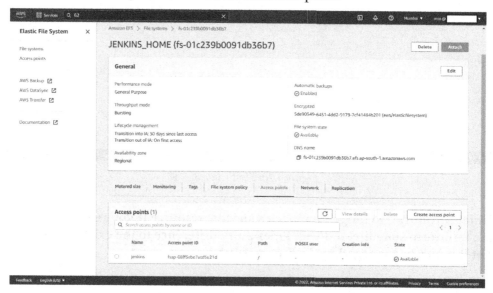

Figure 4.12: EFS Access points

4. Click on **Network** and create mount target that has **Subnet ID** and **Security Group** created using Terraform script.

Figure 4.13: *EFS Network*

5. Create EC2 instance using Terraform and once instance is available, execute the following commands in EC2 instance:

```
#!/bin/bash
sudo yum update -y
sudo yum install nfs-utils
#Mount EFS Mount Access point
sudo mkdir /root/.jenkins
sudo mount -t nfs4 -o nfsvers=4.1,rsize=1048576,w-size=1048576,hard,timeo=600,retrans=2,noresvport fs-0d6103dd-6806be283.efs.ap-south-1.amazonaws.com:/ /root/.jenkins
```

6. Execute **sudo java -jar jenkins.war**.

7. Now that we've got the new EFS mounted for Jenkins state, let's go back to the web browser and create a new job and folder.

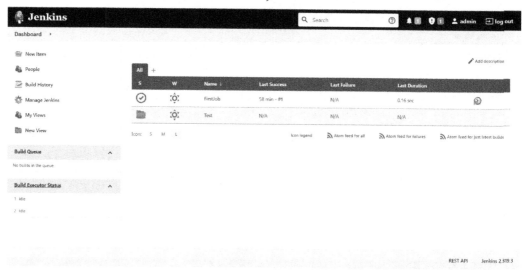

Figure 4.14: Folder in Jenkins

Note: Going back to the browser and accessing EC2 public DNS name + 8080 will take you back to the "Unlock Jenkins" page. Go back through the steps and obtain the admin password, install the suggested plugins, and create an admin account. (This is because we changed the JENKINS_HOME directory to EFS and restarted.)

It might take some time to sync data in EFS. Delete EC2 instance after some time. Create another instance and execute above commands to mount EFS file system and start the Jenkins. You will have same jobs, folders and configuration available.

Consider a new scenario where we have already created VPC and other resources, and now we also want to create EFS using Terraform code.

Remember that, in the earlier steps, we manually created EFS and configured it manually. Now, we will do it with Terraform to understand it better.

We have already created a security group and are aware of subnet ID.

The following code will create EFS, access point, and mount target:

```
# Provides an Elastic File System (EFS) File System resource to
store JENKINS_HOME

resource "aws_efs_file_system" "jenkins_home_efs" {
```

```
    creation_token = "jenkins_home_efs"


  tags = {
    Name = "dev_terraform_jenkins_home"
  }
}
# Provides an Elastic File System (EFS) mount target
resource "aws_efs_mount_target" "jenkins_mount_target" {
  file_system_id   = aws_efs_file_system.jenkins_home_efs.id
  subnet_id        = aws_subnet.public_subnet.id
  security_groups = [aws_security_group.sg_jenkins_efs.id]
}


# Provides an Elastic File System (EFS) access point
resource "aws_efs_access_point" "jenkins_access_point" {
  file_system_id = aws_efs_file_system.jenkins_home_efs.id

  root_directory {
      path = "/"
  }
}
```

Execute Terraform plan+apply. Note EFS and use it in the following userdata file.

Note: Visit https://docs.aws.amazon.com/efs/latest/ug/mounting-fs.html to get more details on Mounting EFS file systems.

Mounting on Amazon EC2 with a DNS name https://docs.aws.amazon.com/efs/latest/ug/mounting-fs-mount-cmd-dns-name.html

Mounting with an IP address https://docs.aws.amazon.com/efs/latest/ug/mounting-fs-mount-cmd-ip-addr.html

Mounting EFS file systems from another account or VPC https://docs.aws.amazon.com/efs/latest/ug/efs-mount-helper.html# manage-fs-access-vpc-peering

Using the amazon-efs-utils Tools https://docs.aws.amazon.com/efs/latest/ug/using-amazon-efs-utils.html

Now, the important thing is to mount a file system when a new EC2 instance launches. We can use the userdata file to store the commands that we executed in the EC2 instance to mount EFS, as shown below.

Create a **userdata.tpl** file with the following content and change the file system ID in the **userdata.tpl** file to the new file system created by terraform script above:

```
#!/bin/bash
sudo yum update -y
sudo yum install nfs-utils
#Mount EFS Mount Access point
sudo mkdir /root/.jenkins
sudo mount -t nfs4 -o nfsvers=4.1,rsize=1048576,w-
size=1048576,hard,timeo=600,retrans=2,noresvport fs-0d6103dd-
6806be283.efs.ap-south-1.amazonaws.com:/ /root/.jenkins
```

Add the **template_file** block in the main terraform file and provide its reference in instance configuration, as follows:

```
#The template_file data source usually loaded from an external
file.
data "template_file" "init" {
  template = file("${path.module}/userdata.tpl")
}


#Create an Instance using latest Packer AMI and apply User Data
- This allows instances to be created, updated, and deleted -
https://registry.terraform.io/providers/hashicorp/aws/latest/
docs/resources/instance
resource "aws_instance" "jenkins-instance" {
  ami                    = data.aws_ami.packeramis.id
  instance_type          = var.instance_type
  key_name               = "terraform"
  vpc_security_group_ids = [aws_security_group.sg_allow_ssh_http.
id]
  subnet_id = aws_subnet.public_subnet.id
  user_data = data.template_file.init.rendered
  tags = {
    Name = "dev_terraform_jenkins_instance"
```

```
    }
}
```

Execute terraform apply in code where we have a script to create security group, userdata, EFS, EFS access point, and EFS mount target.

Execute **sudo java -jar jenkins.war.** Verify EFS Dashboard after some time when size is increased.

Delete the EC2 Instance.

Execute terraform apply.

It will create AWS Instance with Jenkins. Execute **sudo java -jar jenkins. war** in the instance. Visit URL with port 8080.

Create one freestyle job for verification.

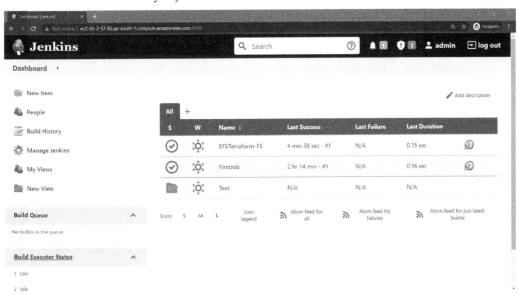

Figure 4.15: Jenkins home page with sample job

8. Now, delete the AWS instance from AWS console and execute terraform apply again.

   The new instance will be created.

```
F:\1.DevOps\2022\Terraform 1.1.6\Chapter 4\Code>terraform plan
-out tf.plan

aws_vpc.devVPC: Refreshing state... [id=vpc-0dfed409e2dc5dcbe]

aws_efs_file_system.jenkins_home_efs: Refreshing state... [id=fs-
0d6103dd6806be283]
```

```
aws_efs_access_point.jenkins_access_point: Refreshing state...
[id=fsap-0e02d20864091fbe3]
.

.

.

Plan: 1 to add, 0 to change, 0 to destroy.


Changes to Outputs:
  ~ aws_instance = "i-0f5b10fe120e7d25f" -> (known after apply)
  ~ public_dns   = "ec2-65-2-57-82.ap-south-1.compute.amazonaws.
com" -> (known after apply)
  ~ public_ip    = "65.2.57.82" -> (known after apply)
```

```
Saved the plan to: tf.plan


To perform exactly these actions, run the following command to
apply:
    terraform apply "tf.plan"

F:\1.DevOps\2022\Terraform 1.1.6\Chapter 4\Code>terraform apply
tf.plan
aws_instance.jenkins-instance: Creating...
aws_instance.jenkins-instance: Still creating... [10s elapsed]
aws_instance.jenkins-instance: Still creating... [20s elapsed]
aws_instance.jenkins-instance: Still creating... [30s elapsed]
aws_instance.jenkins-instance: Creation complete after 32s [id=i-
011f9833063e3ec04]

Apply complete! Resources: 1 added, 0 changed, 0 destroyed.

Outputs:

aws_instance = "i-011f9833063e3ec04"
aws_internet_gateway = "igw-035a33f87495eecf8"
packer_ami = "ami-078a0cdb2b95ae65c"
```

```
public_dns = "ec2-15-207-114-242.ap-south-1.compute.amazonaws.
com"

public_ip = "15.207.114.242"

public_subnet = "subnet-0e66c8c1968c6d5d3"

security_group = "sg-03825c4fa1d9afded"

vpc_id = "vpc-0dfed409e2dc5dcbe"
```

9. It will create AWS Instance with Jenkins. Execute **sudo java -jar jenkins. war** in the instance. Observe that the IP address changes after successful execution of terraform script. Visit **http://ec2-15-207-114-242.ap-south-1. compute.amazonaws.com:8080/**, and you will not have to configure Jenkins. This is because the new EC2 instance is mounted to an EFS created earlier, and Jenkins was already configured. Jenkins Job, which was created earlier, is also available.

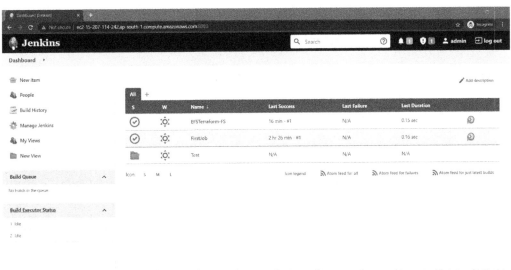

Figure 4.16: *Jenkins home page after the restoration of EC2 instance*

10. Go to EFS, verify both the EFSes, and observe changes in their size over time.

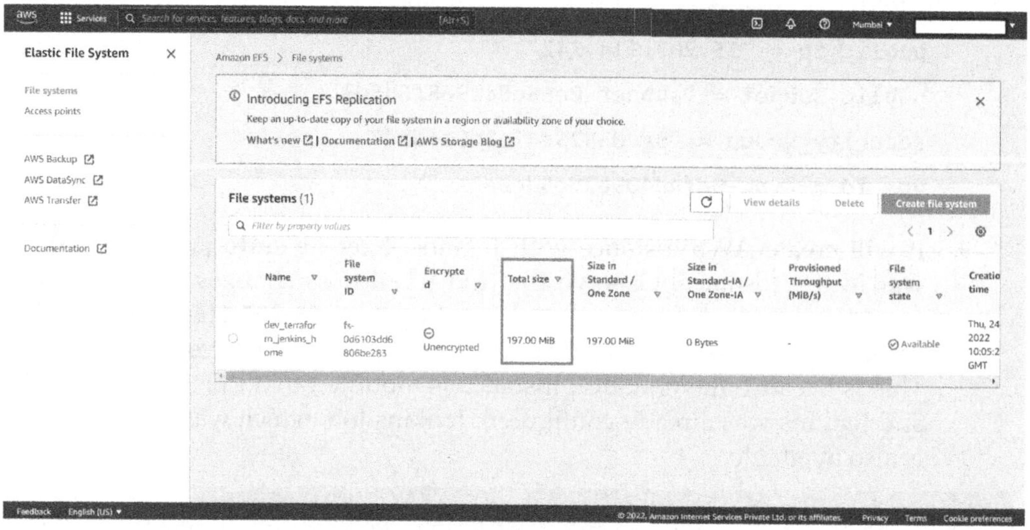

Figure 4.17: JENKINS_HOME in EFS

We will discuss Identity and Access Management in the next section.

Identity and Access Management

Identity and access management service enables authentication and authorization. With permissions and policies, we can control what actions can be performed by a user and which resources can be affected. We can attach a policy to a user or a group, who will be allowed to perform actions that are available in the policy on resources that are indicated in the policy.

Here, we will create jenkins-administrators and jenkins-users groups, create multiple users, and assign those users to specific groups. Create **iam.tf** and execute it with the **terraform apply** command.

```
# Jenkins administrators - IAM group
resource "aws_iam_group" "jenkins-administrators" {
  name = "jenkins-administrators"
}
# Jenkins users - IAM group
resource "aws_iam_group" "jenkins-users" {
  name = "jenkins-users"
}
```

```
# jenkins-admin - IAM user
resource "aws_iam_user" "jenkins-admin" {
  name = "jenkins-admin"
}
# jenkins-dev-team - IAM user
resource "aws_iam_user" "jenkins-dev-team" {
  name = "jenkins-dev-team"
}
# jenkins-test-team - IAM user
resource "aws_iam_user" "jenkins-test-team" {
  name = "jenkins-test-team"
}


#admin user assignment to group - manage IAM Group membership for IAM
Users
resource "aws_iam_group_membership" "jenkins-administrators-users-
assignment" {
  name = "jekins-administrators-users"
  users = [
    aws_iam_user.jenkins-admin.id
  ]
  group = aws_iam_group.jenkins-administrators.id
}
#non-admin users assignment to group
resource "aws_iam_group_membership" "jenkins-users-assignment" {
  name = "jekins-users"
  users = [
    aws_iam_user.jenkins-dev-team.id,
    aws_iam_user.jenkins-test-team.id
  ]
  group = aws_iam_group.jenkins-users.id
}
```

Note: Refer to the following for more details about the resources created in the above terraform script:

- Resource: `aws_iam_group` https://registry.terraform.io/providers/hashicorp/aws/latest/docs/resources/iam_group

- Resource: `aws_iam_group_membership` https://registry.terraform.io/providers/hashicorp/aws/latest/docs/resources/iam_group_membership

- Resource: `aws_iam_group_policy` https://registry.terraform.io/providers/hashicorp/aws/latest/docs/resources/iam_group_policy

- Resource: `aws_iam_user` https://registry.terraform.io/providers/hashicorp/aws/latest/docs/resources/iam_user

- Resource: `aws_iam_user_group_membership` https://registry.terraform.io/providers/hashicorp/aws/latest/docs/resources/iam_user_group_membership

Let's verify users in AWS management console.

1. Go to Identity and **Access management** section in AWS Portal and click on **Users**. Verify users created by the script is available or not.

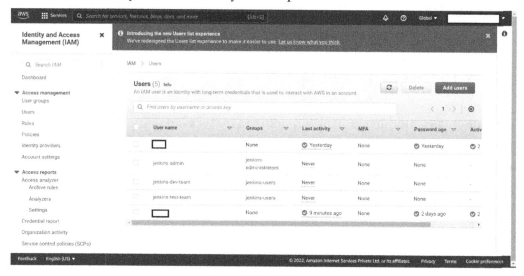

Figure 4.18: IAM users

2. Go to the **Identity and Access Management** section in AWS Portal and click on **User Groups**. Confirm whether the groups created by the script are available.

   Permissions are not defined yet.

Figure 4.19: IAM user groups

3. Let's try to attach different policies to different user groups using the following resource blocks in **iam.tf**:

```
# Attaches a Managed IAM Policy to user(s), role(s), and/or
group(s)-https://registry.terraform.io/providers/hashicorp/aws/
latest/docs/resources/iam_policy_attachment

resource "aws_iam_policy_attachment" "jenkins-administrators-
policy" {

   name       = "jenkins-administrators-policy"

   groups     = [aws_iam_group.jenkins-administrators.id]

   policy_arn = "arn:aws:iam::aws:policy/AdministratorAccess"

}

resource "aws_iam_policy_attachment" "jenkins-users-policy" {

   name       = "jenkins-users-policy"

   groups     = [aws_iam_group.jenkins-users.id]

   policy_arn = "arn:aws:iam::aws:policy/AmazonEC2ReadOnlyAccess"

}
```

4. Execute the **terraform validate** and **terraform apply** commands and verify the Identity and Access Management section again.

Permissions are defined now.

Figure 4.20: Permissions attached to user groups

5. Go to the specific user group and click on the **Permissions** tab. Verify the **Policy Name** as given in the terraform script, and verify the attached entities to the policy, that is, two users should be available in the group.

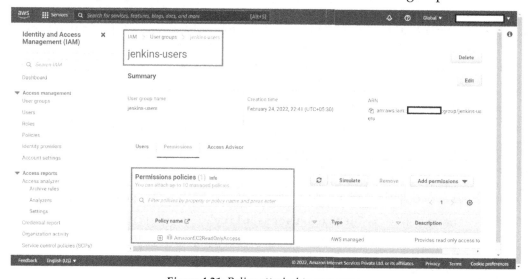

Figure 4.21: Policy attached to user group

6. Configure the console password to one of the users available in the Jenkins-users group. This group has a policy attached that provides read-only access to EC2 resources.

7. Log in with the user available in the Jenkins-users group and try to terminate the EC2 instance.

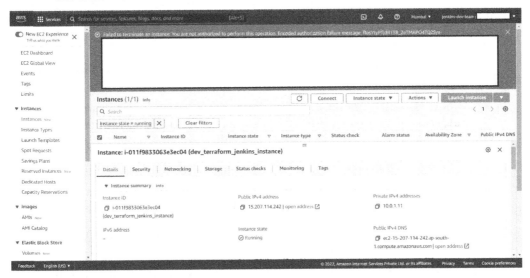

Figure 4.22: Authorization failure based on policy attached to a user group

8. Only authorized actions can be performed on the resources based on a policy with IAM services.

Note: Refer to the following for more details on IAM:

- **What is IAM? https://docs.aws.amazon.com/IAM/latest/UserGuide/introduction.html**

- **Controlling access to AWS resources using policies https://docs.aws.amazon.com/IAM/latest/UserGuide/access_controlling.html**

- **Policies and permissions in IAM https://docs.aws.amazon.com/IAM/latest/UserGuide/access_policies.html**

- **IAM Identities (users, user groups, and roles) https://docs.aws.amazon.com/IAM/latest/UserGuide/id.html**

We will discuss auto scaling and load balancing in the next section.

Auto scaling and load balancing

Amazon EC2 Auto Scaling helps make available a correct number of Amazon EC2 instances to manage the load for your application based on CPU utilization and other metrics. An auto scaling group is a collection of EC2 instances. We can configure a minimum and a maximum number of instances in each auto scaling group. Auto-scaling policies help us launch and terminate EC2 instances as per configured metrics.

> **Note: Refer to the following for more details on Auto Scaling and Elastic Load Balancing in AWS:**
>
> - **What is Amazon EC2 Auto Scaling? https://docs.aws.amazon.com/ autoscaling/ec2/userguide/what-is-amazon-ec2-auto-scaling.html**
>
> - **Tutorial: Set up a scaled and load-balanced application https://docs.aws. amazon.com/autoscaling/ec2/userguide/as-register-lbs-with-asg.html**
>
> - **Launch configurations https://docs.aws.amazon.com/autoscaling/ec2/ userguide/LaunchConfiguration.html**
>
> - **Auto Scaling groups https://docs.aws.amazon.com/autoscaling/ec2/ userguide/AutoScalingGroup.html**
>
> - **What is Elastic Load Balancing? https://docs.aws.amazon.com/ elasticloadbalancing/latest/userguide/what-is-load-balancing.html**
>
> - **How Elastic Load Balancing works https://docs.aws.amazon.com/ elasticloadbalancing/latest/userguide/how-elastic-load-balancing-works.html**
>
> - **Getting started with Elastic Load Balancing https://docs.aws.amazon. com/elasticloadbalancing/latest/userguide/load-balancer-getting-started.html**
>
> - **Migrate your Classic Load Balancer https://docs.aws.amazon.com/ elasticloadbalancing/latest/userguide/migrate-classic-load-balancer. html**
>
> - **Attaching a load balancer to your Auto Scaling group https://docs.aws. amazon.com/autoscaling/ec2/userguide/attach-load-balancer-asg.html**

We will create an Auto Scaling group of EC2 instances that have Nginx installed. Amazon Linux 2 supports Nginx 1.12.2, so we will create Nginx AMI using Packer to create EC2 instances.

Create the JSON file as detailed below (for eu-west-2) and execute **packer build**. Verify provisioners sections on how we are installing Nginx packages in AMI. Refer to *Chapter 3, Terraform Provisioners,* for more details on provisioners.

The following is a script to create an AMI in Amazon EC2 using Packer.

```json
{
    "variables": {
      "aws_access_key": "",
      "aws_secret_key": ""
    },
    "builders": [
      {
        "type": "amazon-ebs",
        "access_key": "{{user `aws_access_key`}}",
        "secret_key": "{{user `aws_secret_key`}}",
        "region": "ap-south-1",
        "source_ami": "ami-0c6615d1e95c98aca",
        "instance_type": "t2.micro",
        "ssh_username": "ec2-user",
        "ami_name": "packer-cf-ami-{{timestamp}}"
      }
    ],
    "provisioners": [
      {
        "type": "shell",
        "inline": [
          "sudo yum update -y",
                "sudo amazon-linux-extras install -y nginx1.12",
                "sudo service nginx start"
        ]
      }
    ]
}
```

Let's create launch configuration using the **aws_launch_configuration** resource and autoscaling group using **aws_autoscaling_group**.

We will also define policies to scale resources up and down. Create **autoscaling. tf** and copy the following script into it:

```
resource "aws_launch_configuration" "nginx_launch_config" {
  image_id        = data.aws_ami.packeramis.id
  instance_type   = var.instance_type
  security_groups = [aws_security_group.sg_allow_ssh_http.id]

  user_data = data.template_file.init.rendered

  lifecycle {
    create_before_destroy = true
  }

}

resource "aws_autoscaling_group" "nginx_autoscaling_group" {
  launch_configuration = aws_launch_configuration.nginx_launch_config.id
  vpc_zone_identifier  = [aws_subnet.public_subnet.id]

  health_check_type    = "ELB"

  min_size = 2
  max_size = 5
  load_balancers           = [aws_elb.nginx-elb.id]
  tag {
    key                 = "Name"
    value               = "dev_terraform_nginx_instance_asg"
    propagate_at_launch = true
  }
}

resource "aws_autoscaling_policy" "nginx_cpu_policy_scaleup" {
    name = "nginx_cpu_policy_scaleup"
    autoscaling_group_name = aws_autoscaling_group.nginx_autoscaling_
group.name
    adjustment_type = "ChangeInCapacity"
    scaling_adjustment = 1
    cooldown = "120"
```

```
}

resource "aws_autoscaling_policy" "nginx_cpu_policy_scaledown" {
    name = "nginx_cpu_policy_scaledown"
    autoscaling_group_name = aws_autoscaling_group.nginx_autoscaling_
group.name
    adjustment_type = "ChangeInCapacity"
    scaling_adjustment = -1
    cooldown = "120"
}
```

Execute the **terraform validate** and **terraform apply** commands. Here, we are assuming that the entire VPC is ready and available or part of the same execution. We have provided **vpc_zone_identifier = [aws_subnet.public_subnet.id]** in nginx-autoscaling-group, which is a public subnet created using terraform script to create VPC.

Let's verify Auto Scaling group in AWS Management Console.

1. Go to the AWS portal and verify the Auto Scaling group in EC2 services based on the configuration in terraform script.

2. Verify the desired and minimum capacity and other details based on the terraform script.

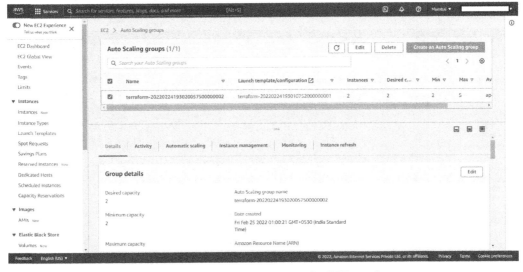

Figure 4.23: Auto scaling groups in AWS portal

3. Click on the **Instance management** tab in the bottom pane and verify the instances available in the Auto Scaling group.

These are the instances created using the configuration available in the launch configuration, where we have mentioned the image ID, instance type, security group, and other details.

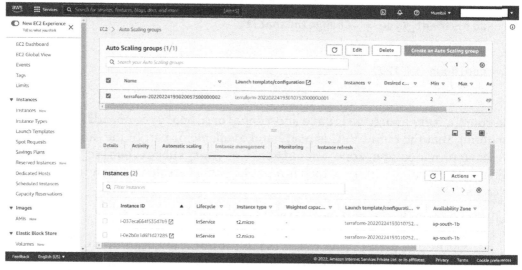

Figure 4.24: Instance management in autoscaling group

4. Click on the launch configuration column link for a specific Auto Scaling group, and verify the launch configuration details.

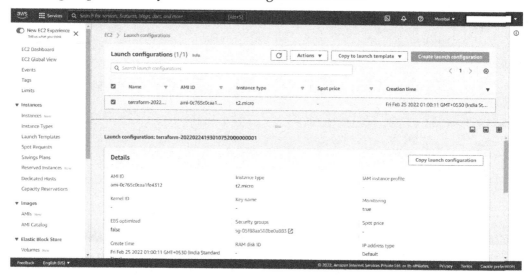

Figure 4.25: Launch configuration for Autoscaling group

5. Scroll down to the bottom pane and click on the userdata link to verify that the same userdata mentioned in our script is available.

Figure 4.26: User data in launch configuration

6. Let's verify that everything is working fine. Select the first instance available and copy the IP address.

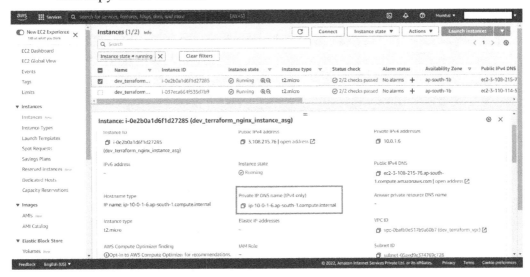

Figure 4.27: First instance in Auto Scaling group

7. Paste the IP address in the browser and visit the Nginx page. Note the hostname that we have added in the Nginx index page using userdata.

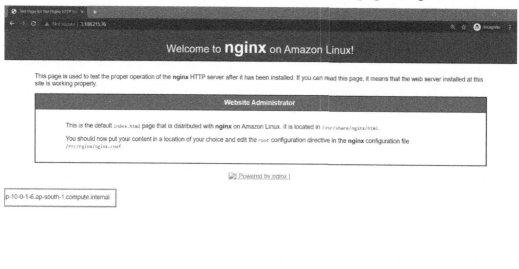

Figure 4.28: Nginx page – Instance 1

8. Select the second instance available and copy the IP address.

Figure 4.29: Second instance in Auto Scaling group

9. Paste the IP address in the browser and visit the Nginx page. Note the hostname that we have added in the Nginx index page using userdata.

Note: The "terraform state" command is used for advanced state management and to modify the Terraform state.

Figure 4.30: Nginx page - Instance 2

10. We have used Nginx just to demonstrate the difference. You can also try tomcat or any specific application to verify Autoscaling and ELB demonstrations.

Note: Choosing the Right Load Balancer on Amazon: AWS Application Load Balancer vs. NGINX Open source vs. NGINX Plus
https://www.nginx.com/blog/aws-alb-vs-nginx-plus

Let's create Elastic load balancer and configure listener as well as health check details. Create a file named **elb.tf**:

```
# Elastic Load Balancer resource, also known as a Classic Load
Balancer - https://registry.terraform.io/providers/hashicorp/aws/
latest/docs/resources/elb

resource "aws_elb" "nginx-elb" {
    name = "nginx-elb"
    subnets = [aws_subnet.public_subnet.id]
    security_groups = [aws_security_group.sg_allow_ssh_http.id]
    listener {
        instance_port    = 80
        instance_protocol = "http"
```

```
        lb_port          = 80
        lb_protocol      = "http"
    }
    health_check {
        healthy_threshold    = 2
        unhealthy_threshold  = 2
        timeout              = 2
        target               = "HTTP:80/"
        interval             = 30
    }
    tags = {
        Name = "nginx_elb"
    }
}
```

Add `load_balancers = [aws_elb.nginx-elb.id]` in the auto scaling group that we created earlier to link ELB and Auto scaling group:

```
resource "aws_autoscaling_group" "nginx_autoscaling_group" {
  launch_configuration = aws_launch_configuration.nginx_launch_
config.id
  vpc_zone_identifier  = [aws_subnet.public_subnet.id]

  health_check_type    = "ELB"

  min_size = 2
  max_size = 5
  load_balancers               = [aws_elb.nginx-elb.id]
  tag {
    key                = "Name"
    value              = "dev_terraform_nginx_instance_asg"
    propagate_at_launch = true
  }
}
```

12. Execute **terraform plan** + Apply to set up the ELB and assign it to the Auto Scaling group. Go to the AWS portal and go to EC2 services. Click on **Load Balancers**. Verify the newly created load balancer in the AWS portal.

Note: The "terraform state mv" command can be used to move resources in a completely different state file. This command will output a backup copy of the state before saving any changes; we cannot disable backup.

Note the DNS name for the load balancer.

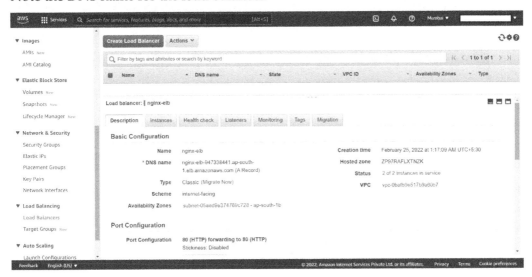

Figure 4.31: AWS load balancers

13. Click on the instances and verify that both instances are from the Auto Scaling group and are in service. Wait for some time if they are out of service. You need to make changes in **Listeners** or **Health check** to troubleshoot issues of instances being out of service.

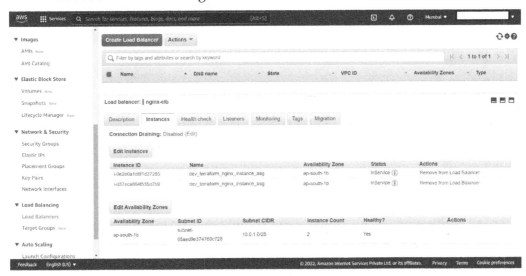

Figure 4.32: ELB instances

14. Visit the DNS name multiple times in the browser, and verify the hostname on the page until it changes. It could take a few requests/attempts.

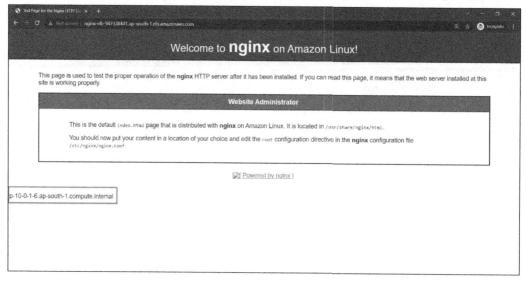

Figure 4.33: Autoscaling group instance serving ELB

15. Note the hostname in the following screenshot as well:

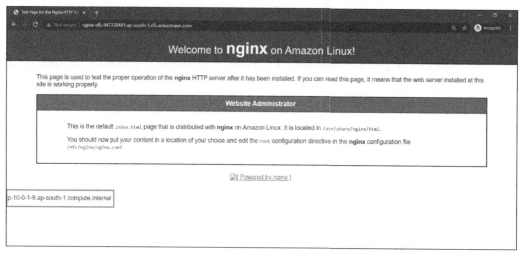

Figure 4.34: Autoscaling group instance serving ELB

Once all verification and execution is completed, we need to remove the dependency of EFS (that we created manually). Once the Access Point and EFS are deleted in the AWS Console UI, use the terraform destroy command to deprovision the infrastructure created using Terraform in AWS Cloud.

Note: Refer to the following for more details about the resources created in the above Terraform script:

- Resource: `aws_launch_configuration` https://registry.terraform.io/ providers/hashicorp/aws/latest/docs/resources/launch_configuration

- Resource: `aws_autoscaling_group` https://registry.terraform.io/ providers/hashicorp/aws/latest/docs/resources/autoscaling_group

- Resource: `aws_autoscaling_policy` https://registry.terraform.io/ providers/hashicorp/aws/latest/docs/resources/autoscaling_policy

- Resource: `aws_elb` https://registry.terraform.io/providers/hashicorp/ aws/latest/docs/resources/elb

Implementing S3 buckets and bucket policies

After all these examples and exercises, we've only scratched the surface of what Terraform can do to help automate and provision services in AWS. If you want to explore more, it's worth implementing other AWS services like S3 and bucket policies. You can also try to create a Bastion Host with Terraform based on EC2 instance creation using Terraform.

Conclusion

In this chapter, we used the packer tool to create Jenkins and Nginx AMIs. We created VPC, subnets, security groups, inbound and outbound rules, route tables, associations, EFS to store **JENKINS_HOME** data, Auto scaling groups, Elastic load balancers, and much more using Terraform script.

In the next chapter, we will use Terraform to manage and maintain resources in the Microsoft Azure cloud.

Points to remember

- The "terraform state" command is used for advanced state management and to modify the Terraform state.

- The "terraform state mv" command can be used to move resources in a completely different state file.

Multiple choice questions

1. Which command is used to automatically updates configurations in the current working directory for readability and consistency?

    a. "terraform validate" command

    b. "terraform fmt" command

    c. "terraform style" command

    d. "terraform plan" command

2. Which command is used to find the configuration for references to providers and tries to load the required plugins?

    a. "terraform plan" command

    b. "terraform validate" command

    c. "terraform init" command

    d. "terraform apply" command

Answers

1. b

2. c

Questions

1. Explain Auto scaling groups in AWS.

2. Explain Elastic Load Balancers in AWS.

3. What is the importance of Security Groups in AWS?

CHAPTER 5
Automating Infrastructure Deployments in Azure Using Terraform

Microsoft Azure is another popular provider that offers more than 200 product and services. Terraform cloud also supports integration with Azure cloud provider so that we can create and update the services and infrastructure in Azure.

We will look into how to create how to use Azure cloud shell for executing Terraform configurations. In this chapter, we will first configure and initialize the Terraform configuration with the Azure Provider. We will then create different resources, like resource groups, virtual network, virtual machine, and virtual machine scale set. We will also update the packer configuration created in the previous chapter to create **azure machine image** (**AMI**) and then create a virtual machine from it. Additionally, we will create a small production-like infrastructure to deploy Java web application and spring boot application.

Structure

We will discuss the following topics in this chapter:

- Using Terraform in Azure Cloud Shell
- Creating resource group in Azure
- Creating virtual network in Azure

- Creating network security groups in Azure

- Creating virtual machine in Azure

- Creating a virtual machine instance with Packer AMI

- Configuring Azure virtual machine scale set

- Creating and deploying an App Services for Java web application

- Managing Application Insights for Java web application

- Creating a database for Java web application

- Creating Application Gateway for Java web application

- Creating Traffic Manager for multi-location web app

- Managing Azure Spring Cloud

Objectives

After studying this chapter, you should be able to create a virtual machine with Packer AMI, and you should be able to create and configure network and subnets. You should also be able to create Azure machine scale set, Azure App Service, and Azure Spring Cloud. Additionally, you should be able to make you infrastructure services secure with Application Gateway WAF and highly available with Traffic Manager.

Using Terraform in Azure Cloud Shell

Let's understand how useful Azure Cloud Shell is! Azure provides authenticated shell access to Azure virtually anywhere from a browser. This shell provides you with two types of command line environment: Bash and PowerShell. Most of the commonly used tools are pre-installed in this environment, so Terraform is already installed and ready to use.

Let's get started with learning how to use this shell:

1. Open a browser and use the link **https://shell.Azure.com** to access the Azure Shell.

2. You will be navigated to the Sign in page, as shown in the following image. Enter your login details for the Azure account you created in *Chapter 1, Setting Up Environment*.

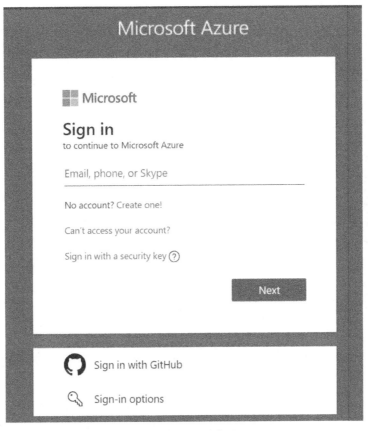

Figure 5.1: Azure login

3. Provide your password on the next page.

Figure 5.2: Enter password

4. Then, enter the code from the message you received on your registered mobile number in the next page, as illustrated in the following screenshot:

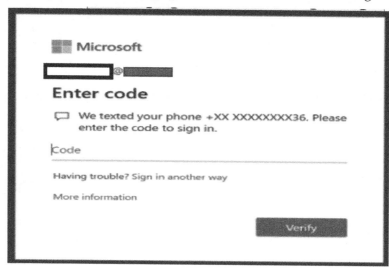

Figure 5.3: Enter the code sent by SMS

5. Now, you should be logged in to Azure Shell, which looks as shown in the following screenshot:

Figure 5.4: Azure Shell

6. You are ready to use the Azure Cloud Shell now. Some tools are already installed in this shell environment; let's run the following command to get the installed version:

```
terraform -v
```

7. Let's create the **main.tf** Terraform file with vi editor using the following code:

```
# Azure Provider source and version being used
terraform {
  required_providers {
    azurerm = {
      source  = "hashicorp/azurerm"
      version = "=2.46.0"
    }
  }
}
# Configure the Microsoft Azure Provider
provider "azurerm" {
  features {}
}
```

Then, save the file.

8. Run the **terraform init** command to initialize the Terraform environment for Azure cloud provider. Once you run this command, you will get logs, as in the following screenshot:

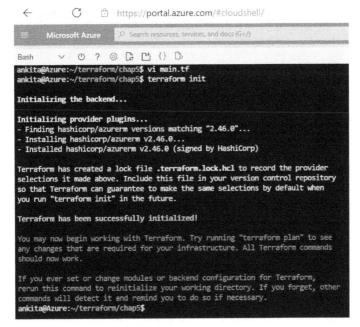

Figure 5.5: Terraform Init in Azure Shell

9. You are now ready to write Terraform code for your infrastructure provisioning.

This is how you can directly use Terraform in Azure Cloud Shell.

In the next section, you will learn how to create resources in Azure with help of Terraform infrastructure code.

Creating resource group in Azure

In all the previous chapters, you have looked at the configuration and infrastructure creation for AWS cloud. You have not seen the provider configuration for Azure cloud provider, so you first need to configure Terraform provider for Azure before starting with actual resource creation.

Configuring Terraform provider for Azure cloud

In the earlier chapters, you have seen the configuration of AWS provider for creating infrastructure in AWS using the access key and secret key. Similarly, you can use Azure Provider for creating infrastructure in Microsoft Azure.

Before starting with configuration for Azure Provider in Terraform, you need a way to authenticate the account.

Authenticating to Azure

Terraform supports multiple ways for authenticating to Azure. Here are the different methods for authentication to Azure:

- The Azure CLI
- Managed service identity
- A service principal and a client certificate
- A service principal and a client secret

However, you will be using the last method for all our recipes in this book, as Terraform recommends using either managed service identity or service principal to use this non-interactively (i.e., in CI servers), which you will be doing in the upcoming chapters. Authenticating with CLI should be used only when working locally.

Now, let's perform the following steps to authenticate Azure using a service principal and a client secret:

1. **Creating a service principal**

   A service principal is an application that provides us with details and authentication tokens like the **client_id**, **client_secret**, and **tenant_id** fields needed by Terraform. This application is created within Azure Active Directory.

   We will also require **subscription_id**, which can be fetched from Azure account details.

   There are two methods for creating a service principal:

   - Using CLI commands
   - Using Azure Portal

   We will do this using CLI commands. Here's the step-by-step process to create service principal in Azure:

   1. We will be performing all the steps in Azure CLI, i.e., Azure shell portal, so navigate to following link in your browser:

      https://shell.azure.com/

      Log in to the account that you want to use for Azure Shell.

   2. On Azure Shell, you will get output for successful login in JSON format, as shown in the following screenshot:

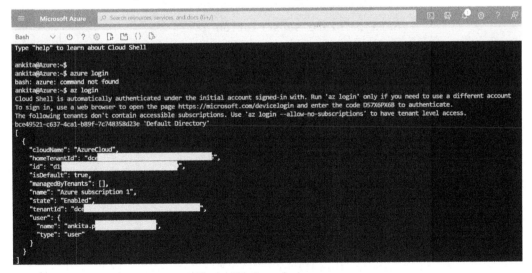

Figure 5.6: Azure login success

   You will find all the details for that user in the JSON output in the previous image, like tenantId, name of subscription, subscription ID, etc.

You can proceed with the creation of service principal once you are logged in on Azure CLI.

Note: If you're using the China, German, or US Government Azure Clouds, you'll need to configure the Azure CLI to work with that Cloud before running the 'az login' command. You can do this by running the following command:

```
az cloud set --name AzureChinaCloud|AzureGermanCloud|AzureUSGovernment
```

3. If you have multiple subscriptions and want to get list of all subscriptions and their details, you can use the following command:

```
az account list
```

You will get output the output in JSON format, as in the following logs. There is currently only one subscription in this account, so there is only one entry in the following JSON output:

```
[
  {
    "cloudName": "AzureCloud",
    "homeTenantId": "xxxx-xxxx-xxxx-xxxx-xxxxxxxxxxxx",
    "id": "d1f3xxxx-xxxx-xxxx-xxxx-xxxxxxxxxxxx",
    "isDefault": true,
    "managedByTenants": [],
    "name": "Azure subscription 1",
    "state": "Enabled",
    "tenantId": "dcecxxxx-xxxx-xxxx-xxxx-xxxxxxxxxxxx",
    "user": {
      "name": "xxxx@xxx.xxx",
      "type": "user"
    }
  }
]
```

In the previous log, you get details for each subscription, as follows:

- **Subscription ID**: In JSON, subscription ID is in the value of key "id". This ID is required to identify a specific subscription.

- **Name of subscription**: In the above-mentioned JSON output, the value is in the key "name".

- **User details**: User-related details, like name and type, are in the object value of key "user".

These details, mainly the subscription ID, can be used in configuration in the following steps.

4. If you want to use a specific subscription, you can set it to the use of subscription ID (i.e., the value of key "id") from the previous JSON output. This can be done with the following command:

```
az account set --subscription="SUBSCRIPTION_ID"
```

You just need to replace "**SUBSCRIPTION_ID**" with the value from the JSON, for example, with something like "**d1f3xxxx-xxxx-xxxx-xxxx-xxxxxxxxxxxx**".

After using this command, you will be using the correct subscription where you want to create service principal and your infrastructure via Terraform.

5. Now, we are ready to create service principal. Service principal from CLI can be created with the following command:

```
az ad sp create-for-rbac --role="Contributor" --scopes="/
subscriptions/SUBSCRIPTION_ID"
```

This command will give you the following output

```
{
    "appId": "557bxxxx-xxxx-xxxx-xxxx-xxxxxxxxxxxx",
    "displayName": "azure-cli-2021-06-04-13-57-13",
    "name": "http://azure-cli-2021-06-04-13-57-13",
    "password": "n.xxxxxxx-xxxxxx-xxxxxxxxxxxxxxx",
    "tenant": "dcecxxxx-xxxx-xxxx-xxxx-xxxxxxxxxxxx"
}
```

This output has values that can be mapped to the following Terraform variables:

- "**appId**" defined above is the "**client_id**" in Terraform variables
- "**password**" defined above is the "**client_secret**" in Terraform variables
- "**tenant**" defined above is the "**tenant_id**" in Terraform variables

Note: You should store the password at a secure location because it will not be available for access later.

6. To test that these values work with Azure authentication, you can execute the following command to log in with the service principal that you just created:

```
az login --service-principal -u CLIENT_ID -p CLIENT_SECRET
--tenant TENANT_ID
```

Replace the value of **CLIENT_ID**, **CLIENT_SECRET**, and **TENANT_ID** from the output in previous step 2.

The output of this login will use the service principal that you created.

```
Cloud Shell is automatically authenticated under the initial
account signed-in with. Run 'az login' only if you need to
use a different account
[
  {
    "cloudName": "AzureCloud",
    "homeTenantId": "dcecxxxx-xxxx-xxxx-xxxx-xxxxxxxxxxxx",
    "id": "d1f3xxxx-xxxx-xxxx-xxxx-xxxxxxxxxxxx",
    "isDefault": true,
    "managedByTenants": [],
    "name": "Azure subscription 1",
    "state": "Enabled",
    "tenantId": "dcecxxxx-xxxx-xxxx-xxxx-xxxxxxxxxxxx",
    "user": {
      "name": "557bxxxx-xxxx-xxxx-xxxx-xxxxxxxxxxxx",
      "type": "servicePrincipal"
    }
  }
]
```

In this output, you will recognize that the user is "**557bxxxx-xxxx-xxxx-xxxx-xxxxxxxxxxxx**", which is the service principal you created. All the other details related to subscription should be familiar, as seen earlier in the user login method.

7. Once logged-in, you should be able to get the list of all available **vm** sizes for specific Azure regions, for example, for the **germanywestcentral** region. Use the following command to verify the login:

```
az vm list-sizes --location germanywestcentral
```

You should now get a list of all the available vm sizes, and you are good to go with Terraform configuration with this service principal you created.

2. **Configuring the service principal in Terraform**

We can configure the service principal in Terraform in two ways:

- By setting environment variables
- By setting Terraform properties in Terraform configuration

Let's take a look at both of them.

- **Setting environment variables**

    You are using Azure shell here in our Terraform implementation, so you can use the following export commands to set the **ARM_CLIENT_ID**, **ARM_CLIENT_SECRET**, **ARM_SUBSCRIPTION_ID**, and **ARM_TENANT_ID** variables.

    ```
    export ARM_CLIENT_ID="<SERVICE-PRINCIPAL-CLIENT_ID >"

    export ARM_CLIENT_SECRET="<SERVICE-PRINCIPAL-PASSWORD>"

    export ARM_SUBSCRIPTION_ID="<AZURE-SUBSCRIPTION_ID>"

    export ARM_TENANT_ID="<AZURE-TENANT_ID>"
    ```

- **Setting Terraform properties in Terraform configuration**

    First, you need to create and define the value of all the variables that you would require. It is recommended to use separate files for all the variables that you use in our infrastructure as code. For this entire chapter, we will use this method of authentication with Terraform variables instead of environment variables.

    Let's first create a **vars.tf** file with the variables defined as follows:

    ```
    # vars.tf

    variable "client_secret" {
        description = "Enter your CLient Secret. Please make
    sure you do not store the value of your client secret in the
    SCM repository"
    }
    variable "client_id" {
    ```

```
    description = "Your client Id."
    default = "<SERVICE-PRINCIPAL-CLIENT_ID>"
}
variable "subscription_id" {
    description = "Your subscription id."
    default = "<AZURE-SUBSCRIPTION_ID>"
}
variable "tenant_id" {
    description = "Your tenant id."
    default = "<AZURE-TENANT_ID>"
}
```

Replace the values of **<SERVICE-PRINCIPAL-CLIENT_ID>**, **<AZURE-SUBSCRIPTION_ID>**, and **<AZURE-TENANT_ID>** with actual value in the above **vars.tf** file. The default value for **client_secret** is not set because this is the password and should not be added to any file that is stored in the repository and accessible. So, value for **client_secret** can be passed from the command line during actual execution or during CI pipeline from a secure location.

Now, add the following code to the already created **main.tf** file to store all the configurations related to provider and add the following code to start with authentication for Azure Provider:

```
# main.tf
# Configure the Microsoft Azure Provider
provider "azurerm" {
  features {}
  subscription_id = var.subscription_id
  client_id       = var.client_id
  client_secret   = var.client_secret
  tenant_id       = var.tenant_id
}
```

This is how you can pass the Azure service principal authentication details to Terraform. In the next point, we will configure the Azure Provider in Terraform file.

3. **Azure Provider configuration in Terraform**

   We have already created a **main.tf** file and added configurations for Terraform to use Azure Provider for creating the infrastructure using the **required_providers** block inside terraform{} block, as shown in the following code (*refer to point 7 under the Using Terraform in Azure Cloud Shell topic*).

   We have already seen a similar block for the configuration of AWS provider block. Your entire **main.tf** file should be like the following code:

```
# main.tf
# Azure Provider source and version being used
terraform {
  required_providers {
    azurerm = {
      source  = "hashicorp/azurerm"
      version = "=2.46.0"
    }
  }
}


# Configure the Microsoft Azure Provider
provider "azurerm" {
  features {}
  subscription_id = var.subscription_id
  client_id       = var.client_id
  client_secret   = var.client_secret
  tenant_id       = var.tenant_id
}
```

4. After this configuration, you need to perform the Terraform initialization step with the **terraform init** command.

   After successful output, you are ready to create a resource group in Azure, but you still need to make the configuration ready to be used in the CI pipeline. To do this, you also need to store and manage the state files from Terraform in storage.

Configuring Terraform state management

You will use standard backend in Terraform configurations for storing the states from Terraform execution; in the case of Azure, the standard backend is called **azurerm**. You need to perform the following steps to set up backend using **azurerm**.

1. **Configuring a storage account**

   You need to create a Azure Storage account before using Azure Storage as a backend.

   The storage account can be created with the following methods:

   - Azure portal

   - PowerShell

   - Azure CLI or

   - Terraform itself

   We will use Azure CLI; you have a bash script that can be used to execute the Azure CLI commands to create the storage account in Azure. Here is the sample bash script **create_azure_storage.sh** to configure the storage account with the Azure CLI:

```bash
#!/bin/bash
# create_azure_storage.sh
RESOURCE_GROUP_NAME=tstate
STORAGE_ACCOUNT_NAME=tstate$RANDOM
CONTAINER_NAME=tstate

# Create resource group
az group create --name $RESOURCE_GROUP_NAME --location
germanywestcentral

# Create storage account
az storage account create --resource-group $RESOURCE_GROUP_NAME
--name $STORAGE_ACCOUNT_NAME --sku Standard_LRS --encryption-
services blob

# Get storage account key
ACCOUNT_KEY=$(az storage account keys list --resource-group
$RESOURCE_GROUP_NAME --account-name $STORAGE_ACCOUNT_NAME --query
'[0].value' -o tsv)
```

```
# Create blob container
az storage container create --name $CONTAINER_NAME --account-name
$STORAGE_ACCOUNT_NAME --account-key $ACCOUNT_KEY

echo "storage_account_name: $STORAGE_ACCOUNT_NAME"
echo "container_name: $CONTAINER_NAME"
echo "access_key: $ACCOUNT_KEY"
```

The above-mentioned script creates the resource group for storage account with the name **tstate** (refer to the Azure CLI command on line 8) in location **germanywestcentral**. Then, it creates storage account with the name **tstate$RANDOM** in the resource group you created (refer to the Azure CLI command on line 11). On line 14, it creates an access key for the storage account **tstate$RANDOM** and assigns the key value to the **ACCOUNT_KEY** variable. This key is required to create a container using CLI command on line 17 in the script. Then, the output should print all the required details, like storage account name, container name, and access key, so you have added the echo command to get this value. Save this file and then execute the following command:

bash ./create_azure_storage.sh

The output of this command is as follows:

```
{
  "id": "/subscriptions/d1f3xxxx-xxxx-xxxx-xxxx-xxxxxxxxxxxx/
resourceGroups/tstate",
  "location": "germanywestcentral",
  "managedBy": null,
  "name": "tstate",
  "properties": {
    "provisioningState": "Succeeded"
  },
  "tags": null,
  "type": "Microsoft.Resources/resourceGroups"
}
{
  "accessTier": "Hot",
  .
  .
```

```
.

      "requireInfrastructureEncryption": null,
      "services": {
        "blob": {
          "enabled": true,
          "keyType": "Account",
          "lastEnabledTime": "2021-06-06T17:25:37.510358+00:00"
        },
        "file": {
          "enabled": true,
          "keyType": "Account",
          "lastEnabledTime": "2021-06-06T17:25:37.510358+00:00"
        },
        "queue": null,
        "table": null
      }
    },
    "extendedLocation": null,
    "failoverInProgress": null,
    "geoReplicationStats": null,
    "id": "/subscriptions/d1f3xxxx-xxxx-xxxx-xxxx-xxxxxxxxxxxx/
resourceGroups/tstate/providers/Microsoft.Storage/
storageAccounts/tstate12345",
    "identity": null,
    "isHnsEnabled": null,
    "keyCreationTime": {
      "key1": "2021-06-06T17:25:37.510358+00:00",
      "key2": "2021-06-06T17:25:37.510358+00:00"
    },

.


.

  "networkRuleSet": {
    "bypass": "AzureServices",
    "defaultAction": "Allow",
```

```
    "ipRules": [],
    "resourceAccessRules": null,
    "virtualNetworkRules": []
  },
  "primaryEndpoints": {
    "blob": "https://tstate12345.blob.core.windows.net/",

        .


    "web": "https://tstate12345.z1.web.core.windows.net/"
  },
  "primaryLocation": "germanywestcentral",

        .


  "sku": {
    "name": "Standard_LRS",
    "tier": "Standard"
  },
  "statusOfPrimary": "available",
  "statusOfSecondary": null,
  "tags": {},
  "type": "Microsoft.Storage/storageAccounts"
}
{
  "created": true
}
storage_account_name: tstate12345
container_name: tstate
access_key: <Some-value-of-access-key>
```

Now, you can use the **tstate12345** storage account and the **tstate** container for our Terraform state management, so note the storage account name, container name, and access key from the log output. These values are needed in the next step when you configure the remote state in Terraform configuration.

2. **Configuring Terraform to use the Storage account**

    Now that you have all the following details related to storage account, you can configure Terraform state backend:

    - **storage_account_name**: This is the name of the Azure Storage account that you created in the previous step.

    - **container_name**: This is the name of the blob container that you created in the previous step.

    - **key**: This is name of the state file to be stored in the blob storage you created.

    - **access_key**: This is storage access key from the above output.

    Each of these properties can be specified in Terraform configuration, but it is recommended not to add the **access_key** to be stored in Terraform configuration file. We recommend defining the environment variable for this **access_key**, as follows:

    ```
    export ARM_ACCESS_KEY=<storage access key>
    ```

    An alternative, and the best way, is to store the value of this key in Azure Key Vault and set the environment variable using the following command:

    ```
    export ARM_ACCESS_KEY=$(az keyvault secret show --name terraform-backend-key --vault-name myKeyVault --query value -o tsv)
    ```

    Now, add the following **azurerm** configuration to the Terraform **main.tf** file to configure the **backend** block in the **terraform** block:

    ```
    backend "azurerm" {

        resource_group_name     = "tstate"

        storage_account_name    = "tstate16782"

        container_name          = "tstate"

        key                     = "terraform.tfstate"

    }
    ```

    Here, you added **resource_group_name**, **storage_account_name**, **container_name**, and key to the backend configuration of **azurerm**. After adding this block, **main.tf** will be updated as follows:

    ```
    # main.tf

    # Azure Provider source and version being used
    ```

```
terraform {
  backend "azurerm" {
    resource_group_name    = "tstate"
    storage_account_name   = "tstate16782"
    container_name         = "tstate"
    key                    = "terraform.tfstate"
  }
  required_providers {
    azurerm = {
      source  = "hashicorp/azurerm"
      version = "=2.46.0"
    }
  }
}


# Configure the Microsoft Azure Provider
provider "azurerm" {
  features {}
  subscription_id = var.subscription_id
  client_id       = var.client_id
  client_secret   = var.client_secret
  tenant_id       = var.tenant_id
}
```

You have made changes to Terraform configuration; you need to execute the **terraform init** command again to apply the changes of backend. You will get the following output after executing this command. This log should tell you the update for your backend and configured backend as **azurerm**:

```
ankita@Azure:~/Chapter-5$ terraform init

Initializing the backend...

.

.

Terraform has been successfully initialized!
```

We have now successfully configured the **azurerm** backend, and all the new Terraform states should be managed and stored in this storage account.

Run the **terraform apply** command to get your state file in your storage account, and you will now find the first state file in the Azure Storage blob.

This Azure blob storage locks the state automatically before write operation for the state in storage container. You can view this in Azure Portal in your account if you want to verify it.

Now, you are all set to start infrastructure creation using Terraform on Azure cloud where multiple people working on your infrastructure code.

Let's create a resource group in Azure with the following steps:

1. Add the following code block at the end of the **main.tf** file that you created in the earlier setup and save it:

```
# main.tf

# Create a resource group

resource "azurerm_resource_group" "test-rg" {

  name     = "test-resources"

  location = "West Europe"

}
```

This code block will create an Azure Resource group with the name **test-rg** in location West Europe.

2. Now, execute the **terraform plan** command to check what is going to be added. You will get the following log:

```
ankita@Azure:~/Chapter-5$ terraform plan
var.client_secret
   Enter your CLient Secret. Please make sure you do not store the
value of your client secret in the SCM repository

   Enter a value: xxxxxxxxxxxxxxxxxxxxxxxxxxxxx

Terraform used the selected providers to generate the following
execution plan. Resource actions are indicated with the following
symbols:
  + create

Terraform will perform the following actions:

  # azurerm_resource_group.test-rg will be created
  + resource "azurerm_resource_group" "test-rg" {
```

```
   + id       = (known after apply)
   + location = "westeurope"
   + name     = "test-resources"
 }

Plan: 1 to add, 0 to change, 0 to destroy.
```

Note: You didn't use the -out option to save this plan, so Terraform can't guarantee to take exactly these actions if you run "terraform apply" now.

You can see that Terraform plans to add one resource group in the Azure cloud provider that we provided.

3. You now have to execute **terraform apply** to create the Azure resource group. You will get a long log, as follows:

ankita@Azure:~/Chapter-5$ terraform apply

var.client_secret

Enter your CLient Secret. Please make sure you do not store the value of your client secret in the SCM repository

Enter a value: xxxxxxxxxxxxxxxxxxxxxxxxxxxxxxxxxxxx

Terraform used the selected providers to generate the following execution plan. Resource actions are indicated with the following symbols:

+ create

Terraform will perform the following actions:

```
  # azurerm_resource_group.test-rg will be created
  + resource "azurerm_resource_group" "test-rg" {
      + id       = (known after apply)
      + location = "westeurope"
      + name     = "test-resources"
    }
```

Plan: 1 to add, 0 to change, 0 to destroy.

Do you want to perform these actions?

Terraform will perform the actions described above.

```
Only 'yes' will be accepted to approve.

Enter a value: yes

azurerm_resource_group.test-rg: Creating...
azurerm_resource_group.test-rg: Creation complete after 0s
[id=/subscriptions/d1f3xxxx-xxxx-xxxx-xxxx-xxxxxxxxxxxx/
resourceGroups/test-resources]

Apply complete! Resources: 1 added, 0 changed, 0 destroyed.
```

Hooray! You have successfully created a resources group in Azure.

4. Verify the creation of resource group in Azure portal. You should be able to find the resource group you created with the name as in the following figure:

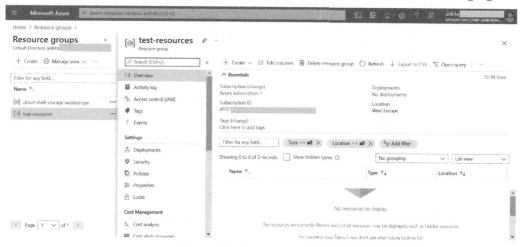

Figure 5.7: Azure resource group

We will use the same resource group for all our infrastructure creation in this chapter. We are now ready to do more recipes using this basic configuration.

Creating a virtual network in Azure

We will create a sample infrastructure, as shown in the following figure:

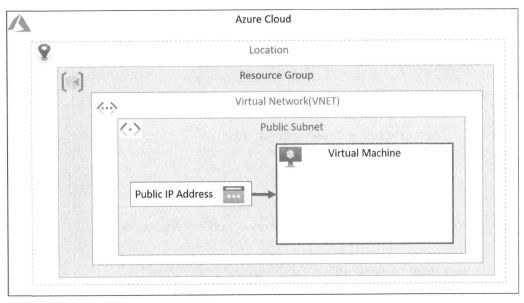

Figure 5.8: *Virtual machine with a virtual network*

In this architecture, you can see that we need an Azure cloud account that we have created. We have also seen how to authenticate with the subscription in the topic #Authenticating to Azure' in Configuring Terraform provider for Azure cloud section above. We will create the following services:

- Resource group

- Virtual network and subnets

- Public IP

- Virtual machine in the network

Whenever working with Azure cloud, always remember to group all your related resources in specific resource groups. We have already seen how to create a resource group in the last section, so you can refer to the same Terraform template for this architecture.

Now, let's start creating a virtual network and subnet with a public IP address. We will go step by step, starting with the virtual network:

1. Before moving to the creation of this environment, let's define the variables that we will use in this setup. Add the **prefix**, **location**, and **dbpassword** variables to the already created **vars.tf** file. The entire file should look as shown in the following code:

```
variable "client_secret" {

    description = "Enter your CLient Secret. Please make sure
you do not store the value of your client secret in the SCM
repository"
}

variable "client_id" {

    description = "Your client Id."

}

variable "subscription_id" {

    description = "Your subscription id."

    default = "xxxxxxxx-xxxx-xxxx-xxxx-xxxxxxxxxxxx"

}

variable "tenant_id" {

    description = "Your tenant id."

    default = "xxxxxxxx-xxxx-xxxx-xxxx-xxxxxxxxxxxx"

}

variable "prefix" {

  description = "The prefix which should be used for all resources
in this Chapter"

  default = "test"

}

variable "location" {

  description = "The Azure Region in which all resources in this
Chapter should be created."

  default = "West Europe"

}

variable "dbpassword" {

  description = "Database Password."

}
```

We have not set the default values for "**client_secret**" and "**dbpassword**", so you will be prompted to enter their values during the execution of the **terraform plan** and **apply** commands. Let's start with creation of the virtual network now.

2. Create **virtual_network.tf** and use the following code to create a VNET:

```
# Virtual network
resource "azurerm_virtual_network" "vnet" {
  name = "${var.prefix}-vnet"
  address_space = ["10.0.0.0/16"]
  location = var.location
  resource_group_name = azurerm_resource_group.test-rg.name
}
```

"**azurerm_virtual_network**" is the **azurerm** module from Terraform. You can define your virtual network required configuration in this resource block, as shown in the above-mentioned example for the creation of network "**vnet**" with address space ["10.0.0.0/16"]. You can also define the **subnet** block in this resource block itself, but we will not use this subnet argument; we will just create it as a separate resource in the next step.

3. We can use following Terraform configuration to create a subnet:

```
# Subnet
resource "azurerm_subnet" "subnet" {
  name = "${var.prefix}Subnet"
  resource_group_name = azurerm_resource_group.test-rg.name
  virtual_network_name = azurerm_virtual_network.vnet.name
  address_prefixes = ["10.0.1.0/24"]
}
```

Subnets represent network segments within the IP space defined by the virtual network. The "**azurerm_subnet**" resource block is used to create/manage a resource called "**subnet**" in the "**test-vnet**" virtual network with address prefixes **["10.0.1.0/24"]**.

There are other optional arguments as well; if required, you can go through the official Terraform documentation for referencing the optional arguments.

Tip on Virtual networks and Subnets

Terraform currently provides the facility to configure subnets with a standalone Subnet resource, and it also allows subnets to be defined in-line within the virtual network resource as argument. At a time, you can only use a virtual network with in-line subnets or subnet resources. Using both will cause a conflict of subnet configurations.

4. We need Terraform configuration to create a public IP address, as shown in the following code:

```
# Public ip
resource "azurerm_public_ip" "publicip" {
  name = "pip1"
  location = var.location
  resource_group_name = azurerm_resource_group.test-rg.name
  allocation_method = "Dynamic"
  sku = "Basic"
}
```

The "**azurerm_public_ip**" resource block in the above-mentioned code will create a "**publicip**" resource within the resource group, and it will create the allocation method as "**Dynamic**" with SKU as "**Basic**".

Sku is an optional argument used to define the SKU that should be used for public IP, and the accepted values are **Basic** and **Standard**.

5. Public IP is created, now we need to assign it with a network interface to a subnet:

```
# Network interface
resource "azurerm_network_interface" "nic" {
  name = "${var.prefix}-nic"
  location = var.location
  resource_group_name = azurerm_resource_group.test-rg.name

  ip_configuration {
    name = "ipconfig1"
    subnet_id = azurerm_subnet.subnet.id
    private_ip_address_allocation = "Dynamic"
    public_ip_address_id = azurerm_public_ip.publicip.id
```

```
        }
    }
```

The "**azurerm_network_interface**" resource block manages the "**test-nic**" network interface for the public IP "**pip1**".

Tip: Azure does not assign a dynamic IP address until the network interface is attached to a running virtual machine (or other resource).

Follow these steps to deploy this configuration now:

1. Execute '**terraform plan**', and you will get the following log:

```
ankita@Azure:~/Terraform/Chapter-5$ terraform plan

var.client_secret

    Enter your CLient Secret. Please make sure you do not store the
    value of your client secret in the SCM repository


    Enter a value: xxxxxxxxxxxxxxxxxxxxxxxxxxxxxxxxxx

Terraform used the selected providers to generate the following
execution plan. Resource actions are indicated with the following
symbols:
    + create

Terraform will perform the following actions:

    # azurerm_network_interface.nic will be created
    + resource "azurerm_network_interface" "nic" {

        ........ . .

    }

    # azurerm_public_ip.publicip will be created
    + resource "azurerm_public_ip" "publicip" {

        . ........ . .

    }

    # azurerm_resource_group.test-rg will be created
    + resource "azurerm_resource_group" "test-rg" {

        ........ .

    }
```

```
# azurerm_subnet.subnet will be created
+ resource "azurerm_subnet" "subnet" {

   ..........

  }


# azurerm_virtual_network.vnet will be created
+ resource "azurerm_virtual_network" "vnet" {

   ..........

  }


Plan: 5 to add, 0 to change, 0 to destroy.
```

```
Note: You didn't use the -out option to save this plan, so
Terraform can't guarantee to take exactly these actions if you
run "terraform apply" now.
```

2. Then, execute '**terraform apply**' to create resources in Azure cloud; the output should be as follows:

```
ankita@Azure:~/Terraform/Chapter-5$ terraform apply
var.client_secret

  Enter your CLient Secret. Please make sure you do not store the
value of your client secret in the SCM repository

  Enter a value: xxxxxxxxxxxxxxxxxxxxxxxxxxxxxxxx

Plan: 5 to add, 0 to change, 0 to destroy.

Do you want to perform these actions?
  Terraform will perform the actions described above.
  Only 'yes' will be accepted to approve.

  Enter a value: yes


azurerm_resource_group.test-rg: Creating...
azurerm_resource_group.test-rg: Creation complete after 0s
[id=/subscriptions/xxxxxxxx-xxxx-xxxx-xxxx-xxxxxxxxxxxx/
resourceGroups/test-resources]
```

```
azurerm_public_ip.publicip: Creating...

azurerm_virtual_network.vnet: Creating...

·

·

azurerm_network_interface.nic: Creation complete after 1s
[id=/subscriptions/xxxxxxxx-xxxx-xxxx-xxxx-xxxxxxxxxxxx/
resourceGroups/test-resources/providers/Microsoft.Network/
networkInterfaces/test-nic]

Apply complete! Resources: 5 added, 0 changed, 0 destroyed.
```

3. Check if the virtual network setup is created from Azure portal with the specified Terraform configuration in the **virtual_machine.tf** file. The following figure shows the network that was created from this configuration:

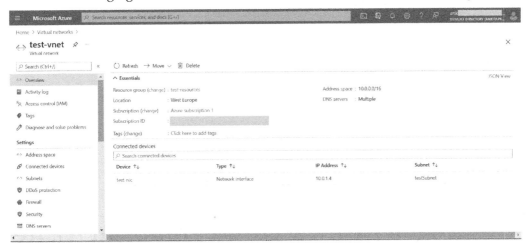

Figure 5.9: Azure virtual network with network interface and subnet

We can also verify the public IP in Azure Portal; it should look as shown in the following figure:

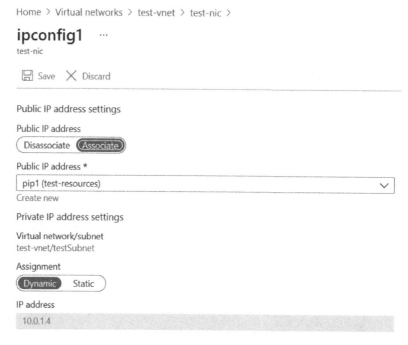

Figure 5.10: Public IP

This was about how we can create a virtual network, subnets, public IP, and network interface from Terraform. In the next section, we will create a network security group.

Creating network security groups in Azure

We have created a network, now we need a way to access different ports on the virtual machine, like HTTP, SSH, FTP, etc. This can be done with the help of different network security configuration, which can be done with network security groups and network security rules.

Let's create a security group for the virtual machine for accessing the http and ssh port of that system. We need to create following services to create a security group for http and ssh port:

- Azure network security group
- Network security rule for HTTP and SSH both
- Subnet network security group association

We can open the HTTP and SSH ports with the following steps:

1. Create Terraform configuration with the following code and also paste it in the **virtual_network.tf** file we created earlier:

```
# virtual_network.tf

# Security Group

resource "azurerm_network_security_group" "frontendnsg" {
  name                = "${var.prefix}SecurityGroup"
  location            = var.location
  resource_group_name = azurerm_resource_group.test-rg.name


  tags = {
    environment = "Production"
  }
}
```

The "**azurerm_network_security_group**" resource block will create the network security group.

We can also define multiple security rules in the **azurerm_network_security_group** resource block itself, but we will not use this **security_rule** argument. Instead, we will just create it as a separate resource in the next step.

2. Create network security rule for HTTP with the help of the following Terraform configuration and paste it in the **virtual_network.tf** file:

```
# virtual_network.tf

# Security rules

resource "azurerm_network_security_rule" "httprule" {
  name                        = "${var.prefix}http"
  priority                    = 100
  direction                   = "Inbound"
  access                      = "Allow"
  protocol                    = "Tcp"
  source_port_range           = "*"
  destination_port_range      = "8080"
  source_address_prefix       = "*"
  destination_address_prefix  = "10.0.1.0/24"
```

```
    resource_group_name          = azurerm_resource_group.test-rg.
name

    network_security_group_name = azurerm_network_security_group.
frontendnsg.name
}
```

The "**azurerm_network_security_rule**" resource block will create a security rule for accessing the http port for which **destination_port_ range** is 8080. This port 8080 will now allow all incoming traffic from all the source port and addresses.

3. Similar to the HTTP rule, we can create a rule for SSH port using this configuration:

```
# virtual_network.tf

# Security rules

resource "azurerm_network_security_rule" "sshrule" {
    name                        = "${var.prefix}ssh"
    priority                    = 101
    direction                   = "Inbound"
    access                      = "Allow"
    protocol                    = "Tcp"
    source_port_range           = "*"
    destination_port_range      = "22"
    source_address_prefix       = "*"
    destination_address_prefix = "10.0.1.0/24"
    resource_group_name          = azurerm_resource_group.test-rg.name

    network_security_group_name = azurerm_network_security_group.
frontendnsg.name
}
```

The "**azurerm_network_security_rule**" resource block will create a security rule for accessing the ssh port for which **destination_port_range** is 22. This SSH port 22 will now allow all incoming traffic from all source port and addresses.

4. The last thing is to associate this security group to the subnet we created; this can be done with the help of thew following Terraform code snippet:

```
# virtual_network.tf

# Subnet - Security Group association
```

```
resource        "azurerm_subnet_network_security_group_association"
"subnetsecuritygroup" {
  subnet_id                    = azurerm_subnet.subnet.id
    network_security_group_id  = azurerm_network_security_group.
frontendnsg.id
}
```

The "**azurerm_subnet_network_security_group_association**" resource block associates the "**testSecurityGroup**" security group with the "**testSubnet**" subnet within the "**test-vnet**" virtual network. The mandatory arguments for this resource block are as follows:

- **network_security_group_id**: This is the ID of the network security group which we want to associate with the subnet. A new resource is to be created if you change this.

- **subnet_id**: This is the ID of the subnet; a new resource is to be created if you change this.

We now have this configuration and just need to apply it to create these resources in the Azure cloud. We will follow these steps to do that:

1. Execute the '**terraform plan**' command to check if every configuration is okay before actually deploying the resources.

2. Then, execute the '**terraform apply**' command.

3. Verify the resources in Azure Portal. The following figure shows the security group and the security rules we created from the previous configuration:

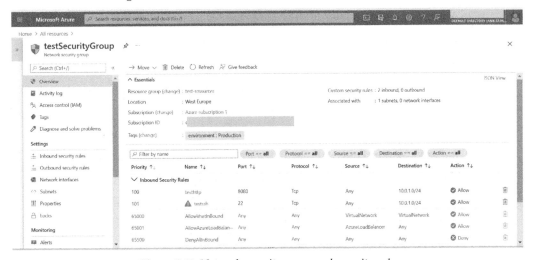

Figure 5.11: Network security group and security rules

We can also verify the association between this security group and the subnet by navigating to the subnets option from the left side of this security group page. This will show us '**testSubnet**', as in the following screenshot:

Figure 5.12: *Security group and subnet association*

Now, the environment is ready to launch a virtual machine.

Creating a virtual machine in Azure

We have the virtual network ready; now, we will launch a new virtual machine from Terraform configuration, as follows:

1. Create the **virtual_machine.tf** file with the following code:

```
# virtual_machine.tf
resource "azurerm_virtual_machine" "vm" {
  # name = "${var.prefix}-vm"
  name                  = "${var.prefix}-vm"
  location              = var.location
  resource_group_name   = azurerm_resource_group.test-rg.name
  network_interface_ids = [azurerm_network_interface.nic.id]
  vm_size               = "Standard_DS1_v2"

  storage_image_reference {
    publisher = "Canonical"
    offer     = "UbuntuServer"
```

```
    sku         = "16.04-LTS"
    version     = "latest"
  }
  storage_os_disk {
    name              = "${var.prefix}osdisk1"
    caching           = "ReadWrite"
    create_option     = "FromImage"
    managed_disk_type = "Standard_LRS"
  }
  os_profile {
    computer_name  = "hostname"
    admin_username = "${var.prefix}admin"
    admin_password = "Password1234!"
  }
  os_profile_linux_config {
    disable_password_authentication = false
  }
  tags = {
    environment = "Production"
  }
}
```

The "**azurerm_virtual_machine**" resource block is used to create a virtual machine.

2. Now, execute the '**terraform plan**' command.

3. Deploy the virtual machine with the '**terraform apply**' command.

4. Verify that the virtual machine is created in Azure Portal. The virtual machine configuration should look as shown in the following screenshot:

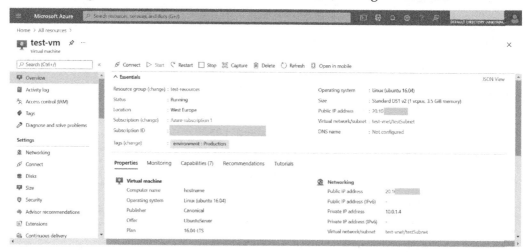

Figure 5.13*: Virtual machine*

We have created a simple virtual machine configuration using Microsoft hosted VM image. In the next section, let's create a virtual machine from a VM image created from packer.

Note: Ensure that you destroy the infrastructure using the 'terraform destroy' command each time before starting with the next topic; else, you will face issues "compute.VirtualMachinesClient# CreateOrUpdate: Disk testosdisk1 already exists in resource group TEST-RESOURCES."

Creating a virtual machine instance with Packer AMI

In the previous chapter, you learned how to create packer configuration for AWS cloud images. Now, you will understand how to deploy an **azure machine image** (**AMI**) to Azure Resource group from a packer configuration.

Pre-requisite: Packer should be installed on the implementation system.

Follow these steps to deploy the virtual machine from an AMI build from packer:

1. Create a resource group called '**ami-rg-store**' in the same Azure subscription (you can create it using Terraform or manually).

2. Create a file named **packer-ami.json** and paste the following packer configuration in this JSON file:

```json
{
  "variables": {
    "az_client_id": "",
    "az_client_secret": ""
  },
  "builders": [{
    "type": "azure-arm",
    "client_id": "{{user `az_client_id`}}",
    "client_secret": "{{user `az_client_secret`}}",
    "tenant_id": "xxxxxxxx-xxxx-xxxx-xxxx-xxxxxxxxxxxx",
    "subscription_id": "xxxxxxxx-xxxx-xxxx-xxxx-xxxxxxxxxxxx",
    "managed_image_resource_group_name": "ami-rg-store",
    "managed_image_storage_account_type": "Standard_LRS",
    "managed_image_name": "jenkins-ami-{{timestamp}}",
    "os_type": "Linux",
    "image_publisher": "Canonical",
    "image_offer": "0001-com-ubuntu-server-focal",
    "image_sku": "20_04-lts-gen2",
    "azure_tags": {
        "dept": "Production",
        "task": "VM Image deployment"
    },
    "location": "West Europe",
    "vm_size": "Standard_DS2_v2"
  }],
  "provisioners": [{
    "execute_command": "chmod +x {{ .Path }}; {{ .Vars }} sudo -E sh '{{ .Path }}'",
    "inline": [
        "apt update -y",
        "sudo apt install -y zip curl wget apt-transport-https openjdk-11-jre openjdk-11-jdk",
        "echo '----Install Jenkins ----'",
        "curl -fsSL https://pkg.jenkins.io/debian-stable/jenkins.
```

```
io.key | sudo tee /usr/share/keyrings/jenkins-keyring.asc > /dev/
null",

      "echo deb [signed-by=/usr/share/keyrings/jenkins-keyring.
asc] https://pkg.jenkins.io/debian-stable binary/ | sudo tee /
etc/apt/sources.list.d/jenkins.list > /dev/null",

      "sudo apt-get update -y",

      "sudo apt-get install -y jenkins"

   ],
   "inline_shebang": "/bin/sh -x",
   "type": "shell"
  }]
}
```

In this JSON configuration, the type is set as "**azure-arm**". Unlike Terraform, packer also needs the authentication details that we have provided in the JSON file itself. Other than Azure resource groups, all the details are related to which type of VM is to be created or what is to be provisioned in this AMI configured in this packer JSON.

3. Build and deploy the AMI to resource group using the following command:

```
packer build packer-ami.json
```

The logs for the creation of this AMI should look as follows (**Note:** some log is removed as it is irrelevant):

```
ankita@Azure:~/Terraform/Chapter-5$ packer build packer-ami.json

azure-arm: output will be in this color.

==> azure-arm: Running builder ...

…..

==> Builds finished. The artifacts of successful builds are:
--> azure-arm: Azure.ResourceManagement.VMImage:

OSType: Linux

ManagedImageResourceGroupName: ami-rg-store

ManagedImageName: jenkins-ami-1624752554

ManagedImageId: /subscriptions/xxxxxxxx-xxxx-xxxx-xxxx-
xxxxxxxxxxxx/resourceGroups/ami-rg-store/providers/Microsoft.
Compute/images/jenkins-ami-1624752554

ManagedImageLocation: West Europe
```

Once the execution is successful, you should make a note of the **ManagedImageName** and **ManagedImageId** values from these logs.

4. Now, let's check if this image is present in the Azure portal in the "**ami-rg-store**" resource group. Refer to the following"**jenkins-ami-1624752554**" image we created:

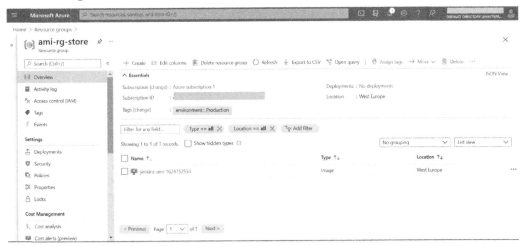

Figure 5.14: AMI created from Packer

5. Create a Terraform virtual machine configuration to use this AMI. Remove the following Terraform configuration block in the **virtual_machine.tf** we created in the earlier section:

```
storage_image_reference {
    publisher = "Canonical"
    offer     = "UbuntuServer"
    sku       = "16.04-LTS"
    version   = "latest"
}
```

Instead, add the new configuration for creating a VM from the packer AMI we created in this file:

```
storage_image_reference {
    id                   = "/subscriptions/${var.subscription_id}/
resourceGroups/ami-rg-store/providers/Microsoft.Compute/images/
{ManagedImageName}"
}
```

The **storage_image_reference** argument block is used to refer to the AMI that is to be used for creating a virtual machine. Replace the value for **ManagedImageName**, which we took note of earlier for the VM image we created from packer. Your new virtual machine configuration should look as follows:

```
# virtual_machine.tf
resource "azurerm_virtual_machine" "vm" {
  name                  = "${var.prefix}-vm"
  location              = var.location
  resource_group_name   = azurerm_resource_group.test-rg.name
  network_interface_ids = [azurerm_network_interface.nic.id]
  vm_size               = "Standard_DS1_v2"
  storage_image_reference {
    id                  = "/subscriptions/${var.subscription_id}/
resourceGroups/ami-rg-store/providers/Microsoft.Compute/images/
jenkins-ami-1624752554"
  }
  storage_os_disk {
    name              = "${var.prefix}osdisk"
    caching           = "ReadWrite"
    create_option     = "FromImage"
    managed_disk_type = "Standard_LRS"
  }
  os_profile {
    computer_name  = "hostname"
    admin_username = "${var.prefix}admin"
    admin_password = "Password1234!"
  }
  os_profile_linux_config {
    disable_password_authentication = false
  }
  tags = {
    environment = "Production"
  }
}
```

6. Execute the '**terraform plan**' command to verify the plan before deploying it to Azure. The logs should look as follows; verify that the AMI ID is updated in the **storage_image_reference** block for this plan.

7. Now, execute '**terraform apply**' to get the log as follows:

```
ankita@Azure:~/Terraform/Chapter-5$ terraform apply

var.client_secret

    Enter your CLient Secret. Please make sure you do not store the
    value of your client secret in the SCM repository

    Enter a value: xxxxxxxxxxxxxxxxxxxxxxxxxxxxxxxxxxxxx

Plan: 1 to add, 0 to change, 0 to destroy.

Do you want to perform these actions?
    Terraform will perform the actions described above.
    Only 'yes' will be accepted to approve.

    Enter a value: yes

azurerm_virtual_machine.vm: Still creating... [30s elapsed]
azurerm_virtual_machine.vm: Creation complete after 46s
[id=/subscriptions/xxxxxxxx-xxxx-xxxx-xxxx-xxxxxxxxxxxx/
resourceGroups/test-resources/providers/Microsoft.Compute/
virtualMachines/test-vm]
Apply complete! Resources: 1 added, 0 changed, 0 destroyed.
```

Note the change in the log as well. It will refer to "**/subscriptions/xxxxxxxx-xxxx-xxxx-xxxx-xxxxxxxxxxxx/resourceGroups/ami-rg-store/providers/Microsoft.Compute/images/jenkins-ami-1624752554**" for creating the virtual machine, not the canonical Ubuntu image.

8. Verify the virtual machine in Azure Portal. Additionally, we have HTTP port accessible from all IP addresses, so we can access Jenkins, which we have installed on port 8080 using the public IP address. Refer to the following figure, which is accessing the public IP at port 8080; this is running Jenkins.

We will not be looking into how to configure Jenkins here as we have already covered that topic in the previous chapter.

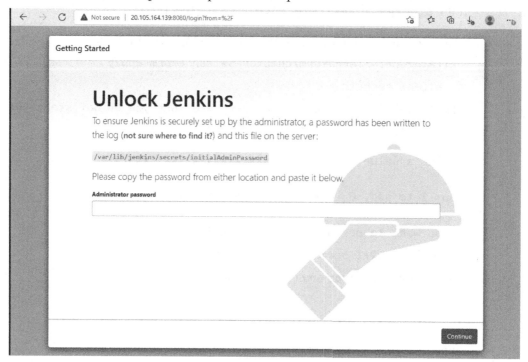

Figure 5.15: Jenkins on virtual machine

This is how we can create AMI from packer and use it to create a virtual machine in Azure.

This is how we can achieve the setup from the architecture we saw in *figure 5.8.*

Configuring Azure Machine scale set

Azure machine scale set helps you create and manage a group of load balanced virtual machines. You can configure this scale set to automatically increase or decrease virtual machine instances in response to demand or on schedule.

We will use the same AMI that we created in the previous topic. Let's start with Terraform configuration for creating this scale set agents:

1. Create the **vitual_machine_scale_set.tf** file and paste the following code in it:

```
# virtual_machine_scale_set.tf

resource "azurerm_linux_virtual_machine_scale_set" "vmss" {
```

```
name                   = "${var.prefix}-vmss"
resource_group_name = azurerm_resource_group.test-rg.name
location               = var.location
sku                    = "Standard_DS2_v2"
instances              = 3
admin_username         = "adminuser"
admin_password         = "p@ssword1234"
source_image_id        = "/subscriptions/${var.subscription_id}/
resourceGroups/ami-rg-store/providers/Microsoft.Compute/images/
{ManagedImageName}"

admin_ssh_key {
  username   = "adminuser"
  public_key = file("~/.ssh/id_rsa.pub")
}
network_interface {
  name    = "internalNI"
  primary = true

  ip_configuration {
    name      = "internal"
    primary   = true
    subnet_id = azurerm_subnet.subnet.id
  }
}

os_disk {
  storage_account_type = "Standard_LRS"
  caching              = "ReadWrite"
}
}

# AutoScale configuration
resource "azurerm_monitor_autoscale_setting" "vmssautoscale" {
  name               = "autoscale-config"
```

```
  resource_group_name = azurerm_resource_group.test-rg.name
  location            = var.location
  target_resource_id  = azurerm_linux_virtual_machine_scale_set.
vmss.id

profile {
  name = "AutoScale"

  capacity {
    default = 3
    minimum = 1
    maximum = 5
  }

  rule {
    metric_trigger {
      metric_name        = "Percentage CPU"
      metric_resource_id = azurerm_linux_virtual_machine_scale_
set.vmss.id
      time_grain         = "PT1M"
      statistic          = "Average"
      time_window        = "PT5M"
      time_aggregation   = "Average"
      operator           = "GreaterThan"
      threshold          = 75
    }

    scale_action {
      direction = "Increase"
      type      = "ChangeCount"
      value     = "1"
      cooldown  = "PT1M"
    }
  }

  rule {
```

```
    metric_trigger {
      metric_name         = "Percentage CPU"
      metric_resource_id = azurerm_linux_virtual_machine_scale_
set.vmss.id
      time_grain          = "PT1M"
      statistic           = "Average"
      time_window         = "PT5M"
      time_aggregation    = "Average"
      operator            = "LessThan"
      threshold           = 25
    }

    scale_action {
      direction = "Decrease"
      type      = "ChangeCount"
      value     = "1"
      cooldown  = "PT1M"
    }
  }
 }
}
```

The "**azurerm_linux_virtual_machine_scale_set**" resource block is used to create the Linux virtual machine scale sets from the packer AMI. Update the value of **ManagedImageName** in the value of **source_image_id** in the preceding code. You will need to create an SSH key for the preceding code. Update the value of **public_key = file("~/.ssh/id_rsa.pub")** to the path of your created public ssh key in the file ("**<PATH-TO-PUBLIC-SSH-KEY>**") at line 14 in the preceding code. Similarly, we have "**azurerm_windows_virtual_machine_scale_set**" to create windows virtual machines.

The "**azurerm_monitor_autoscale_setting**" resource block manages the auto scaling settings for virtual machine scale sets. This also has required mandatory arguments like name, **resource_group_name**, location, profile (specifies profile block), and most importantly, **target_resource_id** (in our case, it's the ID of the virtual machine scale set).

2. Hence, we will forward execute '`terraform apply`' directly to avoid unnecessary repetition of logs. Terraform apply will run '`terraform plan`' before deploying the setup.

3. Lastly, verify this VM Scale set in azure portal; it should look as shown in the following screenshot:

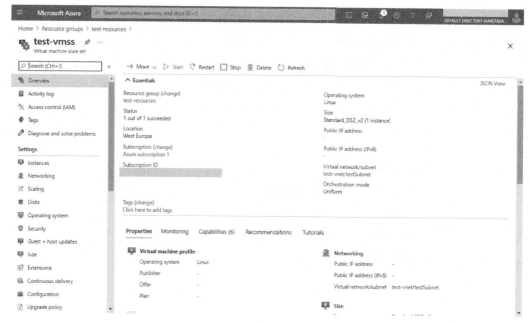

Figure 5.16: Virtual machine scale set

You can view the number of running instances in the instances option of the left panel. You will then see all the instances and their status, as in the following image; we can see only one instance '`test-vmss_0`' running.

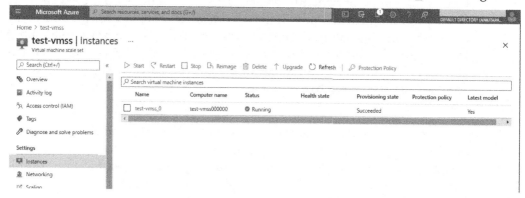

Figure 5.17: Instances in VMSS

This is how you can also configure virtual machine scale sets for Windows. Do not forget to tear down the infrastructure we created using the '`terraform destroy`' command if you are not really using it.

Tip: This virtual machine scale set can be also used as Agent Pool in Azure DevOps.

Creating and deploying an App Service for Java web application

Azure App Services lets you create and manage web and mobile apps for any platform or device quickly and easily, and it enables you to deploy these apps on a scalable and reliable cloud infrastructure.

We have already created simple setups and services. In creation of the App Services, we will see how to create production infrastructure for the App Services.

For a production-based deployment, you always want to protect your App Services from potential attacks, such as SQL injection, **Denial of Service (DDOS)**, and **Cross Side Scripting (XSS)**. You can use Application Gateway with a **web application firewall (WAF)** SKU to do this. We also want your application to support multi-region deployment for high availability, so you can use a Traffic Manager to route the traffic as needed. To achieve this type of deployment, we will create the infrastructure as shown in the following figure:

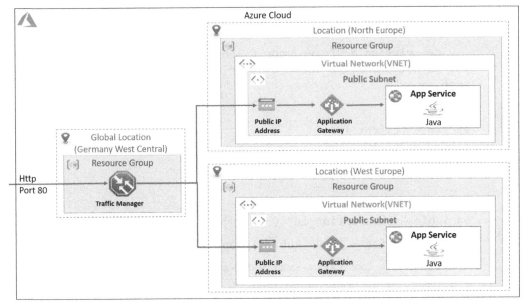

Figure 5.18: Architecture for traffic managed App Service

We will create the following services:

- Define the required variables
- Resource groups (for each North Europe, West Europe, and the Global in Germany West Central)
- Virtual networks, subnets, and public IPs (for each North and West Europe)
- App Services (for each North and West Europe)
- Application Insights (for each North and West Europe)
- Database for Java web application (for each North and West Europe)
- Application Gateway for Java web application (for each North and West Europe)
- Traffic Manager

We will first create Terraform configuration for all these services and then we will deploy it with the help of the '**terraform apply**' command. You can create all the configuration in a single file, but we will create different files for each service in this section.

Let's begin with the setup for this architecture:

1. Create all the variables that you require for this setup and copy the following code with all variables in **vars.tf**:

```
# vars.tf

variable "client_secret" {

    description = "Enter your CLient Secret. Please make sure
you do not store the value of your client secret in the SCM
repository"

}
variable "client_id" {

    description = "Your client Id."

    default = "                        "

}
variable "subscription_id" {

    description = "Your subscription id."

    default = "xxxxxxxx-xxxx-xxxx-xxxx-xxxxxxxxxxxx"

}
variable "tenant_id" {
```

```
    description = "Your tenant id."
    default = "                                    "
}
variable "prefix" {
  description = "The prefix which should be used for all resources
in this Chapter"
  default = "prod"
}
variable "location" {
  description = "The Azure Region in which all resources in this
Chapter should be created."
  default = "West Europe"
}
variable "environment" {
  description = "The Azure Region in which all resources in this
Chapter should be created."
  default = "Production"
}

variable "dbpassword" {
  description = "Enter a strong Database password with at-
least one capitals, one small letters, one number and a special
character. Example : P@ssw0rd in default"
  default = "P@ssw0rd"
}
```

2. Create a **main.tf** file with '**azurerm**' and backend configuration like the following. We assume that you have the backend ready to use as it was covered at the beginning of this chapter.

```
# main.tf
provider "azurerm" {
  features {}
  subscription_id = var.subscription_id
  client_id       = var.client_id
  client_secret   = var.client_secret
  tenant_id       = var.tenant_id
```

```
}


# Azure Provider source and version being used
terraform {
  backend "azurerm" {
    resource_group_name    = "tstate"
    storage_account_name   = "tstate16782"
    container_name         = "tstate"
    key                    = "terraform_app_service.tfstate"
  }
  required_providers {
    azurerm = {
      source  = "hashicorp/azurerm"
      version = "=2.46.0"
    }
  }
}
```

3. Create a new **rg.tf** file and paste the following code in it to create the resource groups:

```
# rg.tf
# Create a resource group north
resource "azurerm_resource_group" "north-prod-rg" {
  name     = "${var.prefix}-north-resources"
  location = "North Europe"

  tags = {
    Environment = var.environment
  }
}


# Create a resource group west
resource "azurerm_resource_group" "west-prod-rg" {
  name     = "${var.prefix}-west-resources"
```

```
  location = "West Europe"

  tags = {
    Environment = var.environment
  }
}

# Create a Resource Groups global
resource "azurerm_resource_group" "global-prod-rg" {
  name     = "${var.prefix}-global-rg"
  location = "Germany West Central"

  tags = {
    Environment = var.environment
  }
}
```

4. Create a **network.tf** file with the following Terraform code to create networks, subnets, and public IPs:

```
# network.tf
# Virtual network North
resource "azurerm_virtual_network" "north-vnet" {
  name = "${var.prefix}-north-vnet"
  address_space = ["10.0.0.0/16"]
  location            = azurerm_resource_group.north-prod-rg.
location
  resource_group_name = azurerm_resource_group.north-prod-rg.name
}

# Virtual network West
resource "azurerm_virtual_network" "west-vnet" {
  name = "${var.prefix}-west-vnet"
  address_space = ["10.0.0.0/16"]
  location            = azurerm_resource_group.west-prod-rg.
location
  resource_group_name = azurerm_resource_group.west-prod-rg.name
```

```
}

# Subnet North
resource "azurerm_subnet" "north-subnet" {
  name = "${var.prefix}-north-subnet"
  resource_group_name = azurerm_resource_group.north-prod-rg.name
  virtual_network_name = azurerm_virtual_network.north-vnet.name
  address_prefixes = ["10.0.1.0/24"]
}

# Subnet West
resource "azurerm_subnet" "west-subnet" {
  name = "${var.prefix}-west-subnet"
  resource_group_name = azurerm_resource_group.west-prod-rg.name
  virtual_network_name = azurerm_virtual_network.west-vnet.name
  address_prefixes = ["10.0.1.0/24"]
}

# Public ip North
resource "azurerm_public_ip" "north-publicip" {
  name = "${var.prefix}-north-pip"
  location           = azurerm_resource_group.north-prod-rg.
location
  resource_group_name = azurerm_resource_group.north-prod-rg.name
  allocation_method = "Dynamic"
}

# Public ip West
resource "azurerm_public_ip" "west-publicip" {
  name = "${var.prefix}-west-pip"
  location           = azurerm_resource_group.west-prod-rg.
location
  resource_group_name = azurerm_resource_group.west-prod-rg.name
  allocation_method = "Dynamic"
}
```

With this, we are ready with the basic infrastructure that we have already learned to create with Terraform. In the following subtopics, we will discuss the creation of Terraform configuration for the main services of the architecture in the previous figure.

Managing Application Insights for Java web application

We have App Service, so need to get the insights from this application. In our setup, we will deploy Java web application to App services, so let's see how to get insights from the Java application.

Create a **app_insight.tf** file and paste the following code in it to create Application Insight:

```
# app_insight.tf
resource "azurerm_application_insights" "north-appinsights" {
    name                = "north-${var.prefix}-appinsights"
    location            = var.location
    resource_group_name = azurerm_resource_group.north-prod-rg.name
    application_type    = "java"
}

output "instrumentation_key_north" {
    value = azurerm_application_insights.north-appinsights.
instrumentation_key
    sensitive = true
}

output "app_id_north" {
    value = azurerm_application_insights.north-appinsights.app_id
}
resource "azurerm_application_insights" "west-appinsights" {
    name                = "west-${var.prefix}-appinsights"
    location            = var.location
    resource_group_name = azurerm_resource_group.west-prod-rg.name
    application_type    = "java"
}
```

```
output "instrumentation_key_west" {
    value = azurerm_application_insights.west-appinsights.
instrumentation_key
    sensitive = true
}

output "app_id_west" {
    value = azurerm_application_insights.west-appinsights.app_id
}
```

The "**azurerm_application_insights**" resource block is used to create application insights for specific application type "**java**". The mandatory arguments for this resource block are as follows:

- **name**: Defines the name of the Application Insight to be created; a new resource is to be created if you change this.

- **resource_group_name**: Defines the name of the resource group in which the Application Insight will be created; a new resource to be created if you change this.

- **location**: This specifies the Azure Region where the Application Insight should exist; a new resource to be created if you change this.

- **Application_type**: Specifies which type of Application Insights to be created for that resource group; valid values are Java for Java web, Node. JS for Node.js, ios for iOS, MobileCenter for AppCenter, store for Windows Store, phone for Windows Phone, web for ASP.NET, and other for General. Note that these values are case sensitive; unmatched values are treated as ASP.NET by Azure. Changing this forces a new resource to be created.

These application insights can be referred to using instrumentation key, like '**azurerm_ application_insights.north_appinsights.instrumentation_key**'.

Creating a database for Java web application

If the Java web application requires the database, then we need to create a database in Azure cloud using the following Terraform code in the **mysql_db.tf** file:

```
# mysql_db.tf
resource "azurerm_mysql_server" "mysqlserver" {
  name                = "${var.prefix}-app-mysqlserver"
  location            = var.location
  resource_group_name = azurerm_resource_group.global-prod-rg.name
```

```
    administrator_login           = "mysqladmin"
    administrator_login_password = var.dbpassword

    sku_name    = "GP_Gen5_2"
    storage_mb = 5120
    version     = "5.7"

    auto_grow_enabled                    = true
    backup_retention_days                = 7
    ssl_enforcement_enabled              = true
    ssl_minimal_tls_version_enforced  = "TLS1_2"
    tags = {
      Environment = var.environment
    }
}

resource "azurerm_mysql_database" "mysqldb" {
  name                    = "${var.prefix}-app-db"
  resource_group_name = azurerm_resource_group.global-prod-rg.name
  server_name             = azurerm_mysql_server.mysqlserver.name
  charset                 = "utf8"
  collation               = "utf8_unicode_ci"
}
```

Here, we have two **resource** blocks. The **resource** block "**azurerm_mysql_ server**" is used to create and configure a MySQL database Server named "**prod- app-mysqlserver**". We have also set the Admin username and password from this Terraform configuration.

The "**azurerm_mysql_database**" resource block is used to create a database named "**prod-app-db**" in the "**prod-app-mysqlserver**" database server we created.

Now, you can access this MySql database from the MySql client using the admin username and password of the MySql server.

Creating App Service

To create an App Service, we first need App Service plan. Let's create Terraform configurations for app service plan and app service with the following steps:

1. Create a file named **app_service.tf** and paste the following code in it for the creation of App service plans for North and West Europe:

```
# app_service.tf

# App Servie plan North

resource "azurerm_app_service_plan" "north-asp" {
  name                = "${var.prefix}-north-asp"
  location            = azurerm_resource_group.north-prod-rg.
location
  resource_group_name = azurerm_resource_group.north-prod-rg.name

  sku {
    tier = "Standard"
    size = "S1"
  }

  tags = {
    Environment = var.environment
  }
}

# App Servie plan West

resource "azurerm_app_service_plan" "west-asp" {
  name                = "${var.prefix}-west-asp"
  location            = azurerm_resource_group.west-prod-rg.
location
  resource_group_name = azurerm_resource_group.west-prod-rg.name

  sku {
    tier = "Standard"
    size = "S1"
  }

  tags = {
    Environment = var.environment
  }
}
```

The "**azurerm_app_service_plan**" resource block creates the Azure App Service plan, which is required to create Azure App Services. This resource block should define the SKU tier and size of the App Service that can be allowed in this App Service plan. In our configuration, we will use the "**Standard**" tier for size "**S1**". The mandatory arguments are **name, resource_ group**, **location**, and **sku** blocks.

2. Now, we can create App Services (in North and West Europe) with the help of the following code; paste this code in the **app_service.tf** file as well to create App Service:

```
# app_service.tf
# App Service North
resource "azurerm_app_service" "north-appservice" {
  name                 = "${var.prefix}-north-java-appservice"
  location             = azurerm_resource_group.north-prod-rg.
location
  resource_group_name = azurerm_resource_group.north-prod-rg.name
  app_service_plan_id = azurerm_app_service_plan.north-asp.id

  site_config {
    java_version           = "1.8"
    java_container         = "TOMCAT"
    java_container_version = "9.0"
  }

  tags = {
    Environment = var.environment
  }

  connection_string {
    name  = "Database"
    type  = "MySQL"
    value = "Server=${var.prefix}-app-mysqlserver;Port=3306;Databa
se=${var.prefix}-app-db;User=mysqladmin;SSLMode=1;UseSystemTrustSt
ore=0;Password=${var.dbpassword}"
  }

  app_settings = {
```

```
      APPINSIGHTS_INSTRUMENTATIONKEY = azurerm_application_
insights.north-appinsights.instrumentation_key

      APPLICATIONINSIGHTS_CONNECTION_STRING = azurerm_application_
insights.north-appinsights.connection_string
  }
}

# App Service West
resource "azurerm_app_service" "west-appservice" {
  name               = "${var.prefix}-west-java-appservice"
  location           = azurerm_resource_group.west-prod-rg.
location
  resource_group_name = azurerm_resource_group.west-prod-rg.name
  app_service_plan_id = azurerm_app_service_plan.west-asp.id

  site_config {
    java_version          = "1.8"
    java_container        = "TOMCAT"
    java_container_version = "9.0"
  }

  tags = {
    Environment = var.environment
  }

  connection_string {
    name  = "Database"
    type  = "MySQL"
    value = "Server=${var.prefix}-app-mysqlserver;Port=3306;Databa
se=${var.prefix}-app-db;User=mysqladmin;SSLMode=1;UseSystemTrustSt
ore=0;Password=${var.dbpassword}"
  }

  app_settings = {
    APPINSIGHTS_INSTRUMENTATIONKEY = azurerm_application_
insights.west-appinsights.instrumentation_key

    APPLICATIONINSIGHTS_CONNECTION_STRING = azurerm_application_
```

```
    insights.west-appinsights.connection_string
  }
}
```

The "**azurerm_app_service**" resource block creates the Azure App Services in the App Service Plans we created earlier, both for North and West Europe. We are focusing on the Java web application, so each of these App Services have **site_config** with **java_version**, **java_container**, and **java_container_version**.

You have two of these resource blocks, one for North Europe Java App Service, and the other for West Europe Java App Service.

Creating Application Gateway for Java web application

Application Gateway in Azure protects your App Service from external attacks and makes it highly available.

Paste the following Terraform code in new file **app_gateway.tf** to create Application Gateways for both App Services (North and West Europe):

```
# app_gateway.tf
# App Gateway North
resource "azurerm_application_gateway" "north-gateway" {
  name                = "${var.prefix}-north-appgateway"
  location            = azurerm_resource_group.north-prod-rg.location
  resource_group_name = azurerm_resource_group.north-prod-rg.name

  sku {
    name     = "WAF_Medium"
    tier     = "WAF"
    capacity = 2
  }

  waf_configuration {
    enabled          = "true"
    firewall_mode    = "Detection"
    rule_set_type    = "OWASP"
    rule_set_version = "3.0"
```

```
    }

  gateway_ip_configuration {
    name      = "${var.prefix}-north-gateway-ip-configuration"
    subnet_id = azurerm_subnet.north-subnet.id
  }

  frontend_port {
    name = "${azurerm_virtual_network.north-vnet.name}-feport"
    port = 80
  }

  frontend_ip_configuration {
    name                 = "${azurerm_virtual_network.north-vnet.name}-
feip"
    public_ip_address_id = azurerm_public_ip.north-publicip.id
  }

  backend_address_pool {
    name = "${azurerm_virtual_network.north-vnet.name}-beap"
    fqdns = ["${azurerm_app_service.north-appservice.name}.
azurewebsites.net"]
  }

  probe {
    name              = "north-probe"
    protocol          = "http"
    path              = "/"
    host              = "${azurerm_app_service.north-appservice.name}.
azurewebsites.net"
    interval          = "30"
    timeout           = "30"
    unhealthy_threshold = "3"
  }

  backend_http_settings {
```

```
    name                       = "${azurerm_virtual_network.north-vnet.name}-
be-htst"
    cookie_based_affinity = "Disabled"
    port                  = 80
    protocol              = "Http"
    request_timeout       = 60
    probe_name            = "north-probe"
    pick_host_name_from_backend_address = true
  }

  http_listener {
    name                          = "${azurerm_virtual_network.north-
vnet.name}-httplstn"
    frontend_ip_configuration_name = "${azurerm_virtual_network.north-
vnet.name}-feip"
    frontend_port_name            = "${azurerm_virtual_network.north-
vnet.name}-feport"
    protocol                      = "Http"
  }

  request_routing_rule {
    name                      = "${azurerm_virtual_network.north-vnet.
name}-rqrt"
    rule_type                 = "Basic"
    http_listener_name        = "${azurerm_virtual_network.north-vnet.
name}-httplstn"
    backend_address_pool_name = "${azurerm_virtual_network.north-vnet.
name}-beap"
    backend_http_settings_name = "${azurerm_virtual_network.north-vnet.
name}-be-htst"
  }

  tags = {
    Environment = var.environment
  }
}
```

```
# App Gateway West
resource "azurerm_application_gateway" "west-gateway" {
  name                = "${var.prefix}-west-appgateway"
  location            = azurerm_resource_group.west-prod-rg.location
  resource_group_name = azurerm_resource_group.west-prod-rg.name

  sku {
    name     = "WAF_Medium"
    tier     = "WAF"
    capacity = 2
  }

  waf_configuration {
    enabled          = "true"
    firewall_mode    = "Detection"
    rule_set_type    = "OWASP"
    rule_set_version = "3.0"
  }

  gateway_ip_configuration {
    name      = "${var.prefix}-west-gateway-ip-configuration"
    subnet_id = azurerm_subnet.west-subnet.id
  }

  frontend_port {
    name = "${azurerm_virtual_network.west-vnet.name}-feport"
    port = 80
  }

  frontend_ip_configuration {
    name                 = "${azurerm_virtual_network.west-vnet.name}-feip"
    public_ip_address_id = azurerm_public_ip.west-publicip.id
  }

  backend_address_pool {
```

```
    name = "${azurerm_virtual_network.west-vnet.name}-beap"
    fqdns = ["${azurerm_app_service.west-appservice.name}.azurewebsites.
net"]
  }

  probe {
    name               = "west-probe"
    protocol           = "http"
    path               = "/"
    host               = "${azurerm_app_service.west-appservice.name}.
azurewebsites.net"
    interval           = "30"
    timeout            = "30"
    unhealthy_threshold = "3"
  }

  backend_http_settings {
    name                               = "${azurerm_virtual_network.
west-vnet.name}-be-htst"
    cookie_based_affinity              = "Disabled"
    port                               = 80
    protocol                           = "Http"
    request_timeout                    = 60
    probe_name                         = "west-probe"
    pick_host_name_from_backend_address = true
  }

  http_listener {
    name                            = "${azurerm_virtual_network.west-
vnet.name}-httplstn"
    frontend_ip_configuration_name = "${azurerm_virtual_network.west-
vnet.name}-feip"
    frontend_port_name              = "${azurerm_virtual_network.west-
vnet.name}-feport"
    protocol                        = "Http"
  }
```

```
    request_routing_rule {

        name                        = "${azurerm_virtual_network.west-vnet.
name}-rqrt"

        rule_type                   = "Basic"

        http_listener_name          = "${azurerm_virtual_network.west-vnet.
name}-httplstn"

        backend_address_pool_name   = "${azurerm_virtual_network.west-vnet.
name}-beap"

        backend_http_settings_name  = "${azurerm_virtual_network.west-vnet.
name}-be-htst"

    }

    tags = {

        Environment = var.environment

    }

}
```

In the preceding code block, we have two blocks of resource "**azurerm_application_
gateway**", which will create and configure Application Gateway with Web Firewall
(WAF) enabled. Additionally, each of these Application Gateways are attached to the
public IP (**north-publicip** and **west-publicip**) we created.

Creating Traffic Manager for multi-location web app

We have App Service in two different regions behind Application Gateway, so we
need to make this highly available globally. This can be done with the help of Traffic
Manager, which will route the traffic as per your requirement.

1. Let's create a Traffic Manager with the help of the following Terraform code;
   paste this code in a new file called **traffic_manager.tf**:

```
# traffic_manager.tf

# Traffic manager for Java Web App

resource "azurerm_traffic_manager_profile" "traffic-manager" {

    name                    = "${var.prefix}-java-webapp-tm"

    resource_group_name     = azurerm_resource_group.global-prod-rg.
name

    traffic_routing_method  = "Performance"
```

```
dns_config {
  relative_name = "${var.prefix}-java-webapp"
  ttl           = 300
}

monitor_config {
  protocol                       = "http"
  port                           = 80
  path                           = "/"
  interval_in_seconds            = 30
  timeout_in_seconds             = 9
  tolerated_number_of_failures = 3
}

tags = {
  Environment = var.environment
}
}
```

2. We have two Application Gateways with public IPs attached to them, so we need to create Traffic manager endpoints for each North and West Europe for directing traffic to these public IPs from Traffic Manager.

You can do this by pasting the following code in the **traffic_manager.tf** file:

```
# traffic_manager.tf
# Endpoint North
resource "azurerm_traffic_manager_endpoint" "north-tm-endpoint" {
  name                = "${var.prefix}-north-global-tm"
  resource_group_name = azurerm_resource_group.global-prod-rg.name
  profile_name        = azurerm_traffic_manager_profile.traffic-manager.name
  target              = azurerm_public_ip.north-publicip.fqdn
  endpoint_location = azurerm_public_ip.north-publicip.location
  type                = "externalEndpoints"
}
```

```
# Endpoint West
resource "azurerm_traffic_manager_endpoint" "west-tm-endpoint" {
    name                = "${var.prefix}-west-global-tm"
    resource_group_name = azurerm_resource_group.global-prod-rg.
name
    profile_name        = azurerm_traffic_manager_profile.traffic-
manager.name
    target              = azurerm_public_ip.west-publicip.fqdn
    endpoint_location = azurerm_public_ip.west-publicip.location
    type                = "externalEndpoints"
}
```

We are done with the development of the Terraform code for all the services required for the architecture shown in *figure 5.18*, so execute the following steps to deploy and verify the creation of this Azure Services:

1. We need to execute '**terraform init**'.

2. Now that we have everything ready in Terraform configuration, let's deploy these services by executing the '**terraform apply**' command.

3. Verify the App Services in Azure Portal. To view the all the App Services, go to **Azure Portal | Search | App Services** and then select **Option**; you will be navigated to a list of all the App Services, as shown in the following figure:

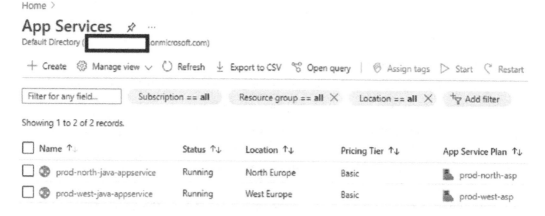

Figure 5.19: App Services

North App Service: We will verify the creation of North Europe; this should look like the following screenshot:

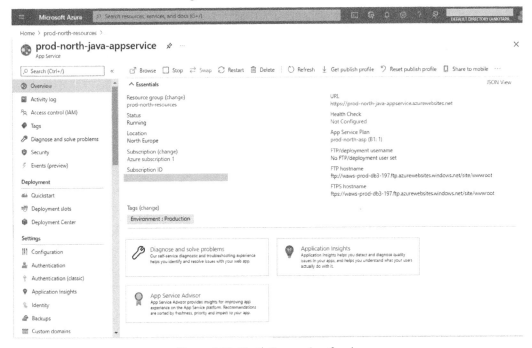

Figure 5.20: *North Europe App Service*

We can access this App Service from the URL given in the App Service page in the preceding figure. Click on the URL, and you will be navigated to the app service tomcat server main page, which says 'Hey, Java Developers!'.

Similarly, we can verify West App Service, which looks similar in the Azure portal but with different configurations.

The URLs of App Services are as follows:

- North Europe: **https://prod-north-java-appservice.azurewebsites. net/**

- West Europe: **https://prod-west-java-appservice.azurewebsites.net/**

So, this shows that both the App Services are created successfully from our Terraform configuration.

4. Verify the MySql database in Azure Portal: go to Azure Portal → Search 'mySql Servers' → Select 'Azure Database for MySQL servers'. You will be navigated to the list of all MySQL Servers. Now, select the server that was

created, i.e., '**prod-app-mysqlserver**', which will look as shown in the following screenshot:

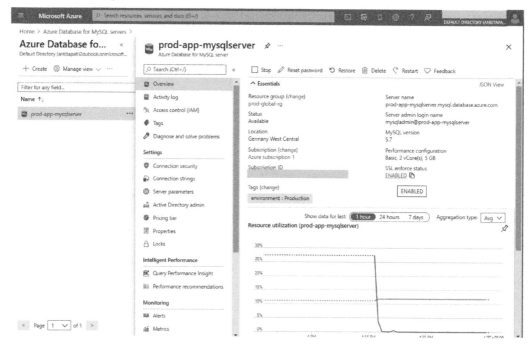

Figure 5.21: MySql server

5. Verify the Application Gateways in Azure Portal: go to Azure Portal → Search '**Application Gateways**' → Select the **Application Gateway**. You will be navigated to the list of all Application Gateways, as shown in the following screenshot:

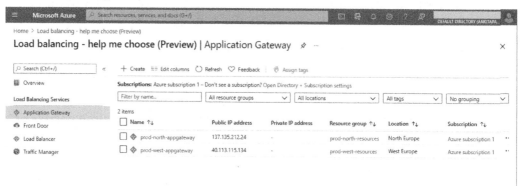

Figure 5.22: Application Gateways

You can see that the public IPs we created are assigned to these Application Gateways. You can further check the details of each by clicking on it to verify that WAF is enabled.

6. Verify the Traffic Manager and its endpoints in Azure Portal: go to Azure Portal → Search '**Traffic Manager profiles**' → Select the created **Traffic Manager Profile**. You will be navigated to the list of all **Traffic Manager profiles**. Click on the one we created from Terraform, which is called '**prod-java-webapp-tm**', and then you will be navigated to a page as shown in the following screenshot:

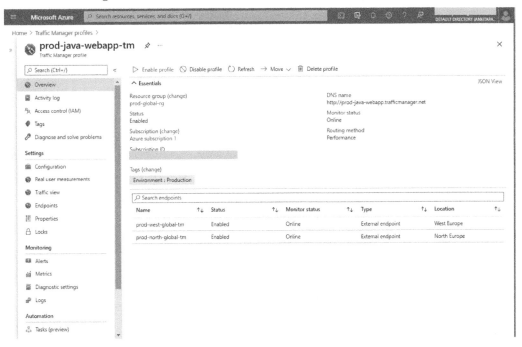

Figure 5.23: Traffic Manager profile

In this profile, you must have two endpoints that we created, and both should have enabled status.

7. In the preceding figure, there is DNS name present for the Traffic Manager profile. It is nothing but the URL to access the App Service. Let's access this DNS name from the browser; it should redirect to the App Service. So, you will see the default page for the App Service, which we saw when we

accessed the App services individually. The following figure verifies the DNS for this Traffic Manager:

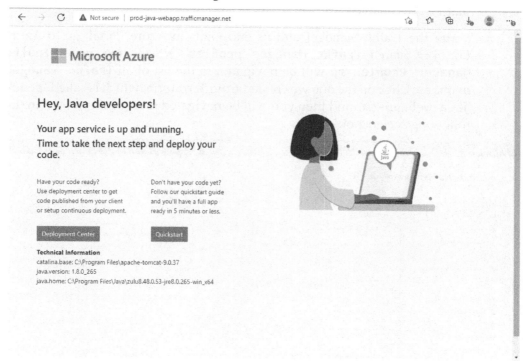

Figure 5.24: *Traffic Manager DNS for the App Services*

We verified our infrastructure, and it is fully ready to deploy a Java web application; we will deploy a sample Java web app in the next topic.

Deploying a Java web application in App Services

We will show the deployment step for North Europe App service, and you must follow the same steps for West Europe App Service.

Pre-requisites

Sample Java Source code in Version Control System (GitHub)

Follow these steps to deploy a Java web application from source code repository:

1. Go to Azure App Service → Select '**prod-north-java-appservice**' → Select '**Deployment Center**' (from left panel option).

2. In the Source dropdown, select the '**Continuous Deployment (CI/CD)**' option, as shown in the following figure:

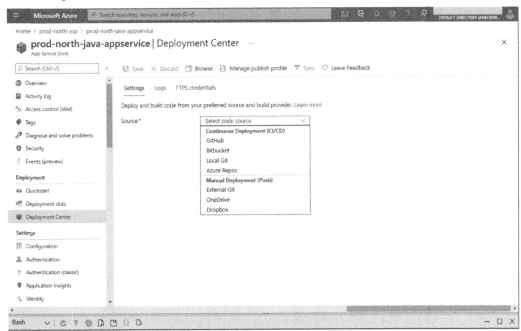

***Figure 5.25**: Deployment source selection*

3. It will ask you to sign-in once you select the version control system, so provide your login details and sign-in. After successful login, enter the required details from your account, like organization, repository, and branch name where the Java application source code is present.

Runtime Stack and version will be automatically added from your App Service Configuration for Tomcat and Java version details.

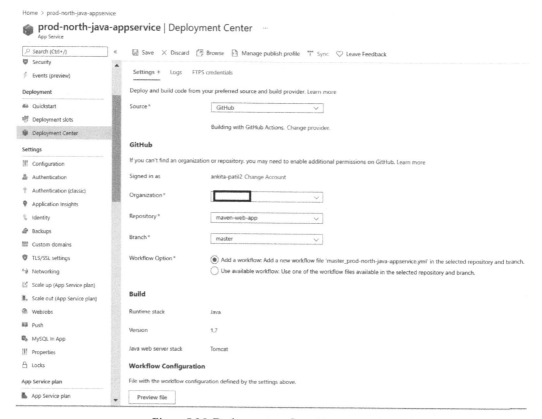

Figure 5.26: Deployment configuration app service

4. Preview the file for Workflow configuration; it should look like the following YML configuration for GitHub Actions.

```
# Docs for the Azure Web Apps Deploy action: https://github.com/
Azure/webapps-deploy
```

```
# More GitHub Actions for Azure: https://github.com/Azure/actions
```

```
name: Build and deploy WAR app to Azure Web App - prod-north-
java-appservice
```

```
on:
```

```
push:
```

```
branches:
```

```
- master
```

```
workflow_dispatch:

jobs:
build:
runs-on: windows-latest

steps:
- uses: actions/checkout@v2

- name: Set up Java version
uses: actions/setup-java@v1
with:
java-version: '1.7'

- name: Build with Maven
run: mvn clean install

- name: Upload artifact for deployment job
uses: actions/upload-artifact@v2
with:
name: java-app
path: '${{ github.workspace }}/target/*.war'

deploy:
runs-on: windows-latest
needs: build
environment:
name: 'production'
url: ${{ steps.deploy-to-webapp.outputs.webapp-url }}

steps:
- name: Download artifact from build job
uses: actions/download-artifact@v2
with:
name: java-app

- name: Deploy to Azure Web App
id: deploy-to-webapp
```

```
uses: azure/webapps-deploy@v2
with:
app-name: 'prod-north-java-appservice'
slot-name: 'production'
publish-profile: ${{ secrets.AzureAppService_PublishProfile_
xxxxxxxxxxxxxxxxxxxxxxxxxxxxxx }}
package: '*.war'
```

This configuration has two jobs: '**build**' and '**deploy**'. These will be triggered after any changes on your master branch and will deploy a java package in the form of a '***.war**' package.

5. Now, click on the **Save** button at the top to save the configurations in GitHub and automatically trigger GitHub Action for this App Service deployment config.

6. To verify the GitHub Actions execution, go to GitHub Repository → **Actions** →Click on the '**Build and Deploy WAR to Azure Web App**' workflow. You will see all the running workflows, as illustrated in the following screenshot:

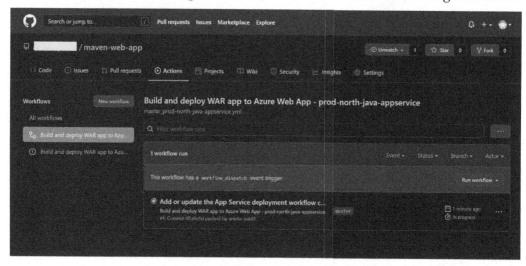

***Figure 5.27**: GitHub Actions - Workflow*

When you click on the first running workflow, you will see the two jobs '**build**' and '**deploy**', as follows:

Figure 5.28: Workflow build and deploy jobs

7. If your GitHub Actions workflow is successfully completed, we can verify the deployment for the North Europe App Service by accessing the URL '**https://test-java-appservice.azurewebsites.net/<APP NAME>**' (in this example, APP NAME is **sample-java**). The URL should redirect you to the first page of your java application. The sample application deployment will look as shown in the following screenshot:

Figure 5.29: Sample Java Application deployed in App Service

8. Now, repeat the steps starting from step 3 to deploy web application to App Service located in West Europe.

We have successfully created an infrastructure for Java App Service and deployed a sample Java application to these services. We have also created a secure and highly available infrastructure, as shown in *figure 5.18*.

Managing Azure Spring Cloud

Azure Spring Cloud is a service used to create and manage Spring Boot Application easily.

Follow these steps to create Spring Cloud service and then deploy a sample Hello Spring Boot application:

1. Create a **vars.tf** file and paste the required variable as the following code. You will need to update the default values for variables like "**client_id**", "**subscription_id**", and "**tenant_id**" in the following code and add additional variables like "**resource_group_name**":

```
# vars.tf
variable "client_secret" {

    description = "Enter your CLient Secret. Please make sure
you do not store the value of your client secret in the SCM
repository"
}
variable "client_id" {

    description = "Your client Id."

    default = " xxxxxxxx-xxxx-xxxx-xxxx-xxxxxxxxxxxx "
}
variable "subscription_id" {

    description = "Your subscription id."

    default = "xxxxxxxx-xxxx-xxxx-xxxx-xxxxxxxxxxxx"
}
variable "tenant_id" {

    description = "Your tenant id."

    default = " xxxxxxxx-xxxx-xxxx-xxxx-xxxxxxxxxxxx "
}
variable "prefix" {

  description = "The prefix which should be used for all resources
```

```
in this Chapter"
  default = "prod"
}

variable "environment" {
  description = "The Azure Region in which all resources in this
Chapter should be created."
  default = "Production"
}

variable "resource_group_name" {
    type        = string
    description = "Core Infrastructure Resource Group"
    default     = "sc-rg"
}
variable "location" {
    type = string
    default = "East US"
}
```

2. Create a **main.tf** file, same as that in the previous topics, which only includes configuration for the terraform {} block and the provider "**azurerm**" {} config (refer to point 3, 'Azure Provider configuration in Terraform', in the *Authenticating to Azure* section for this step).

3. Create a resource group in the **rg.tf** file, just like in the previous topic.

```
# rg.tf
# Create a Spring Cloud Resource Groups global
resource "azurerm_resource_group" "sc-prod-rg" {
  name     = var.resource_group_name
  location = var.location

  tags = {
    Environment = var.environment
  }
}
```

4. Finally, create **spring_cloud.tf**, which will have the configuration for creating application insights and spring-cloud service. Paste the following code in this file and save it:

```
# spring_cloud.tf
# Application insights for spring cloud service
resource "azurerm_application_insights" "sc_app_insights" {
  name                = "sc_insights"
  location            = var.location
  resource_group_name = azurerm_resource_group.sc-prod-rg.name
  application_type    = "web"
}

resource "azurerm_spring_cloud_service" "sc" {
  name                = "sc-service"
  resource_group_name = azurerm_resource_group.sc-prod-rg.name
  location            = var.location

  timeouts {
    create = "60m"
    delete = "2h"
  }

  trace {
    instrumentation_key = azurerm_application_insights.sc_app_
insights.instrumentation_key
  }
}
```

We looked at the application insight "**azurerm_application_insights**" resource block in brief in the previous topic. In this topic, only the value of **application_type** changes to "**web**".

Next, we will take a look at the "**azurerm_spring_cloud_service**" resource block for the creation for Spring Cloud service with name "**sc-service**". The Spring Cloud service manages different spring cloud applications created under them.

5. Also, we need to create a spring app under this spring cloud we created. The following Terraform configuration will create an app called " in Spring Cloud service called '**sc-service**'. Paste this code in **spring_cloud.tf**:

```
# spring_cloud.tf
# Spring Cloud App
resource "azurerm_spring_cloud_app" "sc-app" {
  name               = "hellospring"
  resource_group_name = azurerm_resource_group.sc-prod-rg.name
  service_name       = azurerm_spring_cloud_service.sc.name
}
```

The "**azurerm_spring_cloud_app**" resource block creates and maintains the "**hellospring**" application created in the "**sc-service**" Azure Spring Cloud service. The mandatory arguments are as listed here:

- **name**: This defines the name of the Spring Cloud App to be created. A new resource will be created if this is changed.

- **Resource_group_name**: This defines the name of resource group where the Spring Cloud App is to be created.

- **Service_name**: This will specify the Spring Cloud in which you want to create your application.

With this, we have all the required configuration for the creation of simple Spring Cloud infrastructure without any network configuration.

6. Execute '**terraform apply**'; it will plan and apply these configurations.

7. Verify the creation of Spring Cloud Service: go to Azure Portal → Search and Select '**Azure Spring Cloud**' → Select '**sc-service**' that was created from the preceding Terraform apply command. This spring cloud service should look like as follows:

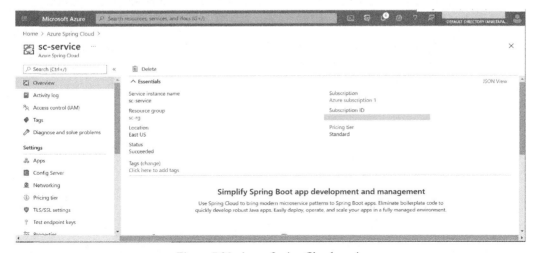

Figure 5.30: Azure Spring Cloud service

Next, deploy a sample Java spring application to this service with the following steps.

Deploying Spring Boot Application to Azure Spring Cloud

For deploying Spring Boot Application, we will need to develop an application that has all the dependencies required for Spring Cloud in its **pom.xml** file. So, we will start with initializing this application.

Pre-requisites

- JDK 8
- Maven
- Azure CLI and Azure Spring Cloud extension:

  ```
  az extension add --name spring-cloud
  ```

Here are the steps for Spring app deployment:

1. Generate a sample Spring Cloud project.

   Let's use the Spring initializer at following link to generate a template for Spring Cloud project:

   https://start.spring.io/#!type=maven-project&language=java&platformVersion=2.3.12.RELEASE&packaging=jar&jvmVersion=1.8&groupId=com.example&artifactId=hellospring&name=hellospring&description=Demo%20project%20for%20Spring%20Boot&packageName=com.example.hellospring&dependencies=web,-cloud-eureka,actuator,cloud-starter-sleuth,cloud-starter-zipkin,cloud-config-client

   Copy the preceding link and access it via a browser; you will be navigated to a page as shown in the following screenshot:

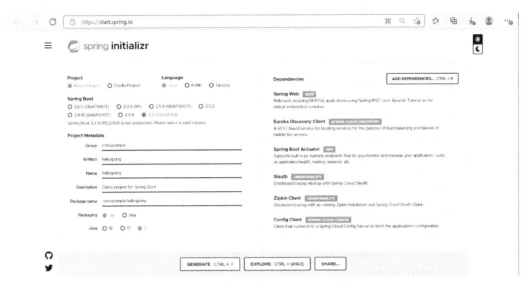

Figure 5.31: Spring Cloud project initializer

You can update **Project** metadata as per your requirements and add more dependencies with the '**Add Dependencies**' option.

2. Click on the **Generate** button once you are done making your changes. Download and extract the downloaded package. For a sample project, create a web controller for a simple web application by adding a Java controller in the **src/main/java/com/example/hellospring/HelloController.java** file with the following code:

```java
// HelloController.java
package com.example.hellospring;

import org.springframework.web.bind.annotation.RestController;
import org.springframework.web.bind.annotation.RequestMapping;

@RestController
public class HelloController {

  @RequestMapping("/")
  public String index() {
   return "Hello, Spring Cloud!";
  }
}
```

Save this file, and your sample Hello Spring project is ready.

3. Build the application using the following maven command from the Spring project root folder:

```
mvn clean package –DskipTests
```

This command should generate a jar file named **hellospring-0.0.1-SNAPSHOT.jar** in the target folder in project root.

4. Deploy this application JAR to the "**hellospring**" Azure Spring Cloud App in the "**sc-service**" Spring Cloud Service using the following commands:

  • Create deployment

```
az spring-cloud app deployment create -n hellospring-deployment --app hellospring -s sc-service -g sc-rg
```

Arguments:

   -n: Name of Deployment

   --app: Spring Cloud Application

   -s: Spring Cloud Service

   -g: Resource group

  • Set deployment

```
az spring-cloud app set-deployment -d hellospring-deployment -n hellospring -s sc-service -g sc-rg
```

Arguments:

   -d: Name of Deployment

   --n: Spring Cloud Application

   -s: Spring Cloud Service

   -g: Resource group

  • Deploy the jar to Spring App

```
az spring-cloud app deploy -n hellospring -s sc-service -g sc-rg --jar-path target/hellospring-0.0.1-SNAPSHOT.jar
```

Arguments:

   -n: Spring Cloud Application

   -s: Spring Cloud Service

-g: Resource group

--jar-path/--artifact-path: Path to jar file of the application to be deployed

5. It takes a few minutes to finish deploying the application. Go to the Apps blade in the Azure portal to verify the deployed Spring application. You will see the status of the application, as shown in the following screenshot. Here, it shows successful as provisioned state:

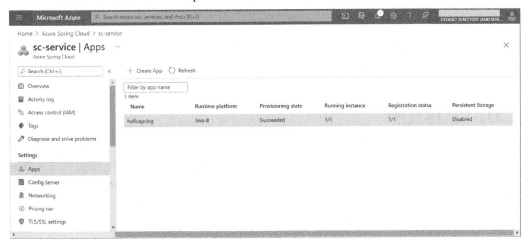

Figure 5.32: Azure Spring Cloud Apps

When you click on '**hellospring**', you will be navigated to Spring App, and you can find the endpoint URL to access this application. This is depicted in the following screenshot:

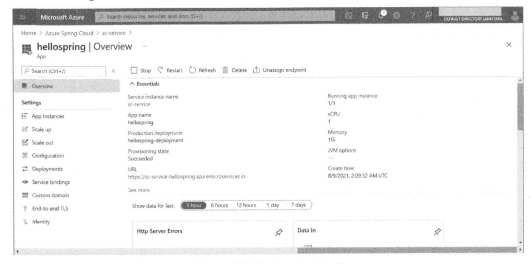

Figure 5.33: Spring App details

6. Verify the deployment by accessing the URL '**https://sc-service-hellospring. azuremicroservices.io**' from the browser; it should look like the following image with '`Hello, Spring Cloud!`'.

Hello, Spring Cloud!

Figure 5.34: HelloSpring URL

This is how we create and deploy Azure Spring Cloud Service and App.

Terraform can also be used to create other Azure cloud services.

Conclusion

In this chapter, we used Azure storage as the backend to manage Terraform states. We also created Jenkins AMI with help of the Packer tool and deployed it in the form of a virtual machine. We created virtual networks, subnets, public IP, security groups, and security rules for accessing the HTTP and SSH ports.

Additionally, we created architecture for managing infrastructure for Azure services like virtual machines, App Service, and Spring Cloud. We also learned how to deploy Java Web app and Spring Boot applications.

In the next chapter, we will learn how to create and work with Terraform modules. Creating Terraform modules makes the Terraform code reusable and avoids duplications in Terraform configuration.

Questions

1. In how many ways can Terraform authenticate with Azure?

2. How do we manage traffic to the app services in different regions?

3. What is Azure App Service?

4. What is Azure Spring Cloud?

CHAPTER 6
Terraform Modules

Some of the eye-catching advantages of **Object-Oriented Programming (OOP)** are modularity for better understanding, troubleshooting, and reuse of code. This methodology is something that's taught from college onward and also in any software development career. **Infrastructure as Code (IaC)** is a great addition to continuous practices of DevOps culture, and IaC also needs optimization to avoid repeated code across teams, applications, or environments.

How can we reuse or share Terraform configurations?

The answer is Terraform modules.

Note: Use "Module First" approach in Terraform configurations for all scenarios to manage infrastructure.

Structure

We will discuss the following topics in this chapter:

- Creating and distributing custom modules
- Managing production-like infrastructure using Terraform
- Creating Amazon VPC using Terraform modules

- Creating EKS cluster using Terraform modules

- Creating Azure network using Terraform modules

- Creating AKS cluster using Terraform modules

- Questions and exercises

Objectives

After studying this chapter, you will know how to create and manage modules using Terraform. We will learn about Terraform modules using the public registry, such as VPC module, EKS module, and AKS module.

Creating and distributing custom modules

In *Chapter 4, Automating Infrastructure Deployments in AWS Using Terraform*, we used the packer tool to create Jenkins and Nginx AMIs. We created VPC, subnets, security groups, inbound and outbound rules, route tables, associations, EFS to store **JENKINS_HOME** data, auto scaling groups, elastic load balancers, and so on using Terraform.

In this section, we will create VPC using our own module and create similar architecture in AWS, as follows:

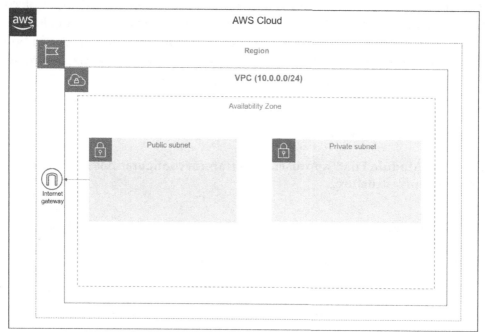

Figure 6.1: *Big Picture - Amazon VPC*

Create the following file and directory structure (refer to *Chapter 4, Automating Infrastructure Deployments in AWS Using Terraform*, for autoscaling, load balancing, and other resource creation using Terraform):

1. ModuleDemo
    1.1. Custommodules
        1.1.1. customvpc
            1.1.1.1. outputs.tf
            1.1.1.2. terraformVPC.tf
            1.1.1.3. vars.tf
    1.2. autoscaling.tf
    1.3. elb.tf
    1.4. id_rsa.pub
    1.5. devVPC.tf
    1.6. securitygroups.tf
    1.7. userdata.tpl
    1.8. vars.tf
    1.9. firstawsami-packer.json

Outputs provides us details about the identifiers of specific resources. The **ModuleDemo/Custommodules/customvpc/outputs.tf** file is created with the following code:

```
output "vpc_id" {
  value = aws_vpc.devVPC.id
}
output "aws_internet_gateway" {
  value = aws_internet_gateway.igw.id
}
output "public_subnet" {
  value = aws_subnet.public_subnet.id
}
```

The **ModuleDemo/Custommodules/customvpc/terraformVPC.tf** file is created with the following code:

```
#Providers are a logical abstraction of an upstream API. They help to
understand API interactions and exposing provider resources such AWS,
Google,

provider "aws" {
  region = var.apac_region
}


# Query all available Availability Zone; we will use specific
availability zone using index - The Availability Zones data source
provides access to the list of AWS Availability Zones which can be
accessed by an AWS account specific to region configured in the provider.
data "aws_availability_zones" "aws_az" {}


# Provides a VPC resource - https://registry.terraform.io/providers/
hashicorp/aws/latest/docs/resources/vpc
resource "aws_vpc" "devVPC" {
  cidr_block          = var.vpc_cidr_block
  enable_dns_hostnames = true # default is false


  tags = {
    Name = "dev_terraform_vpc"
  }
}

# Public Subnet - Provides an VPC subnet resource - https://registry.
terraform.io/providers/hashicorp/aws/latest/docs/resources/subnet.
resource "aws_subnet" "public_subnet" {
  cidr_block            = var.public_cidr
  vpc_id                = aws_vpc.devVPC.id
  map_public_ip_on_launch = true
  availability_zone       = data.aws_availability_zones.aws_az.names[1]

  tags = {
    Name = "dev_terraform_vpc_public_subnet"
  }
}
```

```
# Private Subnet - Provides an VPC subnet resource - https://registry.
terraform.io/providers/hashicorp/aws/latest/docs/resources/subnet.
resource "aws_subnet" "private_subnet" {
  cidr_block            = var.private_cidr
  vpc_id                = aws_vpc.devVPC.id
  map_public_ip_on_launch = false
  availability_zone     = data.aws_availability_zones.aws_az.names[1]


  tags = {
    Name = "dev_terraform_vpc_private_subnet"
  }
}


#To access EC2 instance inside a Virtual Private Cloud (VPC) we need
an Internet Gateway and a routing table connecting the subnet to the
Internet Gateway
# Creating Internet Gateway
# Provides a resource to create a VPC Internet Gateway - https://
registry.terraform.io/providers/hashicorp/aws/latest/docs/resources/
internet_gateway.
resource "aws_internet_gateway" "igw" {
  vpc_id = aws_vpc.devVPC.id

  tags = {
    Name = "dev_terraform_vpc_igw"
  }
}


# Provides a resource to create a VPC routing table - https://registry.
terraform.io/providers/hashicorp/aws/latest/docs/resources/route_table
resource "aws_route_table" "public_route" {
  vpc_id = aws_vpc.devVPC.id

  route {
    cidr_block = var.cidr_blocks
    gateway_id = aws_internet_gateway.igw.id
  }
```

```
   tags = {
     Name = "dev_terraform_vpc_public_route"
   }
}
```

Provides a resource to create an association between a Public Route
Table and a Public Subnet - https://registry.terraform.io/providers/
hashicorp/aws/latest/docs/resources/route_table_association

```
resource "aws_route_table_association" "public_subnet_association" {
  route_table_id = aws_route_table.public_route.id
  subnet_id      = aws_subnet.public_subnet.id
  depends_on     = [aws_route_table.public_route, aws_subnet.public_
subnet]
}
```

The `ModuleDemo/Custommodules/customvpc/vars.tf` file is created with the following code:

```
# Input Variables https://www.terraform.io/language/values/variables
variable "apac_region" {
 default = "ap-south-1"
}
variable "cidr_blocks" {

}
#Network Mask - 255.255.255.0 Addresses Available - 256
variable "vpc_cidr_block" {

}
variable "public_cidr" {

}
variable "private_cidr" {

}
```

The `ModuleDemo/autoscaling.tf` file is created with the following code (remember to input your OwnerID for the AMI ID filter):

```
resource "aws_launch_configuration" "nginx_launch_config" {
```

```
  image_id          = data.aws_ami.packeramis.id
  instance_type     = var.instance_type
  security_groups = [aws_security_group.sg_allow_ssh_http.id]

  user_data = data.template_file.init.rendered

  lifecycle {
    create_before_destroy = true
  }
}

resource "aws_autoscaling_group" "nginx_autoscaling_group" {
  launch_configuration = aws_launch_configuration.nginx_launch_config.id
  vpc_zone_identifier  = [module.customvpc.public_subnet]

  health_check_type      = "ELB"

  min_size = 2
  max_size = 5
  load_balancers             = [aws_elb.nginx-elb.id]
  tag {
    key                = "Name"
    value              = "dev_terraform_nginx_instance_asg"
    propagate_at_launch = true
  }
}

resource "aws_autoscaling_policy" "nginx_cpu_policy_scaleup" {
    name = "nginx_cpu_policy_scaleup"
    autoscaling_group_name = aws_autoscaling_group.nginx_autoscaling_
group.name
    adjustment_type = "ChangeInCapacity"
    scaling_adjustment = 1
    cooldown = "120"
}

resource "aws_autoscaling_policy" "nginx_cpu_policy_scaledown" {
    name = "nginx_cpu_policy_scaledown"
```

```
    autoscaling_group_name = aws_autoscaling_group.nginx_autoscaling_
group.name
    adjustment_type = "ChangeInCapacity"
    scaling_adjustment = -1
    cooldown = "120"
}

#Get latest AMI ID based on Filter - Here AMI created using Packer
data "aws_ami" "packeramis" {
  owners        = ["1xxxxxxxxxxx"] #change the owner ID as per your
account
  most_recent = true

  filter {
    name    = "name"
    values = ["packer-nginx*"]
  }


}

#The template_file data source usually loaded from an external file.
data "template_file" "init" {
  template = file("${path.module}/userdata.tpl")
}
```

The **ModuleDemo/elb.tf** file is created with the following code:

```
# Elastic Load Balancer resource, also known as a Classic Load Balancer
- https://registry.terraform.io/providers/hashicorp/aws/latest/docs/
resources/elb
resource "aws_elb" "nginx-elb" {
    name = "nginx-elb"
    subnets = [module.customvpc.public_subnet]
    security_groups = [aws_security_group.sg_allow_ssh_http.id]
    listener {
        instance_port      = 80
        instance_protocol = "http"
        lb_port            = 80
```

```
        lb_protocol        = "http"
    }
    health_check {
        healthy_threshold   = 3
        unhealthy_threshold = 3
        timeout             = 3
        target              = "HTTP:80/"
        interval            = 30
    }
    tags = {
        Name = "nginx_elb"
    }
}
```

The **ModuleDemo/devVPC.tf** file is created with the following code:

```
provider "aws" {
  region = var.apac_region
}
module "customvpc" {
  source = "./Commmodules/customvpc"
  region = var.apac_region
  cidr_blocks = "0.0.0.0/0"
  vpc_cidr_block = "10.0.1.0/24"
  public_cidr = "10.0.1.0/28"
  private_cidr = "10.0.1.16/28"
}
```

In this code, note the source = "**./Commmodules/customvpc**". We are providing the path of the module here.

The **ModuleDemo/securitygroups.tf** file is created with the following code:

```
# Provides a security group resource - https://registry.terraform.io/
providers/hashicorp/aws/latest/docs/resources/security_group
resource "aws_security_group" "sg_allow_ssh_http" {
  vpc_id = module.customvpc.vpc_id
```

```
  name = "dev_terraform_vpc_allow_ssh_http"


  tags = {
    Name = "dev_terraform_sg_allow_ssh_http"
  }
}


# Ingress Security Port 22 (Inbound) - Provides a security group rule
resource (https://registry.terraform.io/providers/hashicorp/aws/latest/
docs/resources/security_group_rule)
resource "aws_security_group_rule" "ssh_ingress_access" {
  from_port         = 22
  protocol          = "tcp"
  security_group_id = aws_security_group.sg_allow_ssh_http.id
  to_port           = 22
  type              = "ingress"
  cidr_blocks       = [var.cidr_blocks]
}


# Ingress Security Port 80 (Inbound)
resource "aws_security_group_rule" "http_ingress_access" {
  from_port         = 80
  protocol          = "tcp"
  security_group_id = aws_security_group.sg_allow_ssh_http.id
  to_port           = 80
  type              = "ingress"
  cidr_blocks       = [var.cidr_blocks]
}


# Egress Security (Outbound)
resource "aws_security_group_rule" "egress_access" {
  from_port         = 0
  protocol          = "-1"
  security_group_id = aws_security_group.sg_allow_ssh_http.id
  to_port           = 0
```

```
    type            = "egress"
    cidr_blocks     = [var.cidr_blocks]
}
```

The **ModuleDemo/userdata.tpl** file is created with the following code:

```
#!/bin/bash
sudo service nginx start
hostname >> /usr/share/nginx/html/index.html
```

The **ModuleDemo/vars.tf** file is created with the following code:

```
# Input Variables https://www.terraform.io/language/values/variables
variable "apac_region" {
 default = "ap-south-1"
}
variable "cidr_blocks" {
        default = "0.0.0.0/0"
}
variable "instance_type" {
        default = "t2.small"
}
```

The **ModuleDemo/firstawsami-packer.json** file is created with the following code:

```
{
    "variables": {
      "aws_access_key": "",
      "aws_secret_key": ""
    },
    "builders": [
      {
        "type": "amazon-ebs",
        "access_key": "{{user `aws_access_key`}}",
        "secret_key": "{{user `aws_secret_key`}}",
        "region": "ap-south-1",
        "source_ami": "ami-0dafa01c8100180f8",
```

```
      "instance_type": "t2.small",
      "ssh_username": "ec2-user",
      "ami_name": "packer-nginx-ami-{{timestamp}}"
   }
 ],
 "provisioners": [
    {
      "type": "shell",
      "inline": [
              "sudo yum update -y",
              "sudo amazon-linux-extras install -y nginx1.12"
      ]
    }
 ]
}
```

Execute `packer build -var "aws_access_key=XXXXXXXXXXXXXXXXXXXX" -var "aws_secret_key=XXXXXXXXXXXXXXXXXXXX" firstawsami-packer.json`

> **Note:** Terraform uses the source argument in a module block to find the source code for the required module from local paths, the Terraform registry, source code repositories, URLs, Amazon S3 buckets, and so on. The command terraform init uses the source argument to locate modules and download them to the local machine.

Execute the following command to verify newly created resources:

```
terraform init

Initializing modules...
- customvpc in Custommodules\customvpc

Initializing the backend...

Initializing provider plugins...
- Finding hashicorp/aws versions matching "3.40.0"...
- Finding latest version of hashicorp/template...
- Installing hashicorp/template v2.2.0...
```

-
-
-
-

Note **customvpc** in **Custommodules\customvpc** in the preceding output.

```
terraform plan -out=mymodule.tfplan
```

```
terraform apply mymodule.tfplan
```

Test it out in AWS to confirm that the ELB is active and you can access the NGINX instances. It can take a couple of minutes for the DNS entry of the ELB to register.

> **Note: Terraform configuration has minimum one module, i.e, the root module, with resources available in the terraform configuration files in the working directory.**

Let's push code into the GitHub repository and use it in a Terraform file using GitHub URL:

1. We need to make changes in the **devVPC.tf** file - source = "**github.com/ terraform-home/custommoduledemo/Custommodules//customvpc**":

```
provider "aws" {

  region = var.apac_region

}
module "customvpc" {

  source = "github.com/terraform-home/custommoduledemo/
Custommodules//customvpc"

  region = var.apac_region

  cidr_blocks = "0.0.0.0/0"

  vpc_cidr_block = "10.0.1.0/24"

  public_cidr = "10.0.1.0/28"

  private_cidr = "10.0.1.16/28"


}
```

2. Create a new repository in GitHub, as shown in the following screenshot:

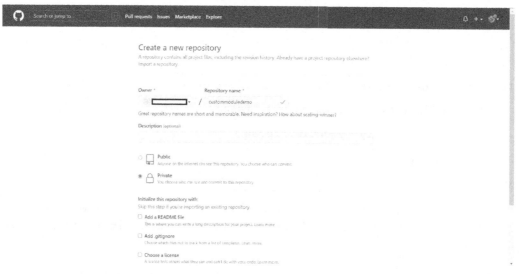

Figure 6.2: GitHub repository for custom modules

3. Go to the **customvpc** directory and execute the following commands to push code into GitHub:

- `cd customvpc`

- `git init .`

- `git add .`

- `git commit -m "first commit"`

    o `git remote add origin https://github.com/<ORG_NAME>/custommoduledemo.git`

    o `git branch -M main`

    o `git push -u origin main`

4. Now, execute **terraform init** and note how our module is used:

```
terraform init

Initializing modules...

Downloading git::https://github.com/terraform-home/
custommoduledemo.git for customvpc...

- customvpc in .terraform\modules\customvpc

Initializing the backend...
```

Note: Terraform Registry is available in public and we can use it to find useful modules to implement proven infrastructure scenarios.

Managing production-like infrastructure using Terraform

Modules are self-contained packages of Terraform configurations files that are easily managed as a group. They promote reusability and stability with incremental and improved learning. There are multiple modules available at **https://registry.terraform.io/browse/modules** for AWS, Azure, and Google Cloud Platforms. We will cover some of the modules in the following sections.

Creating Amazon VPC using Terraform modules

We created our own custom module in the previous section. The existing terraform module is also available in the public registry of Terraform. A Terraform module that creates VPC resources on AWS is available at **https://registry.terraform.io/modules/terraform-aws-modules/vpc/aws/latest**, as shown in the following screenshot:

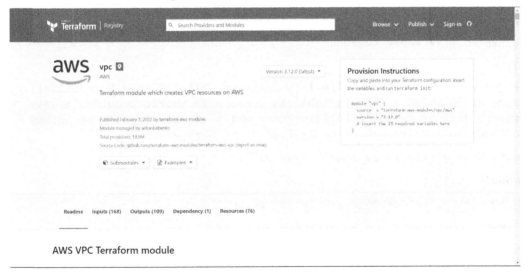

Figure 6.3: *Terraform AWS VPC module*

The **vars.tf** file is created with the following code:

```
variable "vpc_name" {
  default = "terraform_eks_dev_vpc"
  type    = string
}
#Network Mask - 255.255.255.0 Addresses Available - 256
variable "vpc_cidr_block" {
    default = "10.0.0.0/16"
}
variable "apac_region" {
 default = "ap-south-1"
}
```

The **devVPC.tf** file is created with the following code (change it to the latest version for the AWS provider: **https://registry.terraform.io/providers/hashicorp/aws/latest**):

```
#Providers are a logical abstraction of an upstream API. They help to
understand API interactions and exposing provider resources such AWS,
Google, Azure
provider "aws" {
  region = var.apac_region
}
# Query all avilable Availibility Zone; we will use specific availability
zone using index - The Availability Zones data source provides access
to the list of AWS Availability Zones which can be accessed by an AWS
account specific to region configured in the provider.
data "aws_availability_zones" "aws_az" {}
module "vpc" {
  source = "terraform-aws-modules/vpc/aws"
  name                = var.vpc_name
  cidr                = var.vpc_cidr_block
  azs                 = data.aws_availability_zones.aws_az.names
  private_subnets     = ["10.0.1.0/28", "10.0.2.0/28", "10.0.3.0/28"]
  public_subnets      = ["10.0.4.0/28", "10.0.5.0/28", "10.0.6.0/28"]
  enable_nat_gateway  = true
  single_nat_gateway  = true
```

```
  enable_dns_hostnames = true # default is false

  tags = {
    Terraform = "true"
    Environment = "dev"
  }
}
```

The **output.tf** file is created with the following code:

```
output "vpc_id" {
  value       = module.vpc.vpc_id
}


output "region" {
  description = "AWS region"
  value       = var.apac_region
}
```

Execute the following command to verify newly created resources:

```
terraform init
terraform plan -out=devVPC.tfplan
terraform apply devVPC.tfplan
```

> **Note: Manage configuration in local or remote modules to maintain and update configuration easily over time.**

In the next section, we will learn about managing EKS cluster using Terraform modules.

Creating EKS cluster using Terraform modules

Terraform module **terraform-aws-eks** is used to create an **Elastic Kubernetes (EKS)** cluster and associated worker groups on AWS EKS. Visit **https://registry.terraform.io/modules/terraform-aws-modules/eks/aws/latest** for more information. Basic knowledge of Kubernetes is required to go through this section.

The following screenshot shows the EKS cluster using a Terraform module:

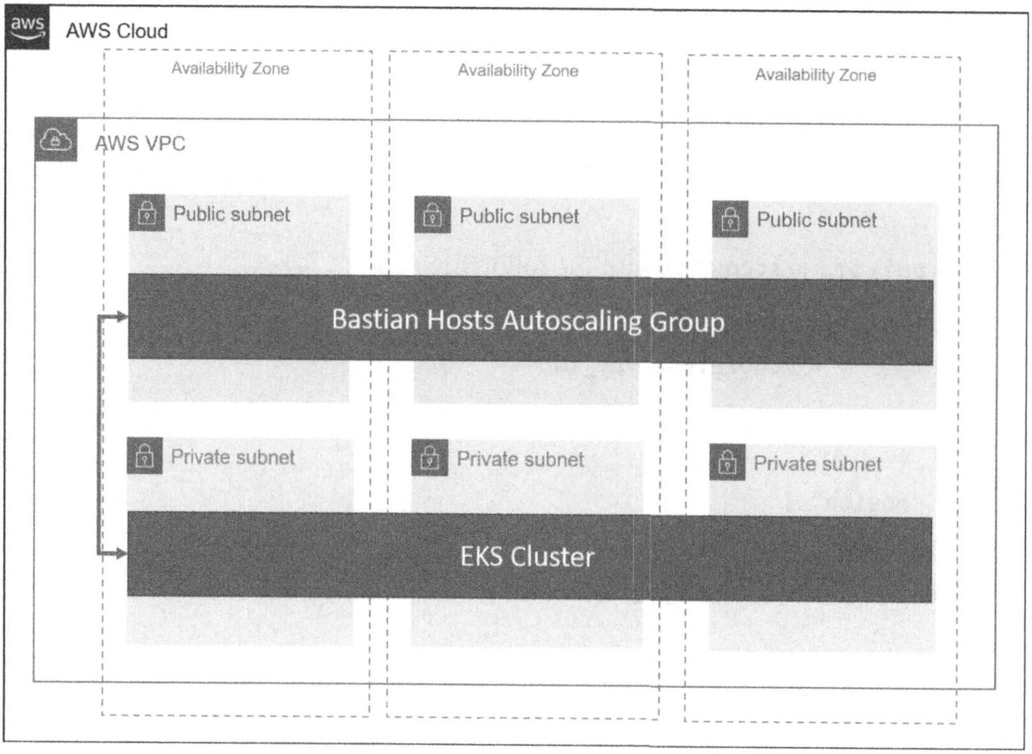

Figure 6.4: EKS cluster using a Terraform module

Let's start creating EKS cluster using Terraform modules using https://learn.
hashicorp.com/tutorials/terraform/eks :

1. Make changes in worker groups and instance type. We will only use small
   instance for worker groups.

```
module "eks" {
  source          = "terraform-aws-modules/eks/aws"
  version         = "17.24.0"
  cluster_name    = local.cluster_name
  cluster_version = "1.20"
  subnets         = module.vpc.private_subnets

  tags = {
    Environment = "dev"
    GithubRepo  = "terraform-aws-eks"
    GithubOrg   = "terraform-aws-modules"
```

```
    }

    vpc_id = module.vpc.vpc_id

    worker_groups = [
      {
        name                          = "worker-group-small"
        instance_type                 = "t2.small"
        asg_desired_capacity          = 2
        additional_security_group_ids = [aws_security_group.worker_
group_mgmt_small.id]
      },
    ]
    .
    .
    .
}
```

2. The next step is to initialize your Terraform workspace using the **terraform init** command, as follows:

```
Initializing modules...

Downloading registry.terraform.io/terraform-aws-modules/eks/aws
17.24.0 for eks...

- eks in .terraform\modules\eks

- eks.fargate in .terraform\modules\eks\modules\fargate

- eks.node_groups in .terraform\modules\eks\modules\node_groups


Initializing the backend...


Initializing provider plugins...

- Finding terraform-aws-modules/http versions matching ">=
2.4.1"...

- Reusing previous version of hashicorp/cloudinit from the
dependency lock file
    .
    .
    .
```

```
- Using previously-installed hashicorp/aws v4.3.0
  .
  .
  .
```

3. Let's create a plan and execute the **terraform plan -out=tf.tfplan** command, as shown in the following code:

```
Plan: 50 to add, 0 to change, 0 to destroy.

- - - - - - - - - - - - - - - - - - - - - - - - - - - - - - - - - - - - - - - - - - - - - - - - - - - -

Saved the plan to: tf.plan

To perform exactly these actions, run the following command to
apply:
    terraform apply "tf.plan"
```

4. Execute **terraform apply tf.tfplan**; you can find output similar to the following after its successful completion:

```
Apply complete! Resources: 50 added, 0 changed, 0 destroyed.

The state of your infrastructure has been saved to the path
below. .
  .
State path: terraform.tfstate
```

5. Wait for around 10 minutes, and you will get the following output:

```
Outputs:

cluster_endpoint = "https://A21C08010055B5BCFC269711620B89C3.yl4.
ap-south-1.eks.amazonaws.com"
cluster_id = "dev-eks-cluster"
cluster_name = "dev-eks-cluster"
cluster_security_group_id = "sg-0d2b85914f8ea7a4b"
  .
  .
  .
kubectl_config = <<EOT
apiVersion: v1
```

```
preferences: {}
kind: Config

clusters:
- cluster:
    server: https://A21C08010055B5BCFC269711620B89C3.yl4.ap-
south-1.eks.amazonaws.com
    certificate-authority-data: XXXXXXXXXXXXXXXXXXXXXXXXXXXXXXXX
```
XXXXXXXXXXXXXXXXXXXXXXXXXXXXXXXXXXXXXXXXXXXXXXXXXXXXXXXXXXXXXX
XXXXXXXXXXXXXXXVFERXdwcmRXSmwKY2O1bGRHVnpNQjRYRFRJeU1ETXdOREUxT-
VRZek9Gb1hEVE15TURNd01URTFNVF16T0Zvd0ZURVRNQkVHQTFVRQpBeE1LYTN-
WaVpYSnVaWFJsY3pDQ0FTSXdEUVlKS29aSWh2Y05BUUVCQlFBRGdnRVBBREND-
QVFvQ2dnRUJBTHpYCjVPWnNNOd3FFcTlVa0p6ZUpuUZkxPa2tXXXXXXXXXXXXXXXX
XXXXXXXXXXXXXXXXXXXXXXXXXXXXXXXXXXXXXXXXXXXXXXXXXXXXXXXXXXXXXXX
XXXXXXXXXXXXXXXXXXXXXXXXXXXXa3J0cG1PbkVFQVlUeeHRBQWZGK3JvRDgx-
SgpZUXlHcTFFkUWllMjh0Y2p1Wm9QejJjWnNhSzNVR0hPUlVVWi9Bdmc1Q1pNR-
1E5MTlBa2V5eGpwWZXXXXXXXXXXXXXXXXXXXXXXXXXXXXXXXXXXXXXXXXXXXXX
XXXXXXXXXXXXXXXXXXXXXXXXXXXXXXXXXXXXXXXXXXXXXXXXXXXXXXXXXdZb
zZhTXJ5dUpQdHJvSDM3ZDNaaUlp1YThYeDDiK0FtNXpSNEg1OUNiQ3M5N2NQREhh-
QVR4RStwMgpMMVFnYlU4K2MzZy91c21xeFM4Q0F3F3RUFXXXXXXXXXXXXXXXXXXXXX
XXXXXXXXXXXXXXXXXXXXXXXXXXXXXXXXXXXXXXXXXXXXXXXXXXXXXXXXXXXXXXX
XXXXXXXXXXXXXXXXXXXXXXXXeGowVnpVeEg0OEVVNQTBHQ1NxR1NJYjMKRFFFQkN-
3VUFBNElCQVFFBck1CaG80R3YrcUJuZDVjUjlicH1PVjJXK21KRKC9FUHZvSHVpYnZi
eFVyVXXXXXXXXXXXXXXXXXXXXXXXXXXXXXXXXXXXXXXXXXXXXXXXXXXXXXXXXXX
XXXXXXXXXXXXXXXXXXXXXXXXXXXXXXXXXXXXXXXXXXXXXXXXXArU31NTWpQb-
mRoSVdCUjEwdTl5ekZ6YjlDY2R1K3lFeTZVS1AvUmIrCswalI1U2tlK1d3S-
jIKY3VRUDVQQODN0a3pPVWJSK0c5N1Bwbkw1L0kXXXXXXXXXXXXXXXXXXXXXXXXXX
XXXXXXXXXXXXXXXXXXXXXXXXXXXXXXXXXXXXXXXXXXXXXXXXXXXXXXXXXXXXXXX
XXXXXXXXXXXXXXXXXXXeE50VXc5NzFiQ1hPVnVMUm0xNFRRCjR2SHMvMFM1U1c1N-
3BJWWNHUGtZKZdWRHZsa0c1ND16N0srdQotLS0tLUVORCBDRVJUSUZJQ0FURS0tL-
S0tCg==
```
```
  name: eks_dev-eks-cluster

contexts:
- context:
    cluster: eks_dev-eks-cluster
    user: eks_dev-eks-cluster
  name: eks_dev-eks-cluster

current-context: eks_dev-eks-cluster

users:
- name: eks_dev-eks-cluster
```
```

```
    user:
      exec:
        apiVersion: client.authentication.k8s.io/v1alpha1
        command: aws-iam-authenticator
        args:
          - "token"
          - "-i"
          - "dev-eks-cluster"

  EOT
  region = "ap-south-1"
```

6. Go to the **C:\Users\<User>\.kube** directory and copy config for backup. Replace content with the **kubectl_config** variable output given earlier.

7. Install kubectl if it is not already installed on your system and keep it on path (environment variable).

8. Execute **kubectl cluster-info**.

   Kubernetes master is running at https://A21C08010055B5BCFC269711620B89C3.yl4.ap-south-1.eks.amazonaws.com

   CoreDNS is running at https://A21C08010055B5BCFC269711620B89C3.yl4.ap-south-1.eks.amazonaws.com/api/v1/namespaces/kube-system/services/kube-dns:dns/proxy" https://A21C08010055B5BCFC269711620B89C3.yl4.ap-south-1.eks.amazonaws.com/api/v1/namespaces/kube-system/services/kube-dns:dns/proxy

9. Now, consider that you get the following error:

   Unable to connect to the server: getting credentials: exec: exec: "aws-iam-authenticator": executable file not found

10. Then, install **aws-iam-authenticator** using the **choco install -y aws-iam-authenticator** command:

    Chocolatey v0.10.15

    Installing the following packages:

    aws-iam-authenticator

    By installing you accept licenses for the packages.

    aws-iam-authenticator v0.5.3 [Approved]

    .

    .

```
.
Chocolatey installed 1/1 packages.

 See the log for details (C:\ProgramData\chocolatey\logs\
 chocolatey.log).
```

11. Execute **kubectl get nodes** to get kubernetes nodes details:

```
NAME                                        STATUS    ROLES     AGE      VERSION
ip-10-0-1-68.ap-south-1.compute.internal    Ready     <none>    113m
v1.20.11-eks-f17b81

ip-10-0-2-70.ap-south-1.compute.internal    Ready     <none>    113m
v1.20.11-eks-f17b81
```

12. Let's deploy the Kubernetes dashboard and visit it in a local browser. Kubernetes Metrics Server is used to gather metrics like cluster CPU and memory usage, but it is not deployed in EKS clusters by default.

Note: Version argument is supported for Terraform Registry modules.

```
module "eks" {
        source = "terraform-aws-modules/eks/aws"
        version = "x.x.x"

        .

}
```

13. Download the metrics server from **https://codeload.github.com/kubernetes-sigs/metrics-server/tar.gz/v0.3.6** and unzip it, as shown here:

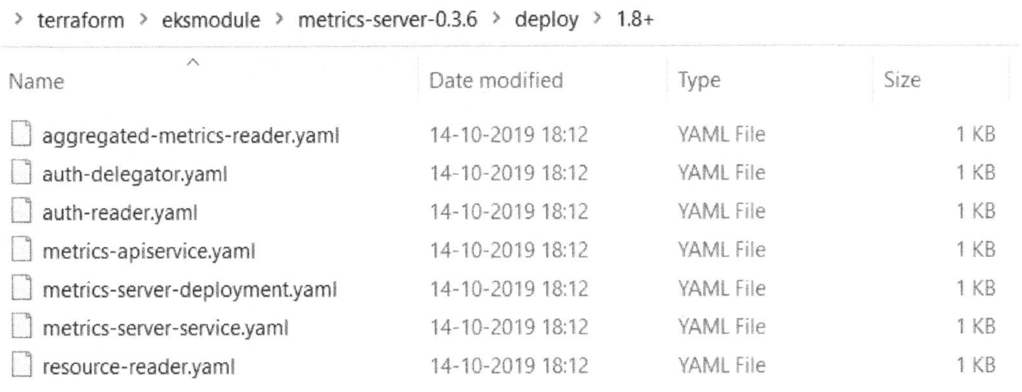

> terraform > eksmodule > metrics-server-0.3.6 > deploy > 1.8+

Name	Date modified	Type	Size
aggregated-metrics-reader.yaml	14-10-2019 18:12	YAML File	1 KB
auth-delegator.yaml	14-10-2019 18:12	YAML File	1 KB
auth-reader.yaml	14-10-2019 18:12	YAML File	1 KB
metrics-apiservice.yaml	14-10-2019 18:12	YAML File	1 KB
metrics-server-deployment.yaml	14-10-2019 18:12	YAML File	1 KB
metrics-server-service.yaml	14-10-2019 18:12	YAML File	1 KB
resource-reader.yaml	14-10-2019 18:12	YAML File	1 KB

Figure 6.5: *Metrics server files*

14. Deploy the metrics server to the cluster by executing **kubectl apply -f metrics-server-0.3.6/deploy/1.8+/**:

15. Verify that the metrics server has been deployed using the **kubectl get deployment metrics-server -n kube-system** command:

NAME	READY	UP-TO-DATE	AVAILABLE	AGE
metrics-server	1/1	1	1	101s

16. Execute **kubectl apply -f https://raw.githubusercontent.com/ kubernetes/dashboard/v2.0.0-beta8/aio/deploy/recommended. yaml** and schedule the resources for the dashboard:

17. Execute the **kubectl proxy** command to start a proxy server that will serve you the dashboard from the browser on a local machine:

```
C:\Kubernetes>kubectl proxy
Starting to serve on 127.0.0.1:8001
```

Figure 6.6: kubectl proxy

18. Access the Kubernetes dashboard at **http://127.0.0.1:8001/api/v1/namespaces/ kubernetes-dashboard/services/https:kubernetes-dashboard:/proxy/**. It will look at follows:

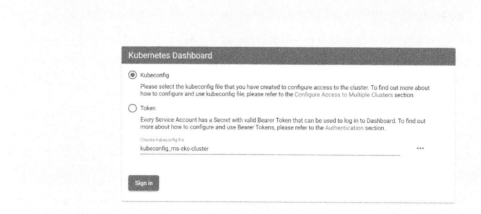

Figure 6.7: EKS cluster dashboard in the local system using proxy

19. We will use Token to login, but how do we get token? Execute the **kubectl -n kube-system get secret** command for this.

20. Find the exact name of the **service-controller-token** shown as follows:

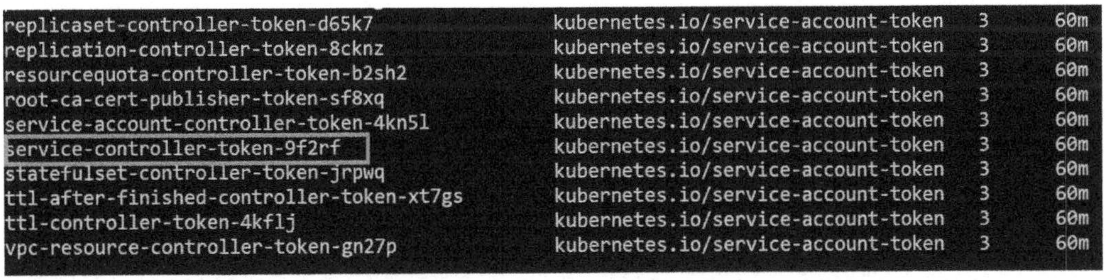

```
replicaset-controller-token-d65k7          kubernetes.io/service-account-token   3    60m
replication-controller-token-8cknz         kubernetes.io/service-account-token   3    60m
resourcequota-controller-token-b2sh2       kubernetes.io/service-account-token   3    60m
root-ca-cert-publisher-token-sf8xq         kubernetes.io/service-account-token   3    60m
service-account-controller-token-4kn5l     kubernetes.io/service-account-token   3    60m
service-controller-token-9f2rf             kubernetes.io/service-account-token   3    60m
statefulset-controller-token-jrpwq         kubernetes.io/service-account-token   3    60m
ttl-after-finished-controller-token-xt7gs  kubernetes.io/service-account-token   3    60m
ttl-controller-token-4kflj                 kubernetes.io/service-account-token   3    60m
vpc-resource-controller-token-gn27p        kubernetes.io/service-account-token   3    60m
```

Figure 6.8: Service-controller-token

21. Execute **kubectl -n kube-system describe secret service-controller-token-9f2rf** to get secret:

Name: **service-controller-token-fbplw**

Namespace: **kube-system**

Labels: **<none>**

Annotations: **kubernetes.io/service-account.name: service-controller**

        kubernetes.io/service-account.uid: 6e293a8b-8817-4f4b-9d97-bad197dbd82e

Type: **kubernetes.io/service-account-token**

Data

====

ca.crt: **1066 bytes**

namespace: **11 bytes**

token: **byxxxxxxxxxxxxxxxxxxxxxxxxxxxxxxxxxxxxxxxxxxxxxxxxxxxxx xxxxxxxxxxxxxxxxxxxxxxxxxxxxxxxxxxxxxxxxxxxxxxxxxxxxxxxxxxxxxxx xxxxxxxxxxxxxxxxxxxxxxxxxxxxxxxxxxxxxxxxxxxxxxxxxxxxxxxxxxxxxxx xxxxxxxxxxxxxxxxxxxxxxxxxxxxxxxxxxxxxxxxxxxxxxxxxxxxxxxxxxxxxxx xxxxxxxxxxxxxxxxxxxxxxxxxxxxxxxxxxxxxxxxxxxxxxxxxxxxxxxxxxxxxxx xxxxxxxxxxxxxxxxxxxxxxxxxxxxxxxxxxxxxxxxxxxxxxxxxxxxxxxxxxxxxxx xxxxxxxxxxxxxxxxxxxxxxxxxxxxxxxxxxxxxxxxxxxxxxxxxxxxxxxxxxxxxxx xxxxxxxxxxxxxxxxxxxxxxxxxxxxxxxxxxxxxxxxxxxxxxxxxxxxxxxxxxxxxxx xxxxxxxxxxxxxxxxxxxxxxxxxxxxxxxxxxxxxxxxxxxxxxxxxxxxxxxxxxxxxxx xxxxxxxxxxxxxxxxxxxxxxxxxxxxxxxxxxxxxxxxxxxxxxxxxxxxxxxxxxxxxxx

XXXXXXXXXXXXXXXXXXXXXXXXXXXXXXXXXXXXXXXXXXXXXXXXXXXXXXXXXXXXXXX
XXXXXXXXXXXXXXXXXXXXXXXXXXXXXXXXXXXXXXXXXXXXXXXXXXXXXXXXXXXXXXX
XXXXXXXXXXXXXXXXXXXXXXXXXXXXXXXXXXXXXXXXXXXXXXXXXXXXXXXXXXXXXXX
XXXXXXXXXXXXXXXXXXXXXXXXXXXXXXXXXXXXXXXXXXXXXXXXXXXXXXXXXXXXXXX

22. Copy the token and enter it in the dashboard. Then, click on **Sign in**, as shown here:

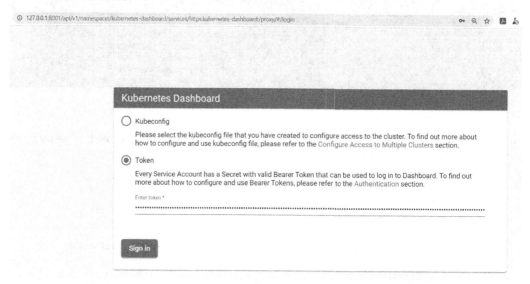

Figure 6.9: *Kubernetes Dashboard login using service-controller-token*

23. Kubernetes Dashboard is available now. Verify the services available in the **Discovery and Load Balancing** section, as illustrated here:

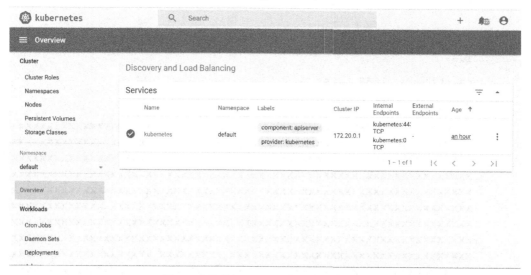

Figure 6.10: *Discovery and Load Balancing*

24. Click on **Cluster** to get all details related to worker groups:

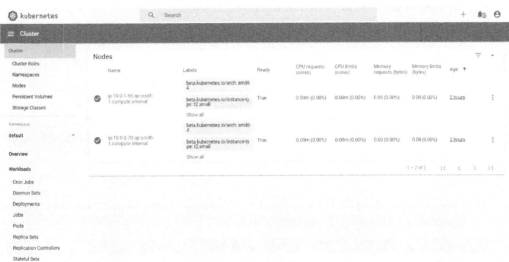

Figure 6.11: Worker groups or nodes

25. Verify the **CPU Usage** and **Memory Usage** by clicking on the **Nodes** section in the Kubernetes Dashboard:

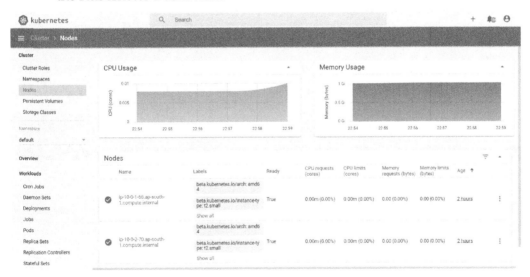

Figure 6.12: Nodes with CPU and Memory usage

26. All resources such as Kubernetes cluster, worker groups, VPC, security groups, and so on are created in Amazon Cloud.

Note: Local modules are in the same or a relative location with Terraform configuration files; hence, they don't support versions.

```
module "customvpc" {

        source = "./Custommodules/customvpc"

        .

        .

}
```

27. Go to the Amazon EKS section in the AWS management portal and verify the cluster created using Terraform module.

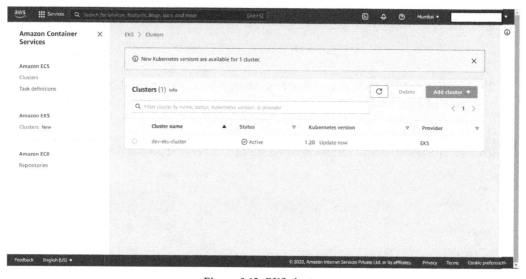

Figure 6.13: EKS cluster

28. Click on the **Overview** section to verify the worker groups created using Terraform module, as shown here:

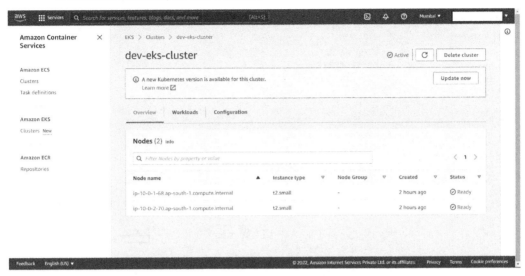

Figure 6.14: *Worker groups in the AWS Management Portal*

29. The **Workloads** section provides details about different deployments in the cluster, as follows:

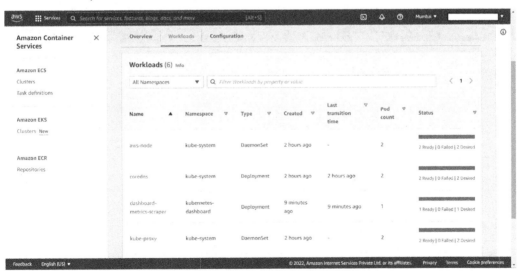

Figure 6.15: *Workload deployments*

30. The **Configuration** section provides details related to the API Endpoint, compute, network, and so on, as shown here:

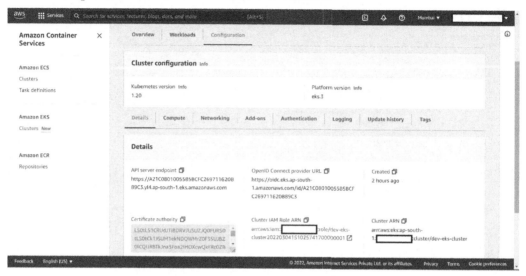

Figure 6.16: Cluster configuration in the AWS Management Console

31. Go to the EC2 section in the AWS Management Console and verify **Auto Scaling groups** for our cluster. Click on the **Instance management** section in the bottom pane to get details about instances running as worker groups.

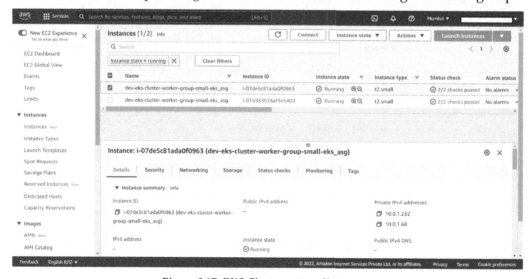

Figure 6.17: EKS Cluster auto scaling group

Note: A module can be either public or private in Terraform. The source argument indicates to find the source code for the required module from local paths, Terraform Registry, source code repositories, URLs, Amazon S3 buckets, and so on.

```
module "customvpc" {
      source = "github.com/terraform-home/moduledemo/Custommodules//
customvpc"

      .

      .

}
module "customvpc" {
      source = "./Custommodules/customvpc"

      .

      .

}
```

In the next section, we will look at creating Azure network using Terraform modules in brief.

Creating Azure network using Terraform modules

The network Terraform module creates a virtual network in Azure with a subnet or a set of subnets passed in as input parameters. Visit **https://registry.terraform.io/ modules/Azure/network/azurerm/latest** for more details.

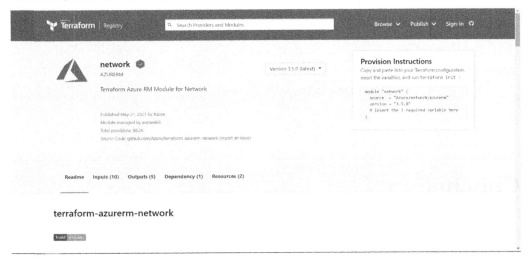

Figure 6.18: Network module

Now that we've covered AWS and the use of modules quite extensively; if you're feeling up to it, you can take the code above and review Azure's documentation to replicate something similar if Azure is your playground of choice.

In the next section, we will learn about creating the AKS cluster using Terraform modules.

Creating AKS cluster using Terraform modules

The `terraform-azurerm-aks` https://registry.terraform.io/modules/Azure/aks/azurerm/latest module deploys a Kubernetes cluster on Azure Kubernetes Services with monitoring support through Azure Log Analytics. Visit https://learn.hashicorp.com/tutorials/terraform/aks?in=terraform/kubernetes for more details.

Implement this section as part of the exercise by following the module documentation.

> **Note: All custom modules require a source argument, which is a meta-argument defined by Terraform. It can be assigned local path or a remote source such as GitHub.**
>
> ```
> module "eks" {
>     source = "terraform-aws-modules/eks/aws"
>         .
>         .
>         .
> }
> module "customvpc" {
>     source = "github.com/terraform-home/moduledemo/Custommodules//customvpc"
>         .
>         .
>         .
> }
> module "customvpc" {
>     source = "./Custommodules/customvpc"
>         .
>         .
>         .
> }
> ```

Conclusion

Modules help us apply OOP concepts like reusability, maintainability, and manageability. Another important aspect is verification and validation, which comes with practice. In this chapter, we covered custom modules and publicly available modules to create Amazon VPC and EKS cluster.

Another benefit of Terraform Modules is that the same modules can be used to build infrastructure for many different infrastructure projects. Hence, good habits and coding practices can be surfaced up within an organization so that consistent outcomes can be delivered across projects more easily.

Modules make life much easier for managing infrastructure. Similarly, Terraform Cloud helps manage one's entire Terraform activities in Cloud with remote state storage and not on your own system or on-premise. We will cover Terraform Cloud in the next chapter.

Points to remember

- Terraform uses the source argument in a module block to find the source code for the required module from local paths, the Terraform registry, source code repositories, URLs, and so on.

- The command terraform init uses the source argument to locate modules and download them to the local machine.

- Terraform configuration has minimum one module.

- Manage configuration in local or remote modules to maintain and update configuration easily over time.

Multiple choice questions

1. **Which is the good place to find existing modules?**

    a. GitHub

    b. Public Terraform Registry

    c. AWS

    d. Azure

2. **State True or False: Terraform configuration has minimum one module with name "root".**

    a. False

    b. True

3. **State True or False: A module can be either protected or private.**

    a. True

    b. False

Answers

1. b
2. b
3. b

Questions

1. What are Terraform Modules and how it is useful?
2. How can we access Modules?
3. Can we store Modules in Code repositories?

CHAPTER 7

Terraform Cloud

Terraform Cloud is an application that allows teams to work on Terraform in a collaborative manner. It reduces the effort of manually executing the Terraform workflow from a local environment each time a change is required in the infrastructure. It has connections supporting different version control systems, including GitHub, Bitbucket, and GitLab.

In this chapter, we will learn how to work with Terraform Cloud application. We will execute Terraform configuration from workspace in Terraform Cloud; the code that we will execute is from *Chapter 5, Automating Infrastructure Deployments in Azure Using Terraform*. Access management of Terraform Cloud is also covered in this chapter.

Structure

We will discuss the following topics in this chapter:

- Introduction to Terraform Cloud
- Workspace in Terraform Cloud
- Executing Terraform configuration in Terraform Cloud
- Access management in Terraform Cloud

Objectives

After studying this chapter, you should be able to create and configure organization, and create workspace and connect it with GitHub. You should also be able to execute Terraform configuration in the workspaces in Terraform Cloud. Additionally, this chapter will provide you with an overview of access management in Terraform Cloud.

Introduction to Terraform Cloud

Terraform Cloud manages Terraform runs in a consistent and reliable environment. It is an application that helps teams use Terraform together. It includes features like easy shared state and secret data management; access controls mechanism is also provided for approving changes to the infrastructure. Terraform Cloud also includes a private registry for sharing Terraform modules.

Here are the features of Terraform Cloud:

- Remote Terraform execution

- Workspace for organizing infrastructure

- Version control integration

- Command line integration

- Private module registry

- Integration of other business systems with API, notification, and run tasks

- Access control and governance

Terraform Cloud is a hosted service at **https://app.terraform.io**. We can sign up free for small teams of up to five members, but a paid plan is also available for larger teams.

Creating an account in Terraform Cloud

Let's create a free account for Terraform Cloud with the following steps:

1. Go to **https://app.terraform.io** and select the **Create your free account** option, as shown in the following screenshot:

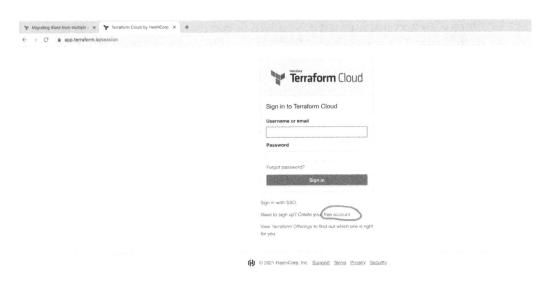

Figure 7.1: Terraform login page

2. Enter the details required as shown in the following screenshot: **Username**, **Email**, **Password** and accept the terms and conditions and privacy policies before clicking on the '**Create account**' button:

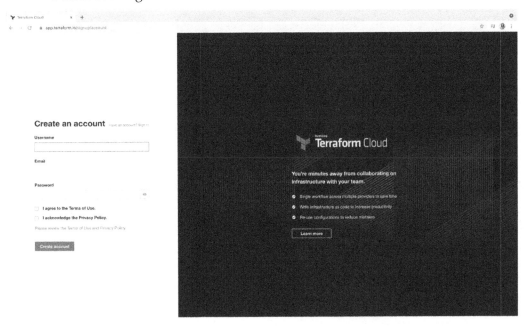

Figure 7.2: Create account in Terraform Cloud

3. Once your account is created, you will be navigated to a window as depicted in the following screenshot, which asks you to confirm the email ID you have provided:

Figure 7.3: Confirm email

4. Go to email and click on the link as shown in the email in the following screenshot:

Figure 7.4: Confirmation mail in email inbox

5. Once you have confirmed your email, you will be navigated to the page shown as follows for getting started:

Figure 7.5: Terraform Cloud welcome page

Setting up Terraform Cloud organization

After signing up, we need to set up workflow for Terraform Cloud. We have two options, as shown in the preceding image: try an example configuration and start from scratch. Try with example has step-by-step instructions that you can easily follow and create an example workflow within a few minutes without any issues.

In this chapter, we will choose the second option, i.e., start from scratch, so that you can learn to create everything from scratch. Let's set up the workflow using the following steps:

1. When you click on the '**Start from scratch**' option after successful signup, you will be navigated to the page as shown in the following figure. Enter the '**Organization name**' in the input box, as shown in following figure, and then click on the '**Create organization**' button:

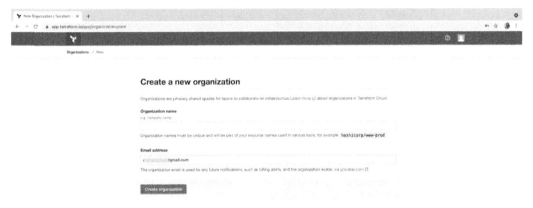

Figure 7.6: Create organization

2.   Now, you will be navigated to a page where you need to choose the workflow type   (refer to the following figure); select the '**Version control workflow**' option here:

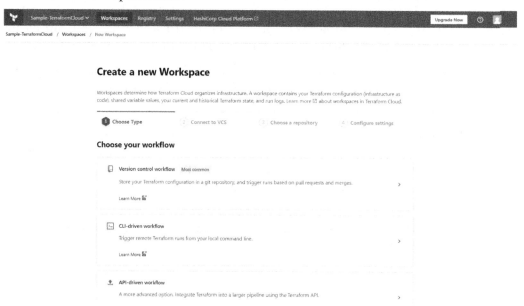

Figure 7.7: Choose workflow type

3.   After choosing this, we can connect the version control system (GitHub, Gitlab, Bitbucket, and Azure DevOps) directly to the organization setting. We will select GitHub for this setup.

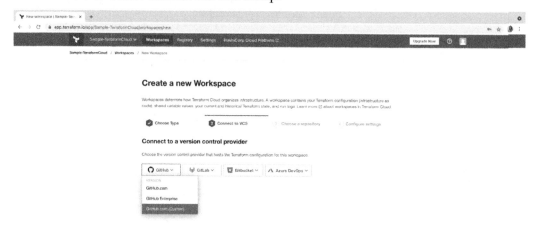

Figure 7.8: Connect to VC provider

4. Now follow the steps shown in the following screenshot to create the connection between your VCS; here, we will use GitHub. So, click on the '**register a new OAuth Application**' hyperlink.

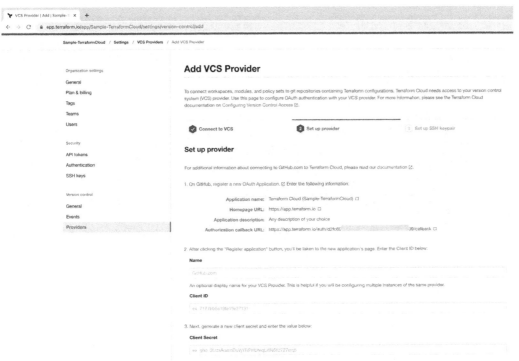

Figure 7.9: *Add VCS provider*

5. If you are not logged in to GitHub already on your browser, clicking '**register a new OAuth Application**' will navigate you to GitHub where you need to login. After login, we will see a page as shown in the following screenshot. Enter all the details in the Terraform Cloud page, as mentioned

in point 1 in the preceding figure, and then click on the green button named '**Register application**'.

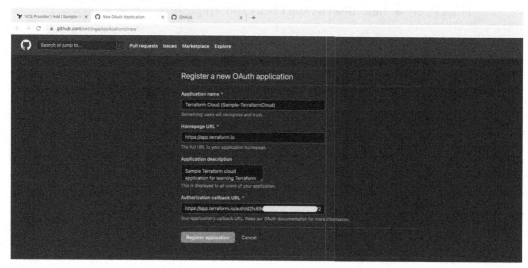

Figure 7.10: Register OAuth app in GitHub

6. After you register the application, you will be navigated to the following page where you will already have a unique '**Client ID**'. You will need this to connect with Terraform Cloud for the identification of your application.

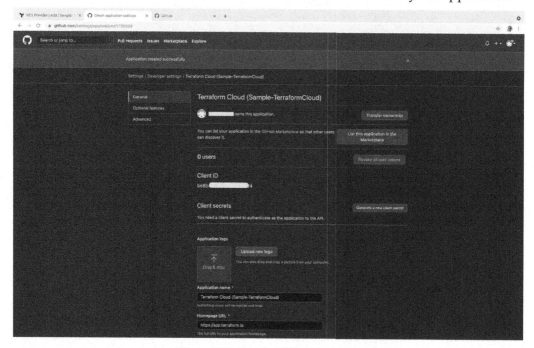

Figure 7.11: OAuth application details

7. Next, we will require a secret for authentication from Terraform Cloud. Click on the `'Generate a new client secret'` button, and a client secret will be generated, like the one with the green tick mark in the following figure. This **Client secrets** is only visible for the first time, so copy and save it for later use.

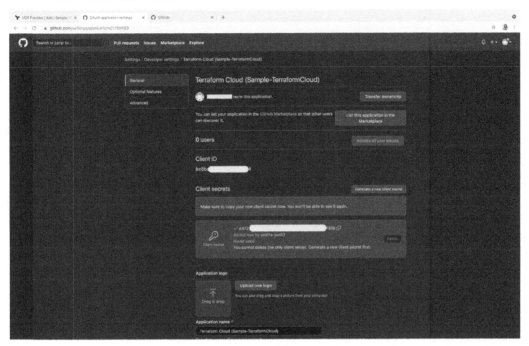

Figure 7.12*: Generate client secret*

Go back to Terraform Cloud once you have a successfully registered application in GitHub.

8. Now that we have all the required information, i.e., **Name**, **Client ID**, and **Client Secret**, fill the setup provider page, as in the following figure. Once

the details are filled, click on the '**Connect and continue**' button to securely add your authentication and connect it with GitHub.

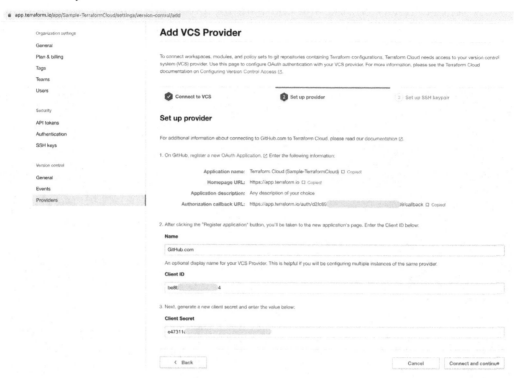

Figure 7.13: VCS provider client details

9. For the first time, you will be asked to authorize your GitHub connection. So, when you click on the '**connect and continue**' button shown in the preceding figure, you will be navigated to authorize your application in GitHub.

All the organizations that are present in your GitHub account will be asked to '**Grant**' access. Here, we have granted access to all organizations that are shown in the following figure. This connection will grant Terraform Cloud Admin access to repository webhooks and services, and it will also have access to all private repositories and full access to personal user data.

Once you have granted access to organizations and verified all the details here, click on the green button named '**Authorize <user>** '. This should successfully authorize and connect you to **https://app.terraform.io** in Terraform Cloud, as shown in the following screenshot:

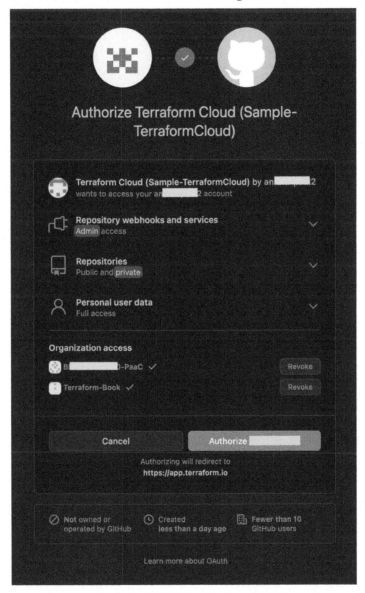

***Figure 7.14**: Authorize OAuth application*

10. If the connection is created successfully, it will ask you to set up SSH keypair optionally, as you can see in the following figure. For now, we will skip this configuration and click on the '**Skip and finish**' button.

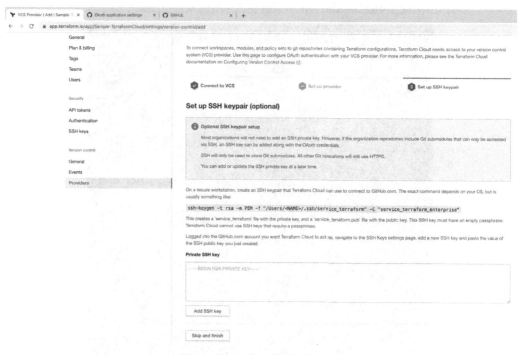

Figure 7.15: Skip SSH key setup

11. With this, you will be navigated to the **VCS Providers** setting page, where you can view the recently configured GitHub.com VCS client connection.

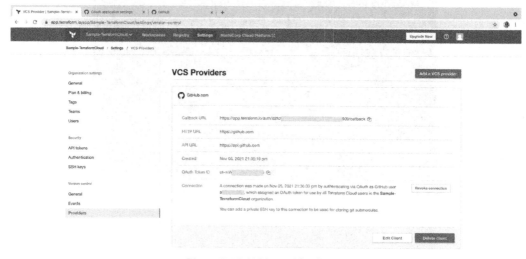

Figure 7.16: VCS provider details

With this, our '**Sample-TerraformCloud**' organization is ready to create a workspace by connecting to GitHub as version control system to maintain the terraform configuration files and trigger the Terraform workflow for these configurations in the GitHub repository.

Now, let's proceed with workspaces in Terraform Cloud in the next section.

Workspace in Terraform Cloud

Terraform configuration has collections of infrastructure resources, and we need to manage them properly in separate directories or workspace.

When we run Terraform locally, it manages each of these collections with a persistent working directory. This persistent directory contains Terraform configuration, Terraform variables, and Terraform state data. We can organize our Terraform configuration for infrastructure resources in separate directories as the Terraform CLI only uses the contents from the current work directory.

Terraform Cloud uses *workspaces* instead of directories to manage infrastructure collections. Each Terraform Cloud workspace functions like a separate working directory. A workspace contains everything required to manage an infrastructure collection. Terraform Cloud workspace and local directory behave similarly, but the way they store their data is different.

Terraform Cloud manages the data in the following way:

Component	Terraform Cloud
Terraform Configuration	Stores in connected version control repository or uploaded via API/CLI
Variables	In workspace
State data	In workspace
Secrets	In workspace (in the form of sensitive variables)

Table 7.1: Component-wise data management in Terraform Cloud

Along with the above data, Terraform Cloud stores the Run history and the backups of the previous state in the form of state versions. Run history is a record of all run activity, like summaries, logs, user comments, and also a reference to the changes that caused the run.

Let's see how the workspaces in Terraform Cloud work, starting with creating a new workspace.

Creating a workspace in Terraform Cloud

Follow these steps to create a workspace in an organization in Terraform Cloud:

1. Go to the '**Workspace**' option in the header bar on the Terraform Cloud web page. You will be navigated to the page as shown in the following figure. Then, click on the '**New workspace**' button in the top-right corner to create a workspace in this organization.

Figure 7.17: Terraform Cloud workspaces

2. As mentioned earlier, we will be using version control in this configuration; select the first option '**Version control workflow**'.

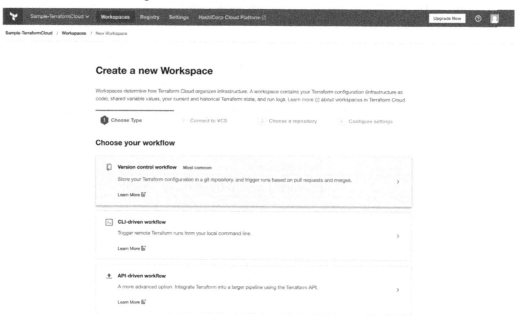

Figure 7.18: Create workspace

3. We have already connected to GitHub while creating the organization, so we just need to select the already created connection '**GitHub**' from the options, as shown in the following screenshot:

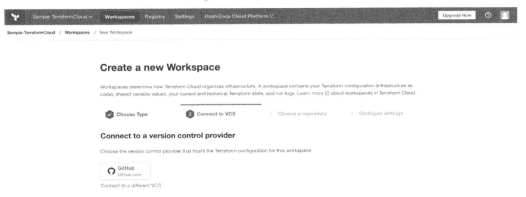

Figure 7.19: *Connect to VC provider GitHub*

4. Once you select GitHub, it will list all the repositories already present in the connected organizations from GitHub.

   For this chapter, ensure that you have a fresh clean repository in GitHub. Create a new repository with the name '**Chapter-7**' in the organization called '**Terraform-Book**' (this creation is not shown here, but you can follow the document at **https://docs.github.com/en/get-started/quickstart/ create-a-repo**), and select '**Terraform-Book/Chapter-7**', as shown in the following screenshot:

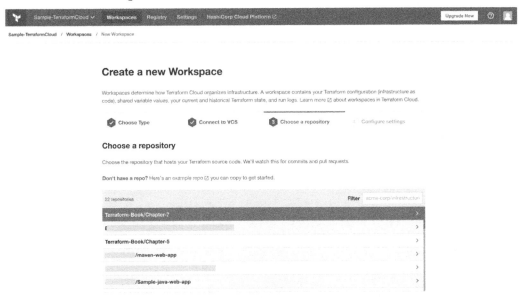

Figure 7.20: *Choose a repository*

5. Once you have selected a repository, you will be navigated to a page as shown in the following figure. Enter the workspace name and description; you can also customize the advanced settings if you want from **Advanced options**. Lastly, click on the '**Create workspace**' button.

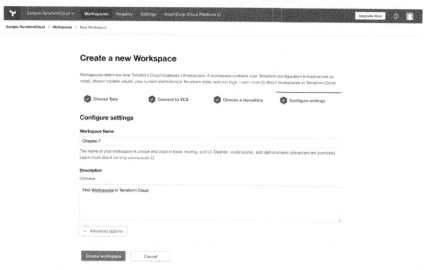

Figure 7.21*: Configure the workspace settings*

6. After successful creation of a workspace, you will be directly navigated into the workspace, as shown in the following screenshot:

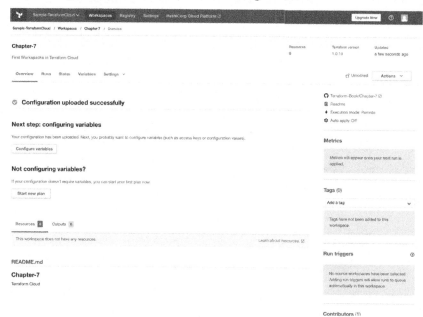

Figure 7.22*: Workspace overview*

The workspace is ready to run the Terraform workflows (Plan, Apply) now. Let's see how to run Terraform configuration in Terraform Cloud in the next section.

Executing Terraform configuration in Terraform Cloud (Runs)

Terraform Cloud always executes Terraform configurations in runs of a Terraform Cloud workspace. If your workspace is not configured with the **Auto apply** method, you will have to manually trigger a Terraform run each time to apply the changes in Terraform configurations version (i.e., change in the configurations).

Each workspace in Terraform Cloud is associated with a particular Terraform configuration, but this configuration can change over time. Hence, Terraform Cloud has to manage Terraform configurations as a series of configuration versions. Mostly, a workspace is linked to a VCS repository, so its configuration versions are tied to revisions/commit ID in the specified VCS branch. In workspaces that are not linked to a VCS repository, new configuration versions can be uploaded via the API or via Terraform CLI.

In Terraform Cloud, each workspace maintains its own queue of runs, and these runs are processed in order. Each new initiated run is added to the end of the queue; a new run won't start until the current one and all previous ones are completed, and all new runs remain in the pending state, as shown in the following figure in run list. When you initiate a run, Terraform Cloud locks the run to a particular configuration version and a set of variable values.

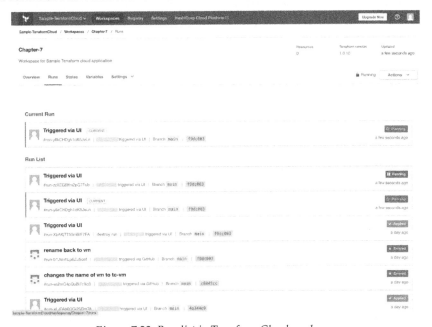

Figure 7.23*: Run list in Terraform Cloud workspace*

New runs can be queued even if the workspace is locked, but they cannot start until the workspace is unlocked. One can also lock a workspace manually from Terraform Cloud, for maintenance purposes or for any other reason.

After knowing these basic details, we are ready to execute runs in Terraform Cloud. However, we need to have auto apply enabled in workspace setting before that, and we also need a basic terraform configuration in version control repository, which is linked to that particular workspace. Let's cover this in the following sections.

Creating Terraform configuration in VC Repository

For executing the Terraform configuration in Terraform Cloud, we need to have Terraform configurations in our linked version control repository. We have a fresh repository attached in our workspace, so we will first add a few Terraform configuration files into the repository.

Follow the given steps to make the repository ready with Terraform configuration.

For this setup, we will be creating a Virtual Machine in Microsoft Azure. Here, we will be using the authentication details, also created in *Chapter 5- Automating Infrastructure Deployment in Azure Using Terraform* (they are subscription ID, tenant ID, client ID, and client secret). All the following code snippets are already created in *Chapter 5- Automating Infrastructure Deployments in Azure Using Terraform*, so we will not be explaining the resources created in these configurations. We will just put these Terraform configurations in the respective '**.tf**' files, as mentioned in the following steps. These files should be created in the GitHub repository (i.e., the repository created for this workspace in this *Chapter 7- Terraform Cloud*).

1. Create a file for variable declaration with the name '**vars.tf**'; create the following code snippet in this file and save it:

```
# vars.tf

variable "client_secret" {

    description = "Enter your CLient Secret. Please make sure
you do not store the value of your client secret in the SCM
repository. This can be added to Terraform Cloud Variables."

}

variable "client_id" {

    description = "Enter your client Id.Please make sure you do
not store the value of your client Id in the SCM repository. This
can be added to Terraform Cloud Variables."

}
```

```
variable "subscription_id" {

    description = "Enter your subscription id. Please make sure
you do not store the value of your subscription id in the SCM
repository. This can be added to Terraform Cloud Variables."

}

variable "tenant_id" {

    description = "Enter your tenant id. Please make sure you do
not store the value of your Tenant id in the SCM repository. This
can be added to Terraform Cloud Variables."

}

variable "prefix" {

  description = "The prefix which should be used for all resources
in this Chapter"

  default = "test"

}

variable "location" {

  description = "The Azure Region in which all resources in this
Chapter should be created."

  default = "West Europe"

}
```

2. Create a '**main.tf**' file with the terraform provider configuration for resource group creation in Azure:

```
# main.tf

# Configure the Microsoft Azure Provider

provider "azurerm" {

  features {}

  subscription_id = var.subscription_id

  client_id       = var.client_id

  client_secret   = var.client_secret

  tenant_id       = var.tenant_id

}

# Azure Provider source and version being used

terraform {

  required_providers {

    azurerm = {
```

```
      source  = "hashicorp/azurerm"
      version = "=2.46.0"
    }
  }
}
# Create a resource group
resource "azurerm_resource_group" "test-rg" {
  name     = "${var.prefix}-resources"
  location = "${var.location}"
}
```

3. Create 'virtual_network.tf' with the following resource blocks:

```
# virtual_network.tf
# Virtual network
resource "azurerm_virtual_network" "vnet" {
  name = "${var.prefix}-vnet"
  address_space = ["10.0.0.0/16"]
  location = var.location
  resource_group_name = azurerm_resource_group.test-rg.name
}
# Subnet
resource "azurerm_subnet" "subnet" {
  name = "${var.prefix}Subnet"
  resource_group_name =  azurerm_resource_group.test-rg.name
  virtual_network_name = azurerm_virtual_network.vnet.name
  address_prefixes = ["10.0.1.0/24"]
}
# Public ip
resource "azurerm_public_ip" "publicip" {
  name = "pip1"
  location = var.location
  resource_group_name = azurerm_resource_group.test-rg.name
  allocation_method = "Dynamic"
  sku = "Basic"
```

```
}
# Network interface
resource "azurerm_network_interface" "nic" {
  name = "${var.prefix}-nic"
  location = var.location
  resource_group_name = azurerm_resource_group.test-rg.name

  ip_configuration {
    name = "ipconfig1"
    subnet_id = azurerm_subnet.subnet.id
    private_ip_address_allocation = "Dynamic"
    public_ip_address_id = azurerm_public_ip.publicip.id
  }
}
# Security Group
resource "azurerm_network_security_group" "frontendnsg" {
  name                = "${var.prefix}SecurityGroup"
  location            = var.location
  resource_group_name = azurerm_resource_group.test-rg.name

  tags = {
    environment = "Production"
  }
}
# Security rules
resource "azurerm_network_security_rule" "sshrule" {
  name                    = "${var.prefix}ssh"
  priority                = 101
  direction               = "Inbound"
  access                  = "Allow"
  protocol                = "Tcp"
  source_port_range       = "*"
  destination_port_range  = "22"
  source_address_prefix   = "*"
```

```
          destination_address_prefix = "10.0.1.0/24"

      resource_group_name         = azurerm_resource_group.test-rg.
name

      network_security_group_name = azurerm_network_security_group.
frontendnsg.name

}
resource "azurerm_network_security_rule" "httprule" {
    name                        = "${var.prefix}http"
    priority                    = 100
    direction                   = "Inbound"
    access                      = "Allow"
    protocol                    = "Tcp"
    source_port_range           = "*"
    destination_port_range      = "8080"
    source_address_prefix       = "*"
    destination_address_prefix  = "10.0.1.0/24"

    resource_group_name         = azurerm_resource_group.test-rg.
name

    network_security_group_name = azurerm_network_security_group.
frontendnsg.name

}

resource "azurerm_subnet_network_security_group_association"
"subnetsecuritygroup" {
    subnet_id                 = azurerm_subnet.subnet.id

    network_security_group_id = azurerm_network_security_group.
frontendnsg.id

}
```

4. Open the last file we created in '**virtual_machine.tf**' and paste the following resource block configuration into it:

```
# virtual_machine.tf

resource "azurerm_virtual_machine" "vm" {

    name                = "${var.prefix}-tc-vm"
    location            = var.location
    resource_group_name = azurerm_resource_group.test-rg.name
```

```
network_interface_ids = [azurerm_network_interface.nic.id]
vm_size                = "Standard_DS1_v2"

# Uncomment this line to delete the OS disk automatically when
deleting the VM
# delete_os_disk_on_termination = true
# Uncomment this line to delete the data disks automatically
when deleting the VM
# delete_data_disks_on_termination = true
storage_image_reference {
  publisher = "Canonical"
  offer     = "UbuntuServer"
  sku       = "16.04-LTS"
  version   = "latest"
}
storage_os_disk {
  name              = "${var.prefix}osdisk1"
  caching           = "ReadWrite"
  create_option     = "FromImage"
  managed_disk_type = "Standard_LRS"
}
os_profile {
  computer_name  = "hostname"
  admin_username = "${var.prefix}admin"
  admin_password = "Password1234!"
}
os_profile_linux_config {
  disable_password_authentication = false
}
tags = {
  environment = "Production"
}
}
```

Now, the repository has the terraform configurations that will create a virtual machine with the name '`test-tc-vm`', along with the virtual network configurations.

Configuring Auto Apply

The next important thing we need to configure is the automatic execution of apply method to the change in plans from the Terraform Cloud workspace we created. This can be done with the following steps:

1. Go to Terraform Cloud workspace (i.e., the one created in workspace with name "Chapter-7"), as shown in the following image:

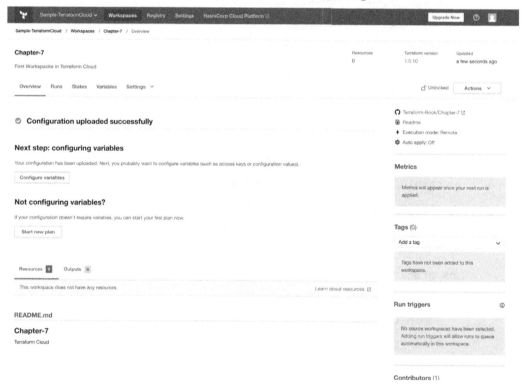

Figure 7.24: Terraform workspace

2. Then, go to the **Settings | General** option from the workspace, as illustrated here:

Overview
Runs
States
Variables
Settings
General
Locking
Notifications
Run Triggers
SSH Key
Version Control
Destruction and Deletion
Latest Run View all runs
Triggered via UI
Policy checks
Upgrade
Estimated cost
Upgrade
Resources 0
Outputs 0

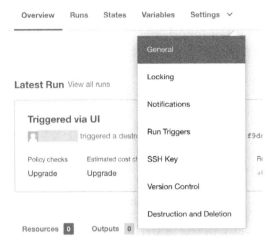

Figure 7.25: *Workspace settings*

3. You will be navigated to a page as shown in the following figure. Scroll down a bit, and you will find the '**`Apply method`**' settings, which, by default, are set to '**`manual apply`**'. This is illustrated in the following screenshot:

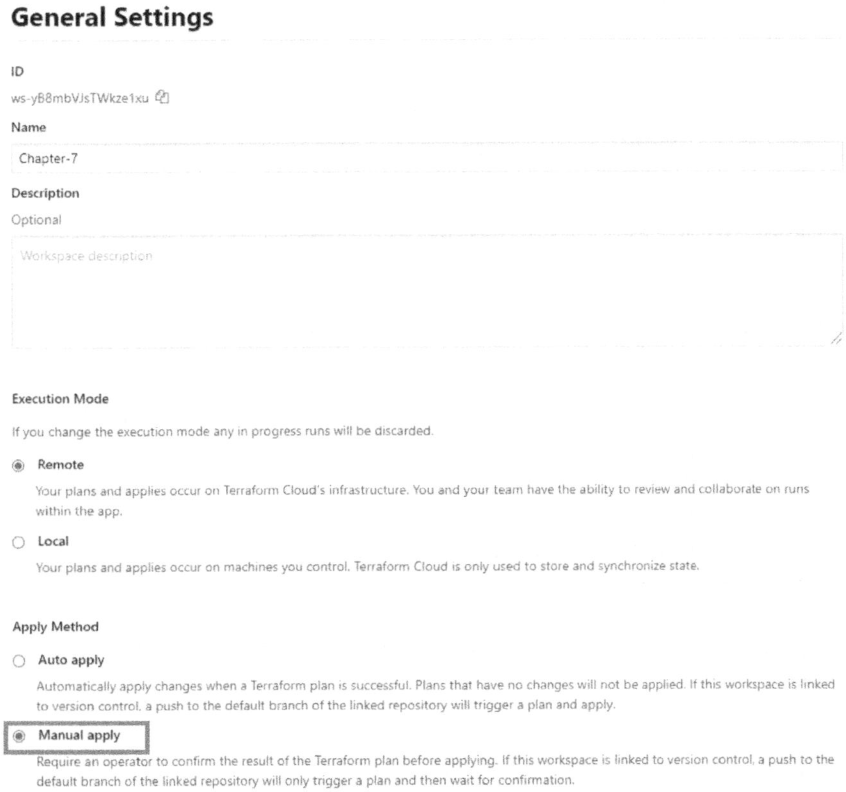

General Settings
ID
ws-yB8mbVJsTWkze1xu
Name
Chapter-7
Description
Optional
Workspace description
Execution Mode
If you change the execution mode any in progress runs will be discarded.
Remote
Your plans and applies occur on Terraform Cloud's infrastructure. You and your team have the ability to review and collaborate on runs within the app.
Local
Your plans and applies occur on machines you control. Terraform Cloud is only used to store and synchronize state.
Apply Method
Auto apply
Automatically apply changes when a Terraform plan is successful. Plans that have no changes will not be applied. If this workspace is linked to version control, a push to the default branch of the linked repository will trigger a plan and apply.
Manual apply
Require an operator to confirm the result of the Terraform plan before applying. If this workspace is linked to version control, a push to the default branch of the linked repository will only trigger a plan and then wait for confirmation.

Figure 7.26: *Apply method in general settings*

4. Change this apply method to '**Auto apply**', as shown in the following figure. This will set our workspace to automatically trigger runs for creating terraform plan and apply them for each change in the Terraform repository.

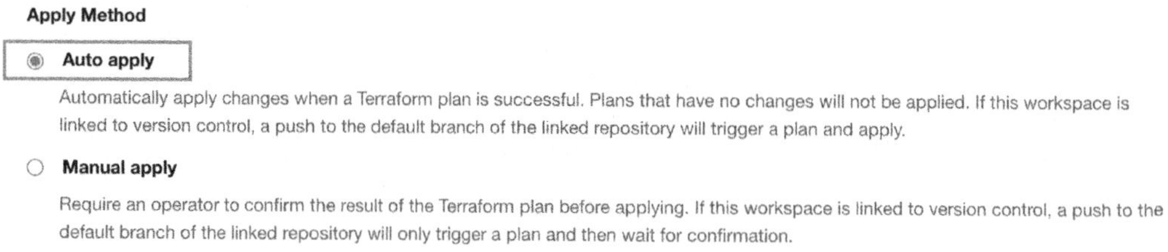

Apply Method

◉ **Auto apply**

Automatically apply changes when a Terraform plan is successful. Plans that have no changes will not be applied. If this workspace is linked to version control, a push to the default branch of the linked repository will trigger a plan and apply.

○ **Manual apply**

Require an operator to confirm the result of the Terraform plan before applying. If this workspace is linked to version control, a push to the default branch of the linked repository will only trigger a plan and then wait for confirmation.

Figure 7.27: Auto apply method

5. Scroll down to the bottom and click on the '**Save settings**' button to save the changes in workspace setting.

Now, we are ready to execute the Terraform configuration in the version control from Terraform Cloud workspace using this runs functionality.

Starting Runs in Terraform Cloud

There are three main types of workflows for managing runs in Terraform Cloud. The selected workflow then determines when and how Terraform runs occur. Here are the three types of workflows:

- **UI/VCS-driven run workflow**: This is the primary mode of operation.

- **API-driven run workflow**: This requires you to create some tooling, but it is more flexible.

- **CLI-driven run workflow**: It uses Terraform's standard CLI tools to execute runs in Terraform Cloud.

We will be using the first type, i.e., **UI/VCS-driven run workflow**, to execute the Terraform configuration we created in the VC repository.

Note: A fresh created workspace with no runs will not accept runs from VCS webhook. We need to at least manually queue one run to confirm that the workspace is ready to accept runs.

Follow these steps to execute the first terraform plan and apply:

1. Go to the **Variables** tab in Terraform Cloud workspace, as shown in the following screenshot. Click on the '**Add variable**' button in Workspace variables.

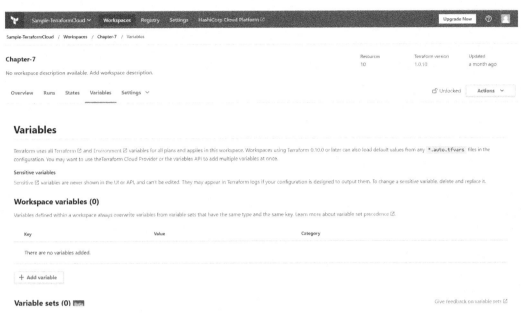

Figure 7.28: Variables

2. Add all the values for the variables needed to apply the Terraform configuration under the **Terraform Variables** option selected, as depicted in the following image. You can also add Environment variables. We will create an infrastructure in Microsoft Azure in our example, so let's add the Subscription ID, Client ID, Client secret, and the tenant ID. Provide the Key, value, and description, and do not forget to check Sensitive checkbox for storing any secret or sensitive values (refer to the following figure).

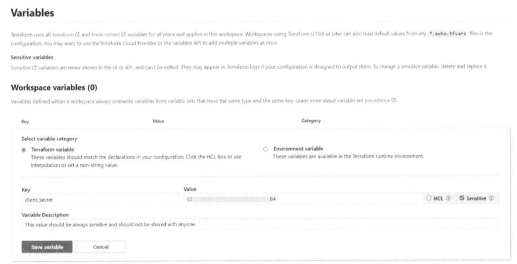

Figure 7.29: Add variable

3. Click on the '**Save variable**' button and also add the rest of the variables.

Figure 7.30: List of variables

4. Now, go to '**Runs**' in the workspace and click on '**Start new plan**' in the '**Actions**' dropdown on the right, as shown in the following screenshot:

Figure 7.31: Start new plan

5. Then, you will get a prompt, as depicted in the following figure; enter a reason (e.g., First run) and then click on the '**Start plan**' button.

Figure 7.32: Reason and type for starting plan

6. You will see that the run is started as in the following figure. It should first show that the plan is queued.

Figure 7.33: Runs

7. **Optional**: (if Auto apply not configure) After successful creation of plan, you will be asked for permission to apply this plan and create/update the infrastructure resources. Click on the '**Confirm and Apply**' button to run the terraform apply on the created plan in the run.

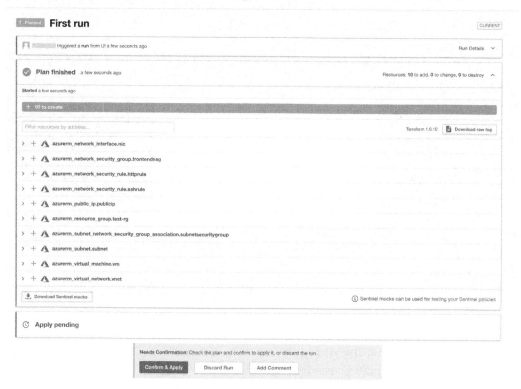

Figure 7.34: Plan finished

8. **Optional**: (if Auto apply not configure) Add a comment if you want, and click on the '**confirm plan**' button to apply and create the infrastructure resources from this plan.

Figure 7.35: Confirm plan

9. Terraform apply runs scripts that will create an infrastructure on successful execution, as shown in the following screenshot:

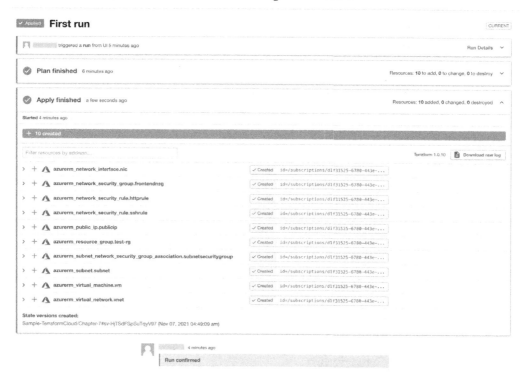

Figure 7.36: Apply finish

10. Now, verify your infrastructure; in our case, we can check if the Azure resource group named '`test-resources`' was created in Azure portal. Additionally, verify that all other resources mentioned in the Terraform configurations are created, as shown in the following screenshot:

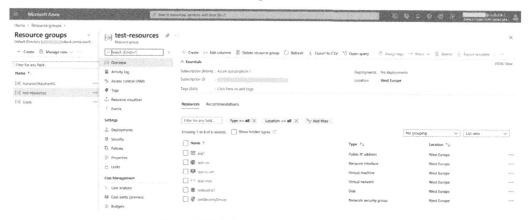

Figure 7.37: Infrastructure created in Azure

If you have noticed, the run we triggered was from UI, not automatically from version control repository. This is also mentioned in the run information and is highlighted in the following   screenshot:

Figure 7.38: Trigger type

Now, let's trigger a run from **version control system (VCS)**. For this, we need to commit a change in the GitHub repository that is linked to this workspace. Follow these steps for this:

1. Go to GitHub repository, i.e., directory with name Chapter-7 (as in the following figure), which is linked in your workspace.

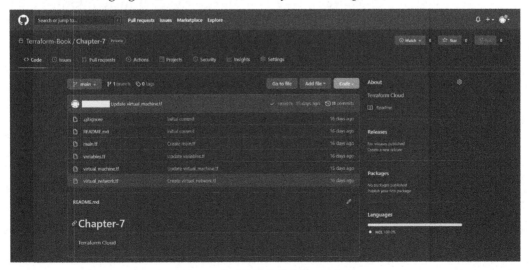

Figure 7.39: GitHub-linked repository

2. Make a change in Terraform configuration in any '**.tf**' file in this repository. For example, we will select **virtual_machine.tf** and update the name of the virtual machine on line 3:

```
name = "${var.prefix}-tc-vm"
```

and change it to:

```
name = "${var.prefix}-vm"
```

3. Scroll to the bottom, add the commit message, and click on the **Commit changes** button.

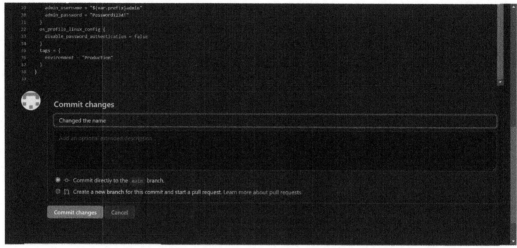

Figure 7.40: Update virtual_machine.tf

4. You commit automatically, so a new run is triggered in Terraform Cloud workspace, as shown in the following screenshot:

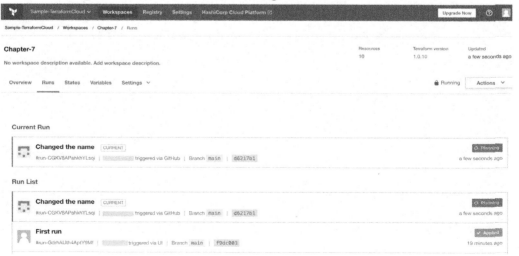

Figure 7.41: Check triggered pending run

5. Similarly to the message 'triggered via UI', now we will be able to see that it is '**triggered a run from GitHub**', as highlighted in the following screenshot:

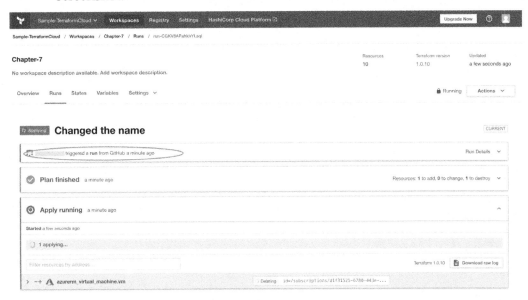

Figure 7.42: GitHub triggered run

6. Verify that the infrastructure in Azure portal Virtual Machine is renamed from '**test-tc-vm**' to '**test-vm**', as illustrated in the following screenshot:

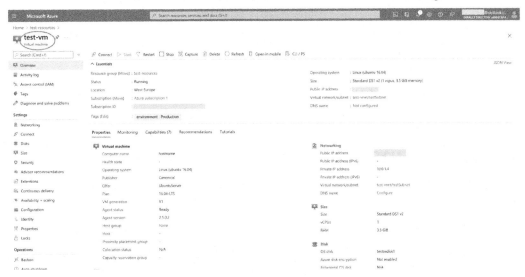

Figure 7.43: Updated VM name

7. After this, we can also view all the created resources in the workspace itself, on the overview page, as shown in the following figure. The resources created are listed here; as you can see, we created 10 resources in Azure.

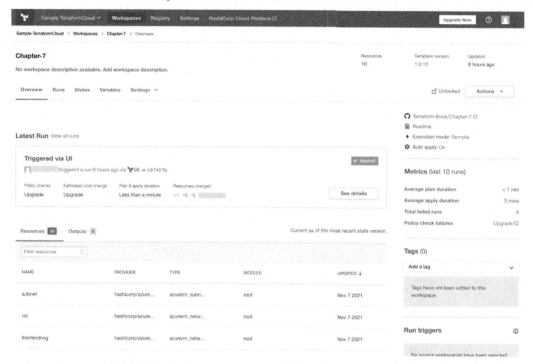

***Figure 7.44:** Verify resources created in Terraform Cloud workspace*

This is how we can execute terraform configuration in Terraform Cloud using UI and VCS-driven workflow.

If you are working in a team, the most important requirement will be to have proper access management in the Terraform Cloud; let's study how we can do this in the next section.

Access Management in Terraform Cloud

In Terraform Cloud, the organizational and the access control model is based on the following three units:

- **Users** are members of a Terraform Cloud organization. They are granted permission on an organization's workspaces based on the teams they belong to.

- **Teams** are groups of users reflecting the organizational structure of your company. A team called organization owners has the permission to create teams and manage their membership and permissions.

- **Organizations** are shared areas for teams to work together on workspaces. An organization can have multiple teams, and organizational owners can set different permissions for teams based on the workspaces they need to have access to.

Let's look at these three units in brief.

Users

A user is individual person who can be a member of multiple organizations. For working with Terraform Cloud, each user needs to create an account. We have already covered this at the start of this chapter.

If your account is created without an invitation from any organization, you do not have any organization in the Terraform Cloud account by default. Alternatively, if you create an account from an organization invite link, you will directly see that particular organization in your account. This invitation is sent by email. A user directly joins the organization if they already have an account with that email, else they need to create an account using that link.

In order to have access to an organization, the owner of that organization will need to add you to one or more teams in that organization. If the user has site admin permission, they can handle the administration of the entire Terraform Cloud instance, including all the organizations.

User settings

Each user has their own default settings when the account is created. We can update it from an option in the top-right corner: click on **User** | **User Settings**, as shown in the following screenshot:

Figure 7.45: User setting

You will be navigated to the page where your will find the profile setting. In the menu on the left, there are various other settings to secure your account.

Profile

Profile has only a few details: **Username**, **Email address**, and **Avatar**. We can update this profile content anytime from this setting.

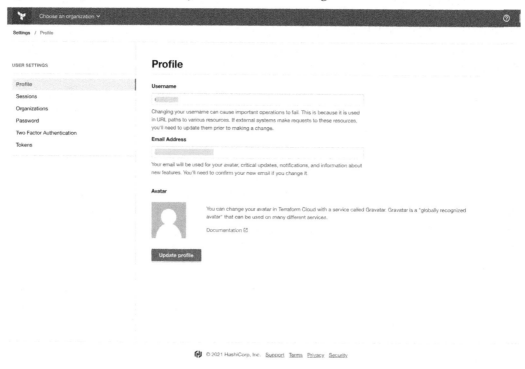

Figure 7.46: User profile

Sessions

This has the details of all your session data, like where we can find the IPs and the system from where our account is logged in. For example, we can now see the following figure show the sessions data for the logged in user account:

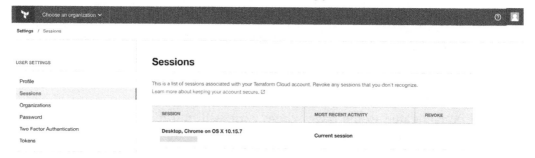

Figure 7.47: Sessions

Organizations

'**Organizations**' on the setting page shows the list of all the organizations that the user belongs to, as shown in the following screenshot:

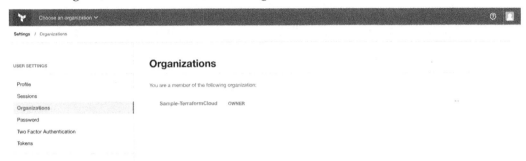

Figure 7.48: *User organizations*

Password

We can update the password if needed from this settings in the **USER SETTINGS**. As depicted in the following figure, you must first provide the current password, then enter the new password twice, and then click on the button.

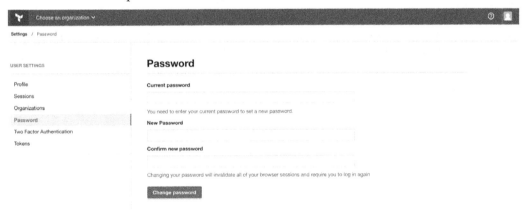

Figure 7.49: *Password settings*

Two-factor authentication

You can enable two-factor authentication if you want additional security. This can be done using an authenticator application or with SMS on the given phone number. The following figure is the setting page for two-factor authentication:

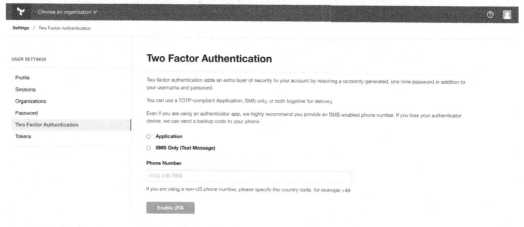

Figure 7.50: *Two-factor authentication settings*

Tokens

Users may require API tokens to perform various actions, like to authenticate the Terraform Cloud API, to authenticate Terraform remote s, and to use Terraform private modules when running Terraform configuration files from a local machine.

These tokens can be created and deleted from the setting page shown in the following screenshot:

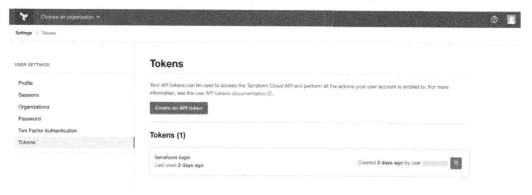

Figure 7.51: *User tokens*

This is how users can manage their accounts in Terraform Cloud.

Teams

A team is group of users within a particular organization. The organization owners can grant workspace permissions to specific teams to manage or delegate the organization's provisioning.

Each team can only have permissions within the same organization. Any user in a team can also belong to teams in other organizations. Users need to be in at least one team of an organization to be a member of that specific organization. Multiple users can be added and removed from teams using these settings.

By default, each organization has a team called '**Team: Owners**', as shown in the following screenshot. The creator of the organization is automatically added to this team after the organization is created. Go to organization '**Sample-TerraformCloud**' → **Settings** → **Teams** ', you will be navigated to the following page to manage team.

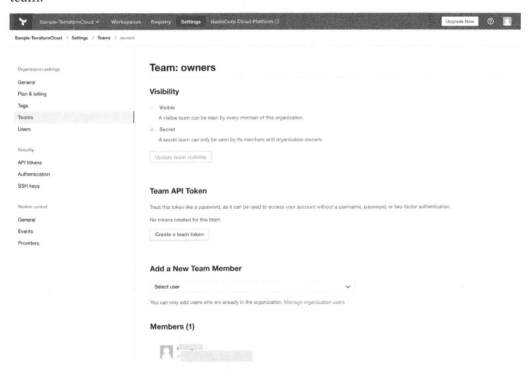

Figure 7.52: Organizational teams

API tokens specific to each team can also be created and used for authenticating the Terraform Cloud API. You can refer to the Terraform Cloud documentation at **https://www.terraform.io/docs/cloud/users-teams-organizations/teams.html** to understand how to manage teams.

If you upgrade the plan to a higher plan like 'Team' or 'Team and Governance', you will be able to create Teams and manage them. Once you upgrade the plan, you will see a page that looks like the following screenshot:

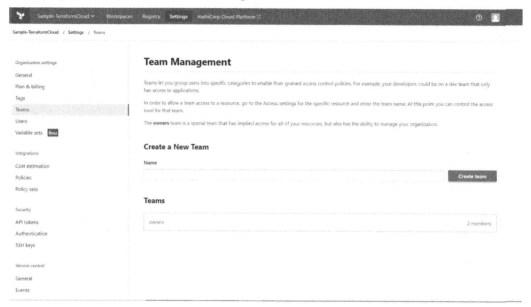

Figure 7.53: Team management

You can now create teams and manage the users and permissions of different teams.

Organizations

Organizations are shared spaces for teams to work together on workspaces in Terraform Cloud. We can select an organization from the top-left dropdown in the header bar of Terraform Cloud portal, as highlighted in the read box of the following screenshot:

Figure 7.54: Select organization

A user can join an organization only if one of the owners invites them via email, but they can leave it from **USER SETTINGS** → **Organizations**; there are three dots, and users can click on them to get the option to leave the organization, as shown in the following screenshot:

Figure 7.55: Leave organization in user settings

We have already seen the how to create an organization in the 'Setting up Terraform Cloud organization' section. Let's navigate through the **Settings** for the selected organization now.

You will find the **Settings** option at the top of the Terraform Cloud page in the navigation header bar. Click on it, and you will be navigated to the organization setting, as shown in the following screenshot:

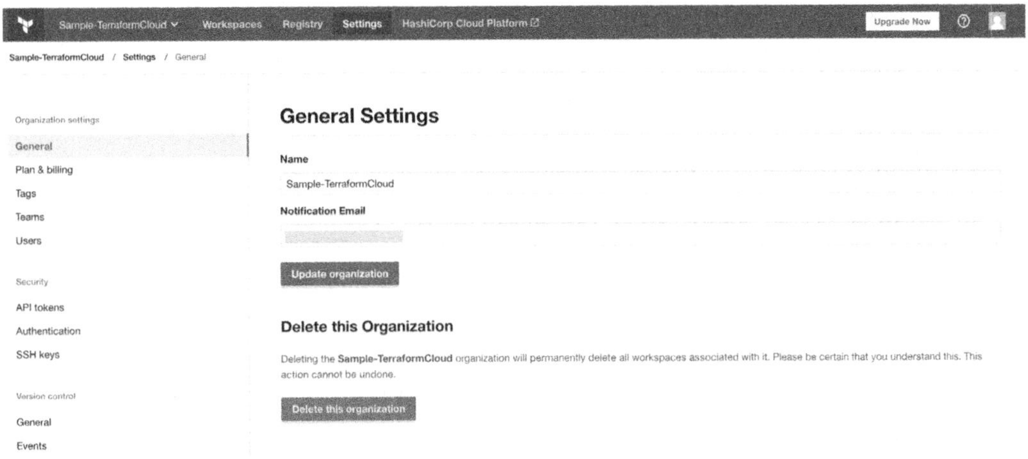

Figure 7.56: Organization settings

There are various organization-specific settings, like **General**, **Plan & billing**, **Tags**, and more, which can be updated. You can view these in the menu options on the left of the settings page. Refer to the documentation at **https://www.terraform.io/docs/cloud/users-teams-organizations/organizations.html** for more details about this setting.

Now, let's come to the main part of access management in the next section: permissions.

Permissions

Terraform Cloud has a team-based access model. We have already mentioned that a user must be in a team with appropriate permissions to access any organization. Access management in Terraform Cloud is split into two levels, as follows:

- Organization-level

- Workspace-level

Now, let's see what permissions can be managed at each of these levels.

Organization level

Each organization has a team called *Team Owners*; these team members have all permissions to the organization. These permissions include all organizational permissions and the highest level of permissions on all workspaces. Here are the permissions for team owners at the organization level:

- Managing workspaces

- Managing policies

- Managing policy overrides

- Managing VCS settings

- Publish private modules (owners only)

- Invite users to organization (owners only)

- Manage team membership (owners only)

- View all secret teams (owners only)

- Manage organization permissions (owners only)

- Manage all organization settings (owners only)

- Manage organization billing (owners only, not applicable to Terraform Enterprise)

- Delete organization (owners only)

- Manage agents (owners only)

All these team permissions can be set as per the team's requirement. To navigate to the following settings page, go to **Settings** | **Teams** and select a '**Developer**' team from the list. This is shown in the following screenshot:

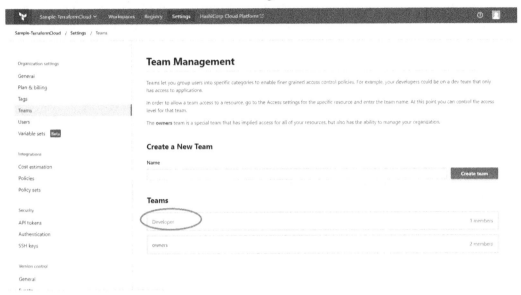

Figure 7.57: Team management

Once you click on the '**Developer**' team, you will be navigated to the following page, where you can update the permissions of this team:

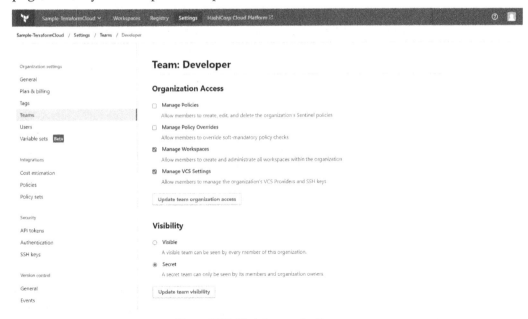

Figure 7.58: Update organization access

Workspace level

Workspace permission can be granted to teams by the admins on per-workspace basis. Admins of the workspace have the highest level of permissions on that workspace. Teams can be granted permissions on a workspace in two ways: fixed permissions set and customer permissions.

The following are the set of permissions that can be granted to teams on per-workspace basis:

- **Runs**
  - o **Read runs**: This permission allows users to view information about Terraform Cloud runs and the configuration versions associated with a run.
  - o **Queue plans**: It allows users to queue Terraform plans in workspace runs. This permission implies the permission to read runs.
  - o **Apply runs**: It allows users to approve and apply Terraform plans, updating the real infrastructure.

- **Lock and unlock workspace**: This permission allows users to manually lock the workspace to temporarily prevent runs.

- **Download Sentinel mocks**: This allows users to download runs data in the workspace in a format that can be used for developing Sentinel policies.

- **Variables**
  - o **Read variables**: It allow users to read the values of Terraform variables and environment variables for the workspace in Terraform Cloud. Sensitive variables are read only, so they cannot be viewed by users.
  - o **Read and write variables**: It allow users to update the values of variables in the workspace. It implies the read variable permission.

- **State versions**
  - o **Read state outputs**: It allows users to access the values of the most recent Terraform state data in the workspace. This permission is required to access the State Version Outputs API endpoint.
  - o **Read state versions**: It allows users to read the complete state files from the workspace. This implies permission to read state outputs.
  - o **Read and write state versions**: It allows users to directly create new state versions in the workspace and implies the permission to read state versions.

You may have noticed the phrase 'implies the permission'; this is because some of the permissions imply other permissions, for example, Queue plan permission also grants the permission to view runs.

Let's see how to manage these permissions in our workspace. Follow the steps listed here to manage workspace permissions:

1. Go to the '**Chapter 7**' workspace, which we have created for this chapter. Then, go to **Settings → Team Access**, as depicted in the following screenshot:

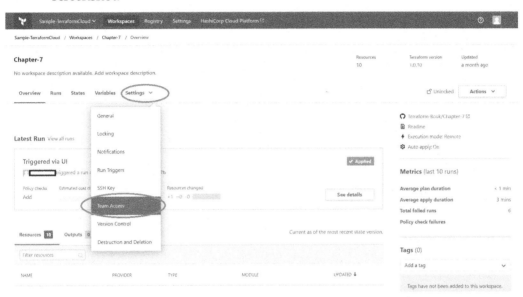

Figure 7.59: Workspace Team Access

2. Let's add a team called '**Developer**' by clicking on the '**Add team and permissions**' button, as shown in the following screenshot:

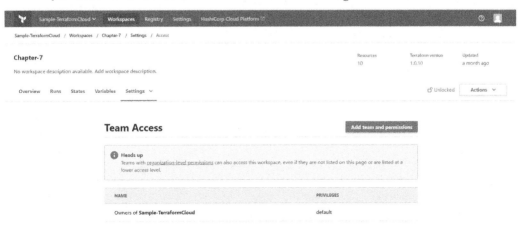

Figure 7.60: Add team and permissions

3. Click on the '**Select team**' button against the team that you want to add; here, we have only one option, i.e., Developer team:

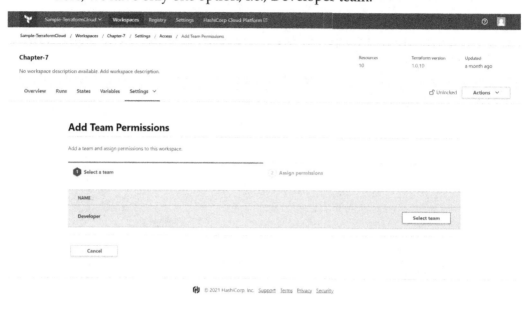

***Figure 7.61**: Select team*

4. You will then be navigated to '**Assign permissions**' where you will see four options to assign. We have covered this at the beginning of this section (refer to the following image). For Developer team, we will be selecting only read access as users should not be able to manipulate the configurations of this workspace.

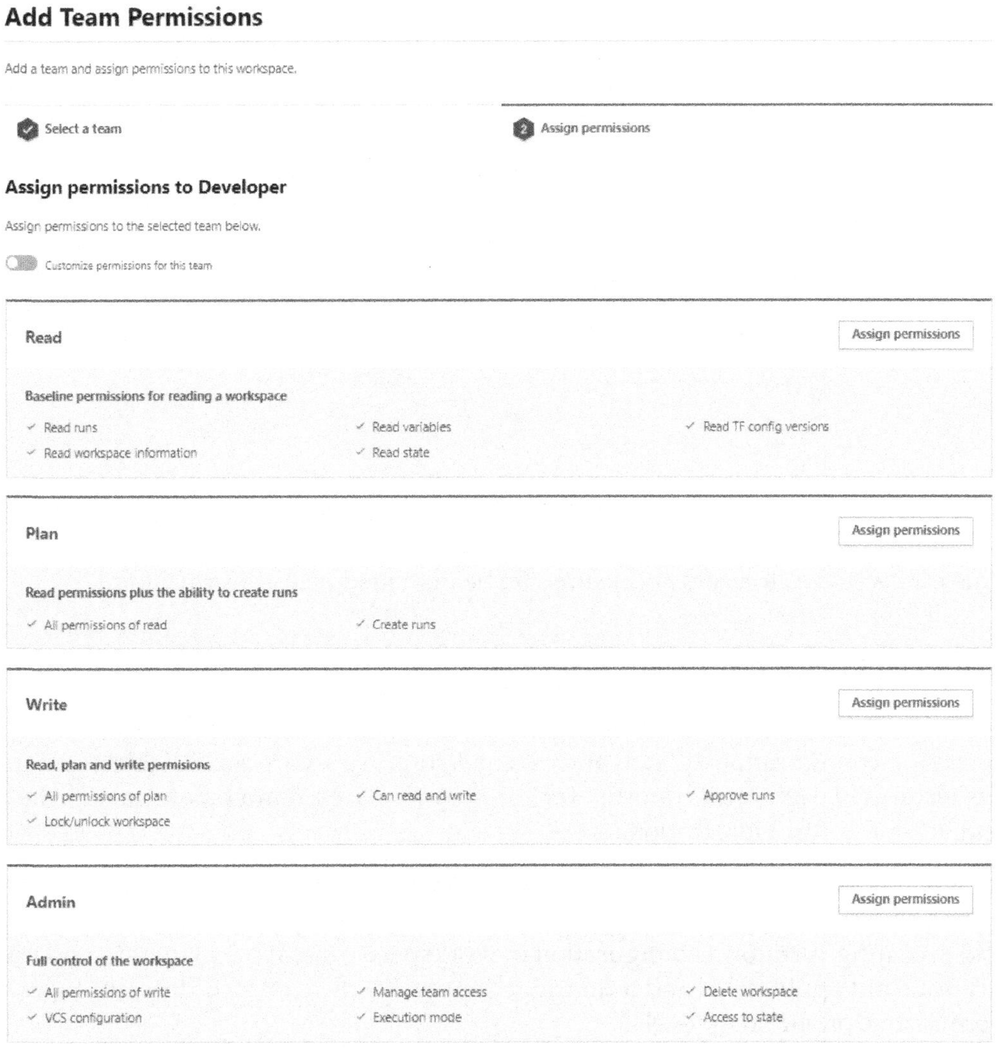

Add Team Permissions

Add a team and assign permissions to this workspace.

✅ Select a team   ② Assign permissions

Assign permissions to Developer

Assign permissions to the selected team below.

⬤ Customize permissions for this team

Read   [Assign permissions]

Baseline permissions for reading a workspace

✓ Read runs   ✓ Read variables   ✓ Read TF config versions
✓ Read workspace information   ✓ Read state

Plan   [Assign permissions]

Read permissions plus the ability to create runs

✓ All permissions of read   ✓ Create runs

Write   [Assign permissions]

Read, plan and write permissions

✓ All permissions of plan   ✓ Can read and write   ✓ Approve runs
✓ Lock/unlock workspace

Admin   [Assign permissions]

Full control of the workspace

✓ All permissions of write   ✓ Manage team access   ✓ Delete workspace
✓ VCS configuration   ✓ Execution mode   ✓ Access to state

Figure 7.62: *Assign permissions to the Team*

5.   Once you select an option and click on the '**Assign permissions**' button, you will be navigated to the '**Team Access**' page again. Here, you will find that Developer team has read access, as shown in the following screenshot:

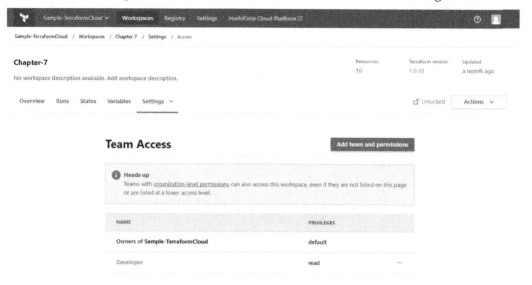

Figure 7.63: Team Access

This is how access to users and teams can be managed in Terraform Cloud.

Conclusion

Terraform Cloud is a platform for teams to collaborate while they are working in Terraform configuration. It plans and executes runs in a secure and reliable manner. It has features like remote terraform execution, workspaces, remote state management, and version control integration.

In this chapter, we covered account creation in Terraform Cloud, creating and setting up organization, creating and configuring workspace in Terraform Cloud, and executing Terraform configuration in workspace runs. We also understood how to create and apply plans and auto trigger apply. Lastly, we listed different types of permissions on different levels.

In the next chapter, we will learn how to integrate Terraform workflow in a continuous integration tool called Jenkins.

Points to remember

- Terraform Cloud provides a feature workspace that separates the infrastructure collection and acts like a separate directory.

- Terraform execution is executed in workspaces where we can execute and apply plan. We can also directly view the state of these runs in their associated workspace.

- Access management in Terraform Cloud is divided into two levels: organization level and workspace level.

Key terms

- **Version Control**: It manages the code and its versions for working with a team to share and manage their code base.

- **Runs**: Terraform Cloud has a feature to create and apply the terraform configuration. This is an important feature to execute infrastructure creation and to update it using Terraform configuration.

- **Workspace**: Workspace is nothing but a separate space in Terraform Cloud to apply Terraform configuration for the collection of related resources.

Multiple choice questions

1. **Which version control systems are supported by Terraform Cloud?**

    a. Bitbucket

    b. GitLab

    c. Azure DevOps

    d. GitHub

    e. All of the above

2. **What happens if you do not have the Auto apply setting configured in workspace settings?**

    a. Run fails after the plan is created

    b. Asks for permission to apply the plan in Run

    c. Applies the run successfully

    d. Does nothing

3. **What type of permission do you need to execute apply on the plans created in runs?**

    a. Read Run

    b. Queue plan

    c. Apply run

    d. None of the above

Answers

1. E
2. B
3. C

Questions

1. What is Terraform Cloud?

2. What are the features provided by Terraform Cloud?

3. List the types of workflows available in Terraform Cloud for the execution of Terraform configuration.

4. Which are the two levels of permissions in Terraform Cloud, and what is the list of permissions associated with these levels?

CHAPTER 8
Terraform and Jenkins Integration

Jenkins 2.0 provided new features, such as Pipeline as code - a new setup experience, and other UI improvements - enhancements with Jenkins interface. The entire user experience underwent a drastic change, and easy navigation to a different section in the job configuration was an eye-catching difference.

Agile development methods came into the picture to deal with the known issues of the traditional development approach. Integrative and incremental development of features brings customer feedback into the development. Customers know what they are going to get after each iteration. It is not an approach where things are considered serially. A lot of communication and effective collaboration (arguably) takes place between stakeholders to understand the requirements or explain the expectations. All stakeholders are continuously involved. To meet the speed of the incremental and iterative model, automation is necessary to speed up things concerning application lifecycle management activities. This is where the challenge comes in: manual processes bring delay in such an incremental and iterative approach in managing infrastructure. The combination of Pipeline as Code and Infrastructure as Code helps create a situation to get the best of both worlds.

Structure

We will discuss the following topics in this chapter:

- Deploying Jenkins automation server
- Jenkins pipeline – best practices
- Terraform in Jenkins declarative pipeline
- Adopting IaC culture in an organization

Objective

After studying this chapter, you will be able to understand how to install Jenkins and SonarQube in Kubernetes Cluster (Amazon EKS) and execute Terraform scripts from Jenkins Pipeline as Code.

Deploying Jenkins Automation Server

Jenkins is an open-source tool that provides integration with the existing tools used in application lifecycle management to automate the entire process based on feasibility. The major change is an introduction and big push for Pipeline as a Code rather than creating pipelines or orchestration using traditional pipelines with plugins like Build Pipeline.

The important thing was to focus on Pipeline as a Code and commit the pipeline into a repository so that versions can be maintained as they are maintained for code. Visualization is an important part of an end-to-end automation pipeline, and Jenkins 2.x focuses on that part significantly.

We need to install AWS CLI to perform this task. Go to **https://docs.aws.amazon. com/cli/latest/userguide/cli-chap-install.html** to get the details on how to install AWS CLI. Once AWS CLI is installed, follow the given steps:

```
C:\Users\<USER_NAME>>aws --version
aws-cli/2.0.43 Python/3.7.7 Windows/10 exe/AMD64
```

Use AWS configure command to set up AWS CLI installation. AWS CLI prompts for four pieces of information, as shown here:

```
C:\Users\<USER_NAME>>aws configure
AWS Access Key ID [****************ABCD]:
AWS Secret Access Key [****************wxYz]:
Default region name [ap-south-1]:
Default output format [None]:
```

The AWS CLI stores this information in a profile named default in the credentials file. By default, the information in this profile is considered when the AWS CLI command is executed, and it has no explicit mention of a profile to use.

Let's consider that Amazon EKS is installed and configured with kubectl. Visit **https://www.eksworkshop.com/** to explore multiple ways to configure VPC, ALB, and EC2 Kubernetes workers and Amazon Elastic Kubernetes Service.

Once the EKS cluster is ready, we can deploy Kubernetes Pods, Service, and Deployment for Jenkins installation.

Before Jenkins deployment on EKS, let's understand some Kubernetes' concepts. That said, a complete discussion on Kubernetes is out of the scope of this book.

Concept	Description

Pod	Pods are the smallest units that you can create and manage in Kubernetes. It is a group of one or more containers. It has shared storage/network resources. We can configure `init` containers that help during the start of a Pod.
	
	Here, we will create Jenkins or Blue Ocean Pod using `image: jenkinsci/blueocean`:
	
	`containers:`
	`- name: blueocean`
	`  image: jenkinsci/blueocean`
	`  ports:`
	`  - name: http-port`
	`    containerPort: 8080`
	`  - name: jnlp-port`
	`    containerPort: 50000`
	
	Reference: https://hub.docker.com/r/jenkinsci/blueocean/

Service	Service helps access an application hosted in pods with IP addresses, and it provides the solution to load the balance. Reference: https://kubernetes.io/docs/concepts/services-networking/service/
Deployment	A deployment provides declarative updates for Pods and ReplicaSets. We will have a configuration file for Deployment and Service. Reference: https://kubernetes.io/docs/concepts/workloads/controllers/deployment/

Concept	Description
Persistent volume	The Kubernetes volume provides an abstraction to share files within a Pod. It helps access data that is stored in many types of volumes. Usually, all data is lost when a pod crashes, but if the volume is associated with the pod, then data is saved in different types of volumes, such as AWS File system or Azure disk. **Persistent Volumes (PV)** exist beyond the lifetime of a pod. A **Persistent Volume Claim (PVC)** is a request for storage by a user, and PVCs consume PV resources. Reference: https://kubernetes.io/docs/concepts/storage/

Table 8.1: Concepts of Kubernetes

Visit https://kubernetes.io/docs/setup/ to get more details on Kubernetes and its concepts and architecture.

The following is the deployment and service YAML to deploy Jenkins in Kubernetes Cluster. Save it with the filename `jenkins-eks-deployment.yml`.

```
apiVersion: v1
kind: Namespace
metadata:
  name: cicd

---

apiVersion: apps/v1
kind: Deployment
metadata:
 name: blueocean-deployment
 namespace: cicd
 labels:
    app: blueocean

spec:
 template:
   metadata:
     name: blueocean-pod
     labels:
```

```yaml
      app: blueocean
   spec:
    containers:
    - name: blueocean
      image: jenkinsci/blueocean
      ports:
      - name: http-port
        containerPort: 8080
      - name: jnlp-port
        containerPort: 50000
 replicas: 1

 selector:
    matchLabels:
        app: blueocean
---
apiVersion: v1
kind: Service
metadata:
 name: blueocean-service
 namespace: cicd
 labels:
    app: blueocean
spec:
 selector:
    app: blueocean
 ports:
  - protocol: TCP
    name: http
    port: 8080
    targetPort: 8080
  - protocol: TCP
    name: agent
```

```
    port: 50000
    targetPort: 50000
type: LoadBalancer
```

Note: Multiple workspaces help manage different environments/sets of infrastructure. They help test the environment without affecting the main/production environment.

Local State: Terraform writes the workspace states in a terraform.tfstate.d directory.

Remote State: Terraform writes the workspace states in Amazon S3 or other supported storage services.

Let's verify the existing workspaces in our Kubernetes Cluster. Execute the kubectl command get namespace:

NAME	STATUS	AGE
cicd	Active	5m7s
default	Active	21m
kube-node-lease	Active	21m
kube-public	Active	21m
kube-system	Active	21m

Execute the kubectl apply command to create deployment and service for Jenkins in the cicd namespace:

```
kubectl create -f jenkins-eks-deployment.yml
```

```
namespace/cicd created
```

```
deployment.apps/blueocean-deployment created
```

```
service/blueocean-service created
```

Execute **kubectl get all -n cicd** to get all resources in the cicd namespace.

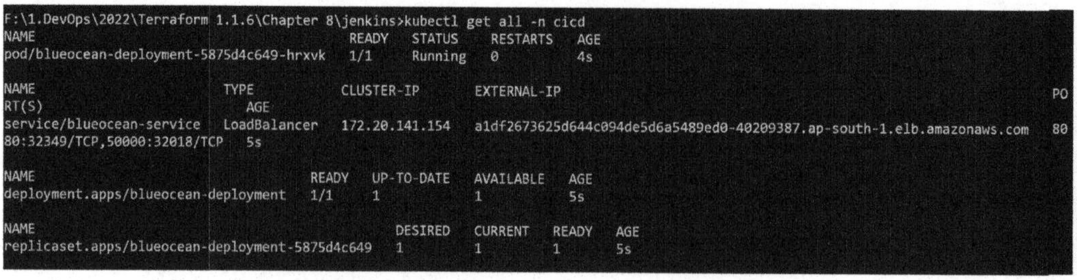

```
F:\1.DevOps\2022\Terraform 1.1.6\Chapter 8\jenkins>kubectl get all -n cicd
NAME                                        READY   STATUS    RESTARTS   AGE
pod/blueocean-deployment-5875d4c649-hrxvk   1/1     Running   0          4s

NAME                         TYPE           CLUSTER-IP       EXTERNAL-IP                                                                            PO
RT(S)                   AGE
service/blueocean-service    LoadBalancer   172.20.141.154   a1df2673625d644c094de5d6a5489ed0-40209387.ap-south-1.elb.amazonaws.com   80
80:32349/TCP,50000:32018/TCP   5s

NAME                                   READY   UP-TO-DATE   AVAILABLE   AGE
deployment.apps/blueocean-deployment   1/1     1            1           5s

NAME                                             DESIRED   CURRENT   READY   AGE
replicaset.apps/blueocean-deployment-5875d4c649   1         1         1       5s
```

Figure 8.1: Kubernetes resources in a namespace

Wait for some time while pod and deployment are ready for Jenkins. Note the EXTERNAL-IP in the following figure:

Noe: Use multiple directories for each set of infrastructure deployment with different environment-specific configurations

Execute logs on the pod name as mentioned earlier in the **kubectl logs blueocean-deployment-5875d4c649-hrxvk** command to get admin password for Jenkins. Note the Administrator password.

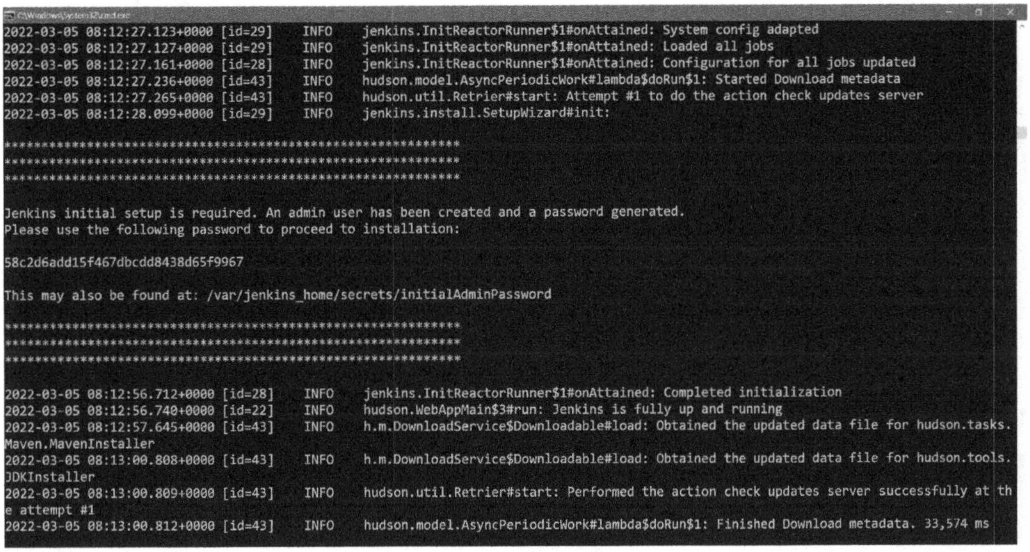

Figure 8.2: Kubernetes Pod logs

Use the EXTERNAL-IP / domain name to visit Jenkins in the browser. Provide the Administrator Password noted in the previous step and click on Continue:

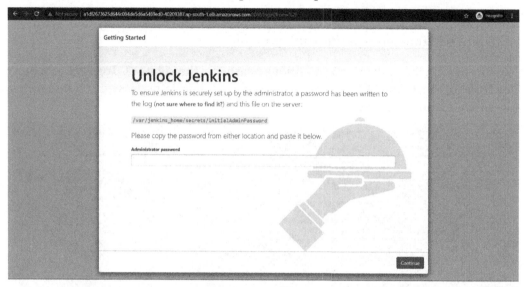

Figure 8.3: Unlock Jenkins

Click on Install suggested plugins:

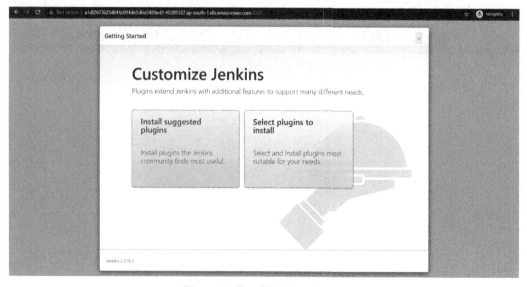

Figure 8.4: Install Jenkins plugins

Wait for all suggested plugins to be installed successfully.

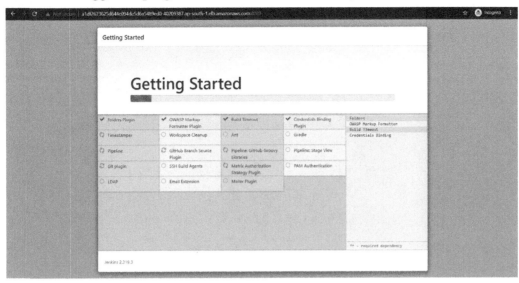

Figure 8.5: *Installation of plugins*

Create admin credentials and click on **Save and Continue**.

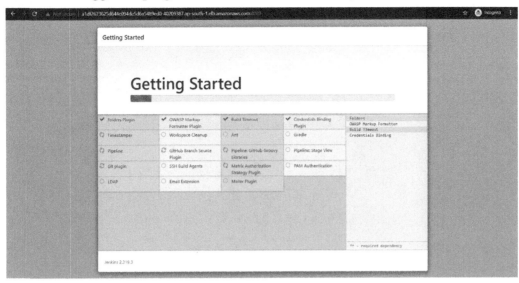

Figure 8.6: *Jenkins user creation*

Confirm the Jenkins URL and click on **Save** and **Finish**.

Figure 8.7: Jenkins instance configuration

Click on **Start using Jenkins**.

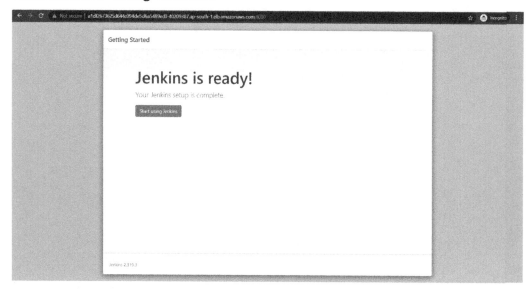

Figure 8.8: Jenkins setup completed

Verify the Jenkins dashboard:

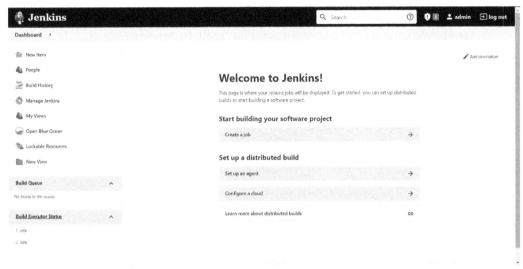

Figure 8.9: Jenkins dashboard

Go to the Manage Jenkins section, click on **Configure System**, and verify the Home directory.

We are using Pod Storage as of now, so all data will go away in case Pod crashes or is recreated.

Use EFS to store the Jenkins Home directory.Open 2049 port in the security group that is attached to subnets configured in Network section in EFS.

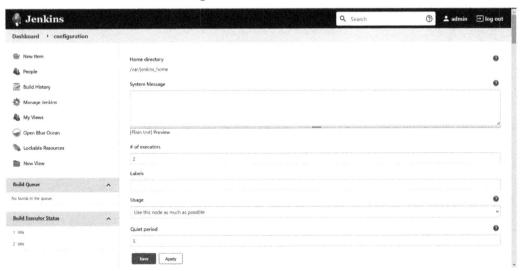

Figure 8.10: Jenkins configuration

Let's create Amazon Elastic File System and note the file system ID and File System Access Point:

1. Go to AWS management console and navigate to Amazon Elastic File System.

2. Click on **Create file system**:

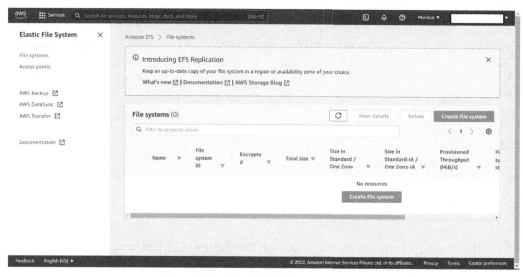

Figure 8.11: Elastic file system

3. Provide **Name** and click on **Create**:

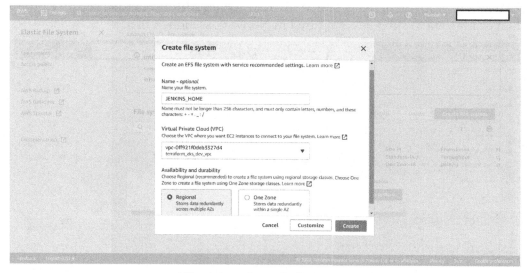

Figure 8.12: Create the file system

4. Note the file system ID available in the fs-xxx0x000 format, as shown in the following figure:

Figure 8.13: Elastic file system

5. Note the file system access point available in the fsap-0x000xx0x0x00000x format:

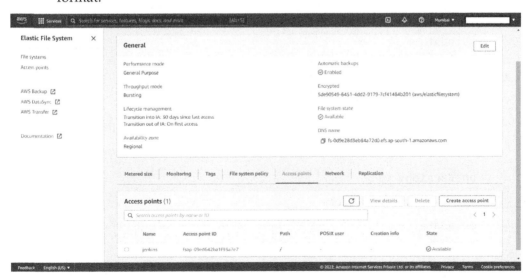

Figure 8.14: EFS access point

6. We need to run the following command to deploy the Amazon EFS CSI driver:

```
kubectl create -k "github.com/kubernetes-sigs/aws-efs-csi-driver/
deploy/kubernetes/overlays/stable/?ref=master"

serviceaccount/efs-csi-controller-sa created

serviceaccount/efs-csi-node-sa created

clusterrole.rbac.authorization.k8s.io/efs-csi-external-
provisioner-role created

clusterrolebinding.rbac.authorization.k8s.io/efs-csi-provisioner-
binding created

deployment.apps/efs-csi-controller created

daemonset.apps/efs-csi-node created

csidriver.storage.k8s.io/efs.csi.aws.com created
```

Note: Read more details on Amazon EFS CSI driver https://docs.aws.amazon. com/eks/latest/userguide/efs-csi.html

7. Here is the YAML for storage class:

```
kind: StorageClass

apiVersion: storage.k8s.io/v1

metadata:

  name: efs-sc

provisioner: efs.csi.aws.com
```

8. In the PV file, use the file system ID and file system access point.

The following is the YAML for Persistent Volume:

```
apiVersion: v1

kind: PersistentVolume

metadata:

  name: jenkins-efs-pv

spec:

  capacity:

    storage: 10Gi

  volumeMode: Filesystem

  accessModes:
```

```
        - ReadWriteMany
    persistentVolumeReclaimPolicy: Retain
    storageClassName: jenkins-efs-sc
    csi:
      driver: efs.csi.aws.com
      volumeHandle: fs-0d9e28d3eb84a72d0::fsap-09ed642ba1f93a7e7
```

9. Here is the YAML for PVC:

```
apiVersion: v1
kind: PersistentVolumeClaim
metadata:
  name: jenkins-efs-claim
spec:
  accessModes:
    - ReadWriteMany
  storageClassName: jenkins-efs-sc
  resources:
    requests:
      storage: 10Gi
```

The following is the YAML for Jenkins on EKS Deployment:

```
apiVersion: apps/v1
kind: Deployment
metadata:
 name: blueocean-deployment
 labels:
    app: blueocean
spec:

  template:
    metadata:
      name: blueocean-pod
```

```
          labels:
              app: blueocean
        spec:
         securityContext:
          fsGroup: 1000
          runAsUser: 0
         containers:
         - name: blueocean
           image: jenkinsci/blueocean
           ports:
           - name: http-port
             containerPort: 8080
           - name: jnlp-port
             containerPort: 50000
           volumeMounts:
            - name: jenkins-home
              mountPath: /var/jenkins_home
         volumes:
            - name: jenkins-home
              persistentVolumeClaim:
                claimName: jenkins-efs-claim

    replicas: 1

    selector:
       matchLabels:
           app: blueocean
---
apiVersion: v1
kind: Service
metadata:
 name: blueocean-service
```

```
    labels:
        app: blueocean
spec:
    selector:
        app: blueocean
    ports:
      - protocol: TCP
        name: http
        port: 8080
        targetPort: 8080
      - protocol: TCP
        name: agent
        port: 50000
        targetPort: 50000
    type: LoadBalancer
```

10. We only need to deploy the above-mentioned files in the EKS cluster using the kubectl apply command.

11. Once deployment is successful, all JENKINS_HOME data from the EKS/ Kubernetes pod will be stored in the Amazon Elastic File System.

Even in the case of pod failure, the new pod will be created, and Jenkins will be up and running as it was in the previous state. This is because Jenkins pod will access data from the Elastic File System available in AWS.

In the next section, we will discuss Jenkins best practices.

Jenkins Pipeline – Best Practices

The following are some of the best practices while creating a pipeline or orchestration:

* Use Blue Ocean to create Jenkinsfile and a multibranch pipeline for its efficient usage.

* Use a script in the DSL to make automation work if the domain-specific language construct is not available.

* Combine commands in a single step, or use a script file for multiple command execution.

- Avoid using a Scripted pipeline as it has its learning curve and is not easy to understand. The scripted pipeline is difficult to manage and maintain over time, and people who manage it find it difficult to hand it over to new people as this may be difficult to learn quickly.

- Use Blue Ocean, Snippet generator to generate Jenkinsfile for the declarative pipeline quickly, as shown in the following figure:

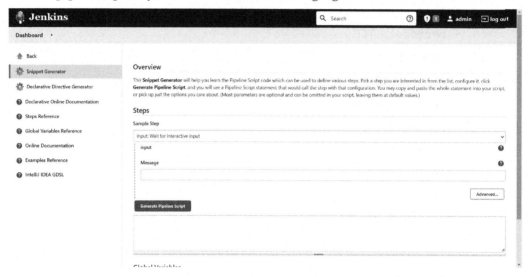

Figure 8.15: Pipeline syntax

Click on **Generate Pipeline Script** after configuration, as shown in the following figure:

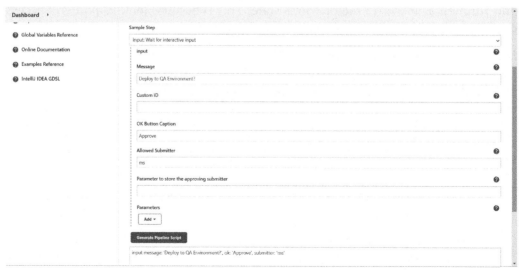

Figure 8.16: Generate Pipeline Script

This helps create a pipeline quickly in the initial stages.

- Create and configure Jenkinsfile for different branches based on the requirements, and make it a practice to utilize pipelines in daily operations to cultivate people's mindset.

- Role-based access forpipeline management and maintenance.

- Configure branches for pipeline execution on the basis of the needs. Use Filter by name (with wildcards) in Branch Sources to keep specific branches in the Jenkins pipeline execution:

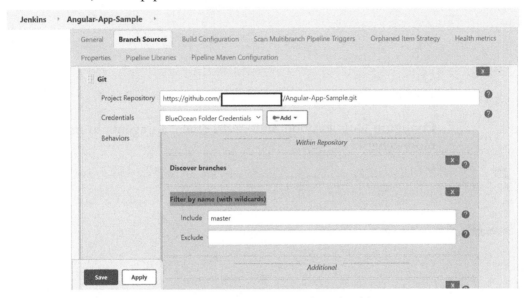

Figure 8.17: *Filter by name (with wildcards)*

It filters specific branches only; hence, it limits resource usage.

- Use controller agent architecture in the pipeline, and use multiple agents for execution so that parallel execution is possible.
  - Use Docker containers or Kubernetes pods as an agent to execute Jenkins pipeline, as follows:

```
pipeline {
 agent {
  kubernetes {
    idleMinutes 5  // how long the pod will live after no
jobs have run on it
    yamlFile 'build-agent-pod.yaml'
```

```
        // path to the pod definition relative to the root of our
project
        defaultContainer 'node'
                // define a default container if more than a few
stages use it, will default to jnlp container
    }
}
stages {

    .

    .

    .

    }
}
```

   o   Configure tools location and environment in agents to make things
       more generic:

Figure 8.18: Node configuration

- Use publish coverage report plugin to publish unit test results; it supports Cobertura, Jacoco, and Istanbul report formats.

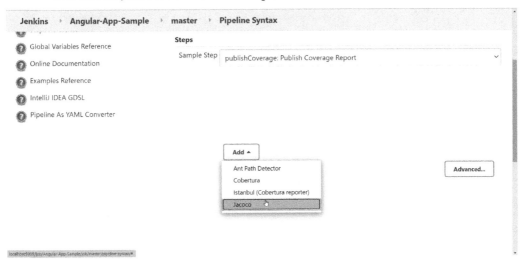

Figure 8.19: *Publish coverage report*

The report provides detailed information of the coverage areas:

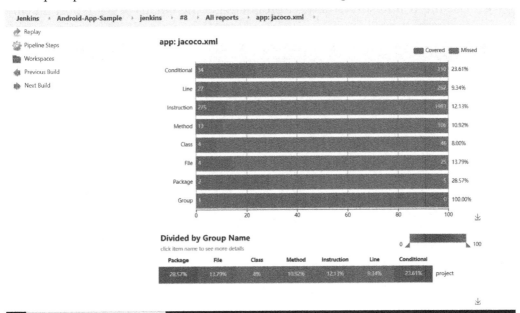

Figure 8.20: *Coverage report*

- Use Quality Gate for code coverage for Unit tests execution. Use thresholds based on business requirements, and ensure to keep them in effect at the beginning:

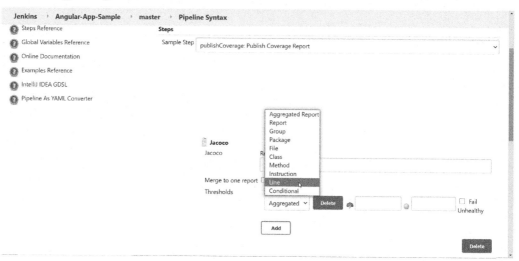

Figure 8.21: *Coverage threshold*

- Use the Test Results Analyzer plugin to get the details of the report on Unit test execution:

Figure 8.22: *Test Results Analyzer plugin*

- Use folders to manage pipelines better. We can configure Project-based security at the folder level in folder configuration as well:

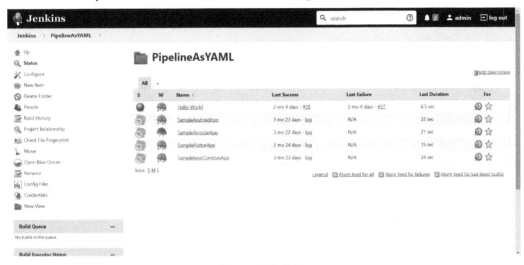

Figure 8.23: Folder

- It is important to backup JENKINS_HOME regularly if it is not stored in Cloud File Systems like Amazon Elastic File Systems.

- Use Jenkins environment variables in Declarative pipeline script for creating effective pipelines.

- It is important to provide training to all team members on how CI/CD implementation will help them save time and how Pipeline as Code is more effective for automating Application Life Cycle Management phases.

- In an organization, automated deployment in most of the environments is not feasible due to many processes that need to be followed for audit purposes. Hence, it is important to introduce Input parameter in the pipeline that allows manual intervention before pipeline stage execution is performed.

In the next section, we will discuss the installation of SonarQube that we will integrate with Jenkins for Static Code Analysis in the next chapter.

Installing SonarQube on Amazon EKS

SonarQube is an open-source tool to implement DevOps Practice - Continuous Code Inspection of quality. It helps perform Static Code Analysis of code to detect bugs, vulnerabilities, and code smells on multiple programming languages. The following is the Deployment and Service YAML; we will use this installation in the next chapter for creating an end-to-end pipeline for application lifecycle management:

```yaml
apiVersion: apps/v1
kind: Deployment
metadata:
 name: sonarqube-deployment
 labels:
    app: sonarqube
spec:
 template:
   metadata:
    name: sonarqube-pod
    labels:
       app: sonarqube
   spec:
    containers:
    - name: sonarqube
      image: sonarqube:latest
      resources:
       requests:
         cpu: 500m
         memory: 1024Mi
       limits:
         cpu: 2000m
         memory: 2048Mi
      ports:
      - name: sonar-port
        protocol: TCP
        containerPort: 9000
 replicas: 1

 selector:
   matchLabels:
       app: sonarqube
---
```

```
apiVersion: v1
kind: Service
metadata:
 name: sonarqube-service
 labels:
    app: sonarqube
spec:
 selector:
    app: sonarqube
 ports:
  - name: sonar-port
    protocol: TCP
    port: 9000
    targetPort: 9000
 type: LoadBalancer
```

Let's use kubectl apply to create SonarQube deployment and service:

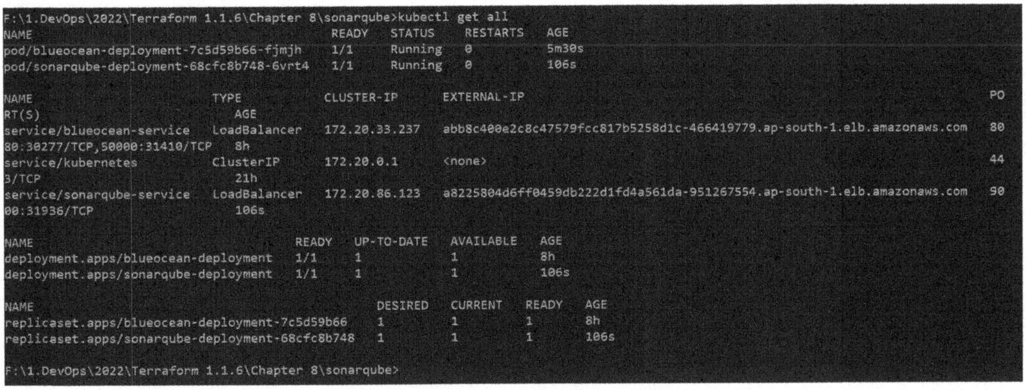

F:\1.DevOps\2022\Terraform 1.1.6\Chapter 8\sonarqube>kubectl apply -f sonarqube-eks-deployment.yml

deployment.apps/sonarqube-deployment created

service/sonarqube-service created

Let's verify the created resources using the kubectl get command. Note the EXTERNAL-IP of SonarQube service:

Figure 8.24: Kubernetes resources for SonarQube and Jenkins

Visit the EXTERNAL-IP of SonarQube service in the browser.

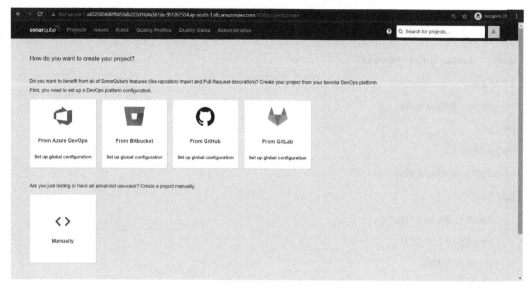

Figure 8.25: SonarQube dashboard

Verify a little note of Embedded Database in the bottom section of the SonarQube dashboard:

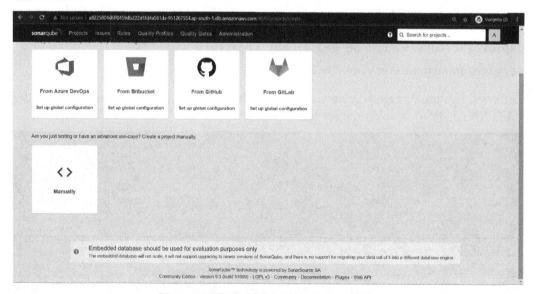

Figure 8.26: Embedded database in SonarQube

Try to use the Postgres database in SonarQube rather than the Embedded Database.

Terraform in Jenkins Declarative Pipeline

Let's execute Terraform scripts using Jenkins. As of now, we will use a custom agent with a Windows operating system that has Terraform installed on it and the rest of the configurations related to AWS CLI are also done.

1. Go to **Manage Jenkins** | **System Configuration** | **Manage Nodes and Clouds** | Click on **New Node**.

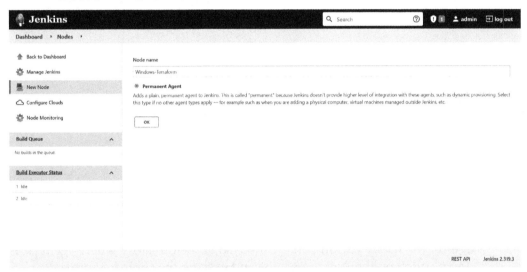

Figure 8.27: New Node

2. Provide details such as executor, remote root directory, labels, usage, and launch method, as follows. Then, click on **Save**.

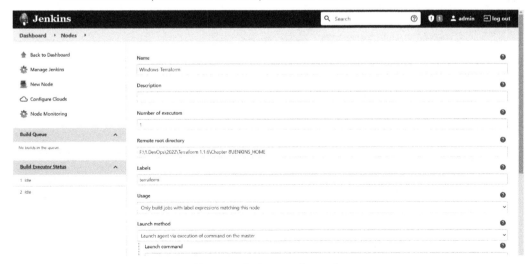

Figure 8.28: Agent node creation

An agent is created but not connected with Jenkins.

3.   Click on the newly created Agent.

Figure 8.29: Offline Agent

4.   Copy the script for Run from the agent command line. Download the **agent.jar** file by clicking on the link. Go to the directory where agent.jar is downloaded on the Agent machine and execute the copied command.

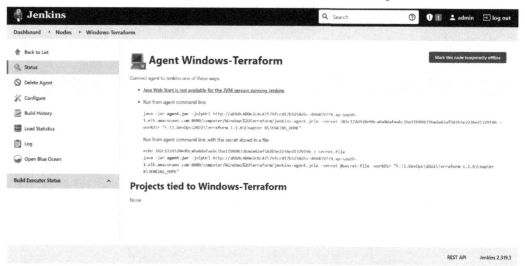

Figure 8.30: Command to connect Agent to Jenkins

```
java -jar agent.jar -jnlpUrl http://
abb8c400e2c8c47579fcc817b5258d1c-466419779.
ap-south-1.elb.amazonaws.com:8080/computer/
Windows%2DTerraform/jenkins-agent.jnlp -secret
382c122d520e96ca6a8dafaabc1ba11b896726ada42af582b5e2236e21329196
-workDir "F:\1.DevOps\2022\Terraform 1.1.6\Chapter 8\JENKINS_HOME"
```

5. Verify the confirmed connectivity.

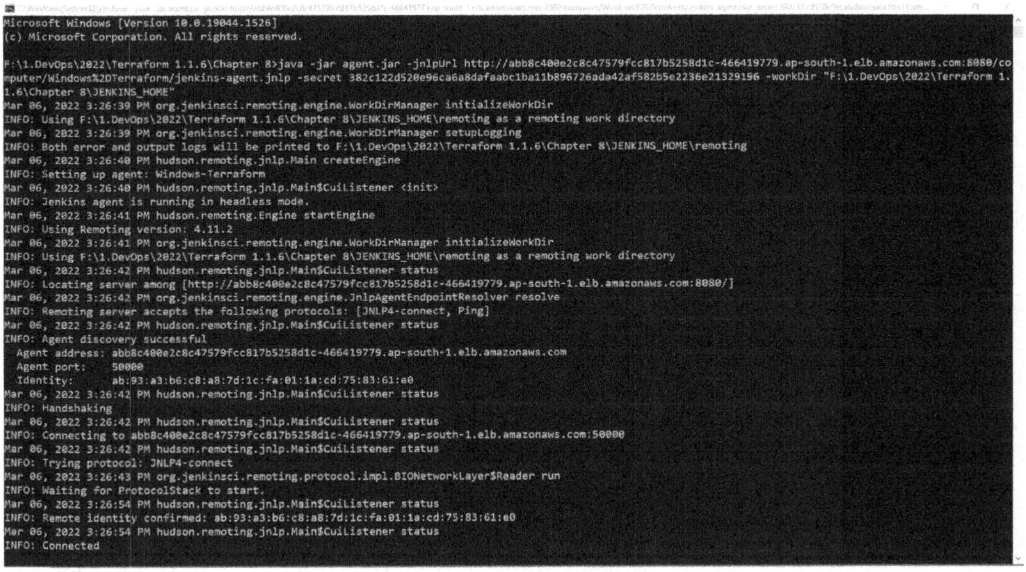

Figure 8.31: Connected Agent

6. Go to **Manage Jenkins | System Configuration | Manage Nodes and Clouds**, and click on the Node name to get the following message:

Figure 8.32: Connected Agent in Jenkins Dashboard

7. Go to **Manage Jenkins** | **System Configuration** | **Manage Nodes and Clouds**, and verify all available nodes.

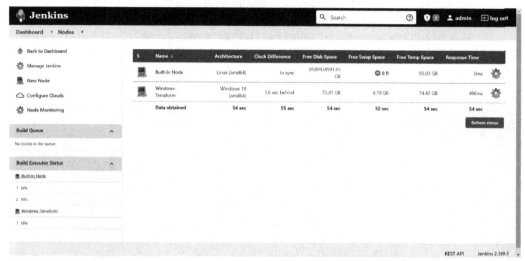

Figure 8.33: Available nodes

8. On Jenkins Dashboard, click on New Item, enter an item name, and select Free-style job project. Click on Ok.

   The pipeline project configuration page will open.

9. We want to restrict the execution of the pipeline in the agent that we configured earlier. Select Restrict where this project can be run, and enter terraform in the Label Expression field.

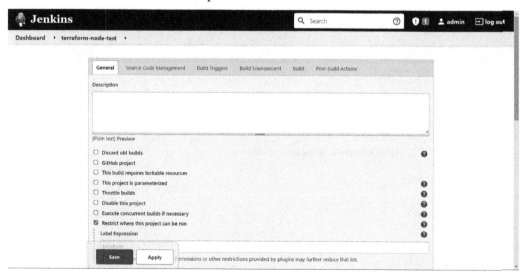

Figure 8.34: Pipeline project

10. Select the Execute Windows Batch Script build step, enter the **terraform -version** command, and click on **Save**.

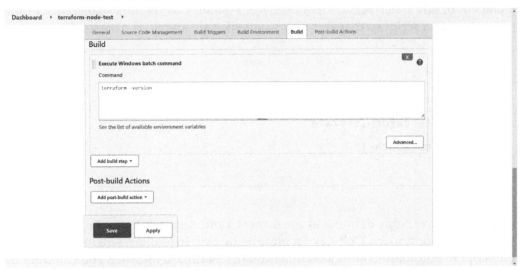

Figure 8.35: Command to verify terraform availability on Connected Agent

Note: Default workspace can't be deleted.

11. Click on **Build Now**. Go to Console Output in Jenkins and verify the execution of the **terraform -version** command.

Figure 8.36: Console Output

We created a custom module for Amazon VPC creation in *Chapter 6, Terraform Modules*. Let's try to execute the same script from the Jenkins. Note that we are not using Git or any other version management system. Use the following block in the main terraform script so that Terraform state files are stored in Amazon S3:

```
terraform {
 backend "s3" {
  bucket = "tfstate-bucket"
  key    = "terraform.tfstate"
  region = "ap-south-1"
 }
}
```

Jenkins pipeline helps define and implement Continuous Integration, Continuous Testing, and Continuous Delivery Pipeline using DSL in Jenkins. Jenkinsfile contains the script to automate Continuous Integration, Continuous Testing, and Continuous Delivery, or it is available in Jenkins Pipeline Job. The visible benefit of creating a Jenkinsfile to contain Pipeline as Code is its version control in the repository. Hence, Infrastructure as Code has a sister named Pipeline as Code.

There are two ways to create a Pipeline:

- Jenkins Dashboard
- Jenkins file

It is a best practice to use Jenkinsfile. Let's understand some basic Pipeline concepts:

- **Pipeline (Declarative)**: It models CICD Pipeline or contains stages or phases of Application Lifecycle Management.

- **Agent or Node**: It is a system (virtual or physical) utilized in the Controller/Master Agent Architecture of Jenkins. Jenkins execution takes place on the Controller/Master or Agent Node.

- **Stage**: It is a collection of tasks. For example, Compilation of Source files, Unit Test Execution, and publishing Junit test reports. We can represent it as a Block. To understand it more easily, consider it as a Source Code Analysis or Continuous Integration or Continuous Testing or Continuous Delivery.

- **Step**: It is a Task. Multiple Tasks make a stage, like execution of script, execution of maven command, execution of SonarQube analysis command, and execution of Gradle command.

Declarative Pipeline follows a declarative programming model. Declarative Pipelines are written in domain-specific language in Jenkins that is clear and easy to understand.

The following is a sample Declarative Pipeline:

```
pipeline {
    /* Stages and Steps */
}
pipeline {
    agent any
    stages {
        stage('SCA') {
            steps {
                //
            }
        }
        stage('CI') {
            steps {
                //
            }
        }
        stage('CD') {
            steps {
                //
            }
        }
    }
}
```

> **Note:** Check out the following references for more information about Jenkins Pipelines:
> - Pipeline: https://www.jenkins.io/doc/book/pipeline/
> - Getting started with Pipeline: https://www.jenkins.io/doc/book/pipeline/getting-started/
> - Pipeline Syntax: https://www.jenkins.io/doc/book/pipeline/syntax/

The following is the pipeline code:

```
pipeline {
    agent
    {
        label "terraform"
    }

    stages {
        stage('terraform-init') {
            steps {
                bat '''terraform -version
                cd F:\\1.DevOps\\2022\\Terraform 1.1.6\\Chapter 8\\
ModuleDemoG
                aws s3api create-bucket --bucket tfstate-bucket0703
--region ap-south-1 --create-bucket-configuration LocationConstraint=ap-
south-1
                terraform init'''
            }
        }
        stage('terraform-validate') {
            steps {
                bat '''terraform -version
                cd F:\\1.DevOps\\2022\\Terraform 1.1.6\\Chapter 8\\
ModuleDemoG
                terraform validate'''
            }
        }
        stage('dev-plan') {
            steps {
                bat '''terraform -version
                cd F:\\1.DevOps\\2022\\Terraform 1.1.6\\Chapter 8\\
ModuleDemoG
                dir
                terraform workspace new dev
                terraform workspace list
                terraform workspace select dev
                terraform plan -out=dev-tfplan'''
            }
        }
```

```
        }
        stage('dev-build') {
            steps {
                bat '''terraform -version
                cd F:\\1.DevOps\\2022\\Terraform 1.1.6\\Chapter 8\\
ModuleDemoG

                terraform workspace select dev
                dir
                terraform apply -auto-approve dev-tfplan'''
            }
        }
        stage('staging-plan') {
            steps {
                bat '''terraform -version
                cd F:\\1.DevOps\\2022\\Terraform 1.1.6\\Chapter 8\\
ModuleDemoG

                dir
                terraform workspace new staging
                terraform workspace list
                terraform workspace select staging
                terraform plan -out=staging-tfplan'''
            }
        }
        stage('staging-build') {
            steps {
                bat '''terraform -version
                cd F:\\1.DevOps\\2022\\Terraform 1.1.6\\Chapter 8\\
ModuleDemoG

                terraform workspace select staging
                dir
                terraform apply -auto-approve staging-tfplan'''
            }
        }
        stage('Destroy Approval') {
            steps {
                bat '''cd F:\\1.DevOps\\2022\\Terraform 1.1.6\\Chapter
8\\ModuleDemoG

                terraform workspace show'''
```

```
            input 'Do you want to destroy Infrastructure?'
        }
    }
    stage('terraform-destroy') {
        steps {
            bat '''cd F:\\1.DevOps\\2022\\Terraform 1.1.6\\Chapter
8\\ModuleDemoG
            dir
            terraform workspace select dev
            terraform destroy -auto-approve
            terraform workspace select staging
            terraform destroy -auto-approve'''
        }
    }
}
}
```

The following is a short description of the above-mentioned pipeline stages:

- The '**terraform-init**' stage creates an s3 bucket that will be used to store terraform state files for different workspaces. It also executes the terraform init command.

- The '**terraform-validate**' stage validates terraform scripts.

- The '**dev-plan**' stage creates a new dev workspace and creates a plan for the new workspace.

- The '**dev-build**' stage creates resources in the newly created dev workspace.

- The '**staging-plan**' stage creates a new staging workspace and creates a plan for the new workspace.

- The '**staging-build**' stage creates resources in the newly created staging workspace.

- The 'Destroy Approval' stage provides a scenario where manual approval is required before performing the next stage execution in the pipeline.

- The '**terraform-destroy**' stage executes the terraform destroy command in both workspaces.

Note: Terraform has a single workspace named "default"; we can't create more workspaces based on requirements.

Save the Pipeline job configuration and click on `Build Now`.

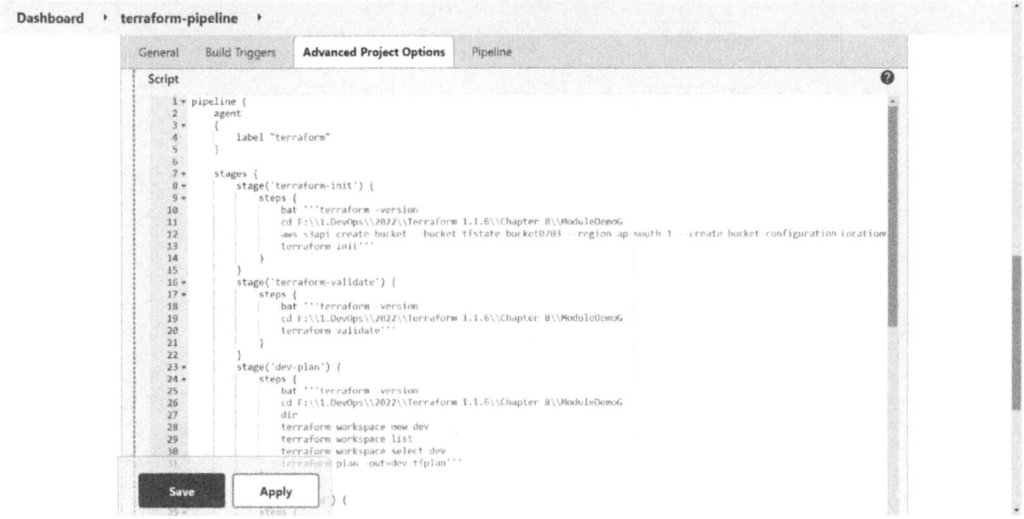

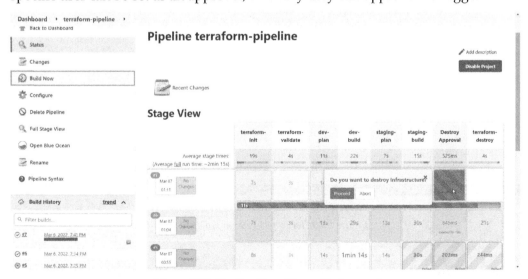

Figure 8.37: Pipeline script

Manual approval can be a click on `Jenkins Dashboard`, shown as follows, or a specific user can be set as an approver, and only they can approve the trigger.

Figure 8.38: Pipeline Stage View with Approval

Given here is a successful Pipeline execution in Jenkins Dashboard:

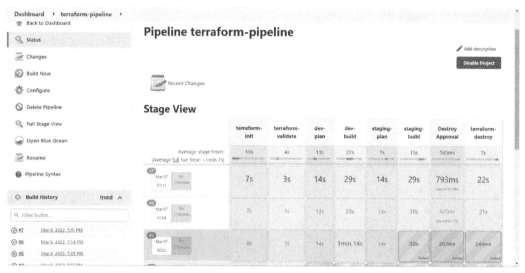

Figure 8.39: Pipeline Stage View

Let's verify the bucket in Amazon S3, as follows:

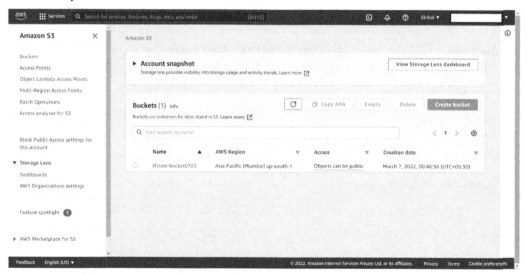

Figure 8.40: Terraform state in Amazon S3

Note: The format of the Terraform state files is JSON.

We have used workspaces, so we see the env directory in the bucket:

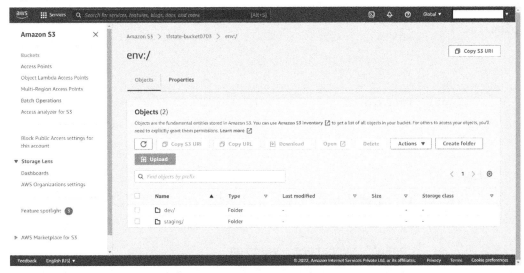

Figure 8.41: Terraform state in Amazon S3 based on workspace

The following are the workspace-based directories that we created using Jenkins Pipeline:

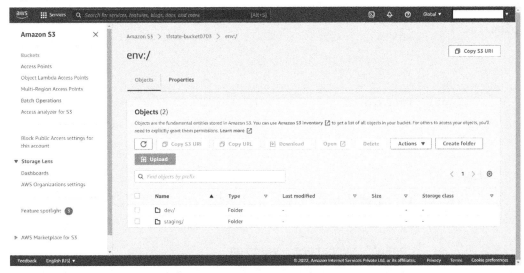

Figure 8.42: Terraform workspaces in Amazon S3

Go to dev or staging directory and verify the Terraform state file.

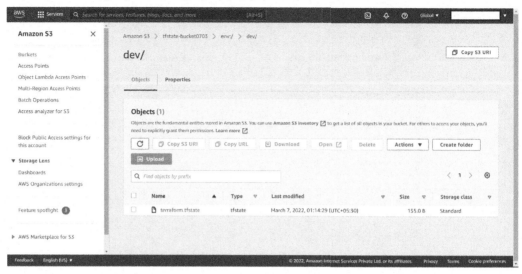

Figure 8.43: *Terraform state in Amazon S3 as per workspace*

The pipeline is in GitHub, along with the complete Terraform script and custom Module, and the pipeline has minor changes, shown as follows. We are not explicitly providing the files' location; a relative path is used.

```
pipeline {

    agent

    {

        label "terraform"

    }


    stages {

        stage('terraform-init') {

            steps {

                bat '''terraform -version

                aws s3api create-bucket --bucket tfstate-bucket --region
ap-south-1 --create-bucket-configuration LocationConstraint=ap-south-1

                terraform init'''

            }

        }
```

```
stage('terraform-validate') {
    steps {
        bat '''terraform -version
        terraform validate'''
    }
}
stage('dev-plan') {
    steps {
        bat '''terraform -version
        dir
        terraform workspace new dev
        terraform workspace list
        terraform workspace select dev
        terraform plan -out=dev-tfplan'''
    }
}
stage('dev-build') {
    steps {
        bat '''terraform -version
        terraform workspace select dev
        dir
        terraform apply -auto-approve dev-tfplan'''
    }
}
stage('staging-plan') {
    steps {
        bat '''terraform -version
        dir
        terraform workspace new staging
        terraform workspace list
```

```
                terraform workspace select staging
                terraform plan -out=staging-tfplan'''
            }
        }
        stage('staging-build') {
            steps {
                bat '''terraform -version
                terraform workspace select staging
                dir
                terraform apply -auto-approve staging-tfplan'''
            }
        }
        stage('Destroy Approval') {
            steps {
                bat '''terraform workspace show'''
                input 'Do you want to destroy Infrastructure?'
            }
        }
        stage('terraform-destroy') {
            steps {
                bat '''dir
                terraform workspace select dev
                terraform destroy -auto-approve
                terraform workspace select staging
                terraform destroy -auto-approve'''
            }
        }
    }
}
```

Terraform script uses a relative path to refer to the custom module that exists in GitHub, as follows:

```
module "customvpc" {
  source = "./Custommodules//customvpc"
  region = "ap-south-1"
  cidr_blocks = "0.0.0.0/0"
  vpc_cidr = "10.0.1.0/24"
  public_cidr = "10.0.1.0/28"
  private_cidr = "10.0.1.16/28"
}
```

In the next section, we will understand the importance of infrastructure as code in brief.

Adopting Infrastructure as Code (IaC) Culture in an Organization

Infrastructure as Code (IaC) is one of the most popular Continuous/DevOps Practices due to its flexibility and easy learning curve. It helps manage infrastructure as we manage normal code using version control, and it fits in the pipeline seamlessly based on the tools we are using. Infrastructure as code started its footprints with virtualization and cloud environments. Speed, uniformity, quality, less manual intervention, control, and management are some of the reasons why IaC is gaining popularity by the day. It allows teams to manage infrastructure efficiently in different environments.

In the long run, culture evolves and helps improve speed, quality, and productivity gains. It provides a single source of truth about infrastructure and environments.

Conclusion

Jenkins is one of the most popular open-source tools to manage DevOps practices implementation using Pipeline as Code and Infrastructure as Code. In this chapter, we covered how Jenkins can be installed in the Kubernetes cluster and understood how to make it robust and highly available. We also installed SonarQube in the **Kubernetes cluster (EKS)** with Postgres as Database and covered how to execute Terraform script using Jenkins Pipeline as Code.

We will utilize Jenkins and SonarQube installed in this chapter in the EKS to create an end-to-end automation pipeline in the next chapter.

Points to remember

- Jenkins 2.0 provided new features, such as Pipeline as code - a new setup experience, and other UI improvements - enhancements with Jenkins interface.

- Pods are the smallest units that you can create and manage in Kubernetes.

- Service helps to access an application hosted in pods with IP addresses, and it provides the solution to load the balance.

- A deployment provides declarative updates for Pods and ReplicaSets.

- Multiple workspaces help to manage different environments/sets of infrastructure.

- **Local State**: Terraform writes the workspace states in a terraform.tfstate.d directory.

- **Remote State**: Terraform writes the workspace states in Amazon S3 or other supported storage services.

- **Pipeline (Declarative)**: It models CICD Pipeline or contains stages or phases of Application Lifecycle Management.

- **Agent or Node**: It is a system (virtual or physical) utilized in the Controller/Master Agent Architecture of Jenkins. Jenkins execution takes place on the Controller/Master or Agent Node.

- **Stage**: It is a collection of tasks. For example, Compilation of Source files, Unit Test Execution, and publishing Junit test reports. We can represent it as a Block. To understand it more easily, consider it as a Source Code Analysis or Continuous Integration or Continuous Testing or Continuous Delivery.

- **Step**: It is a Task. Multiple Tasks make a stage, like execution of script, execution of maven command, execution of SonarQube analysis command, and execution of Gradle command.

Multiple choice questions

1. **State True or False: "Default workspace can't be deleted."**

   a. True

   b. False

2. **State True or False: "Terraform writes the workspace states in a terraform. tfstate.d directory while managing state locally"**

   a. True

   b. False

3. **State True or False: "Terraform writes the workspace states in Amazon S3 or other supported storage services while managing state remotely."**

   a. True

   b. False

Answers

1. a
2. a
3. a

Questions

1. What is the usage of workspaces?

2. Which are the components of Kubernetes?

3. Where we can manage State files?

4. How deployment and replicasets helps in application availability?

CHAPTER 9

End-to-End Application Management Using Terraform

Terraform is an open-source infrastructure as code tool, and it is used to manage multiple cloud services of different cloud service providers such as AWS and Amazon. Package deployment happens in multiple environments, such as dev, qa, staging, and production. It is also important to manage end-to-end activities in an automated way in today's agile world. Continuous Integration and Continuous Delivery pipeline helps us achieve automation. We have already installed Jenkins and integrated it with Terraform in *Chapter 8, Terraform and Jenkins Integration*.

In this chapter, we are going to use a sample application (you can use a simple Angular-based application) and perform static code analysis, execute unit tests, calculate code coverage, execute build, create resources using Terraform, and upload distribution folder or package directory to Amazon S3 to have deployment of static website hosting. We also need to ensure that Jenkins is highly available, and that data is preserved in case of Jenkins installation failures.

Structure

We will discuss the following topics in this chapter:

- Implementing a sample project with **Infrastructure as Code (IaC)** using Terraform in cloud

- Questions and exercises

Objective

After studying this chapter, you should be able to use Jenkins and Terraform to automate end-to-end activities involved in application lifecycle management. It will provide a picture of how automation can help you gain productivity and time, and it will also provide a scenario to work for improving the existing architecture as a self-exercise.

Implementing Sample Project with IaC using Terraform in Cloud

In this chapter, we will create CI/CD pipeline for our sample application. We will create resources in AWS environment and deploy a package using Terraform, as shown in the following figure:

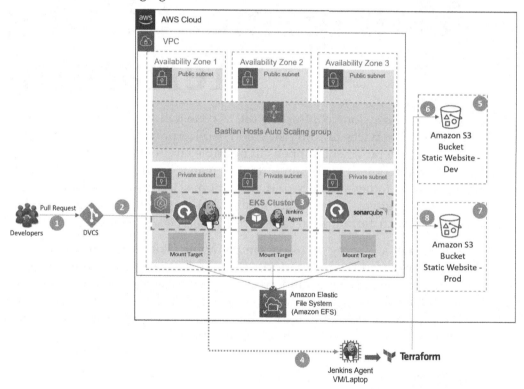

Figure 9.1: *Big picture*

This is the flow of execution in the above architecture:

1.　Developers create a new feature or fix bug and commit code.

2. The Jenkins pipeline is triggered.

3. Continuous Integration pipeline execution on Kubernetes pod, that is, Jenkins agent.

4. Continuous Delivery pipeline execution on Terraform agent.

5. Create resources of Dev environment.

6. Deploy build package in Amazon S3 bucket (Dev environment).

7. Create resources of Prod environment.

8. Deploy build package in Amazon S3 bucket (Prod environment).

In this chapter, we will create/reuse the following resources and execute end-to-end pipeline or CI/CD pipeline:

1. Kubernetes cluster in Amazon EKS (refer to the Creating EKS Cluster Using Terraform Modules section in Chapter 6, Terraform Modules).

2. We will create Amazon EFS and configure Jenkins to use EFS to store JENKINS_HOME data to make Jenkins highly available.

3. Jenkins and SonarQube installation/deployment in Kubernetes cluster is covered in Chapter 8, Terraform and Jenkins Integration.

4. Configure Kubernetes cluster in Jenkins as Cloud in Configure Clouds section so that pods can be utilized as Jenkins Agents.

5. Configure a virtual machine or laptop as a Jenkins agent where Terraform is installed.

   a. We will use this agent to create resources in AWS cloud to deploy a static website.

6. Once the above configuration is available, execute CI/CD pipeline – Jenkinsfile.

   b. Perform the following actions in Kubernetes Agent:

      i. Static code analysis using SonarQube

      ii. Unit test execution

      iii. Code coverage calculation

      iv. Build

      v. Stash build artifact

   c. Perform the following actions in Terraform Agent:

    i.   Download/unstash build artifact

    ii.   Create a plan for the creation of Dev environment

    iii.   Create resources of Dev environment

    iv.   Prod deployment approval

    v.   Create a plan for the creation of Prod environment

    vi.   Create resources of Prod environment

Cloud platforms provide a pay-as-you-go model, which helps create uniform environments, unlike before. We can have dev, qa, and staging environments that are similar to production, and it helps the development team troubleshoot issues and fix them faster. Terraform helps development teams create resources in different cloud service providers easily and quickly.

In this chapter, we will manage uniform infrastructure across different environments using common files and different variables files specific to the environments. We will pass different variables, such as region and Amazon S3 bucket name, where we will upload the distribution directory. We will have two environments: dev and prod.

The following is the directory structure in Windows operating system for Terraform scripts to create an environment without the duplication of code:

Figure 9.2: Directory structure

The following is the content of **dev.tfvars** in the dev directory:

```
bucket_name = "angular-sample-app-dev"
tfstate-dir = "dev/terraform.tfstate"
```

Given here is the content of **prod.tfvars** in the prod directory:

```
bucket_name = "angular-sample-app-prod"
tfstate-dir = "prod/terraform.tfstate"
```

This is a **vars.tf** file:

```
variable "apac_region" {
      default = "ap-south-1"
}

#Keep Empty to initialize it in terraform.tfvars; keep terraform.tfvars
in git ignore list so secret information is not available

variable "bucket_name" {}

variable "tfstate-dir" {}

variable "mime_types" {
  default = {

    html  = "text/html"
    css   = "text/css"
    js    = "application/javascript"
    map   = "application/javascript"

      jpg   = "image/jpeg"

      ico   = "image/ico"
  }
}
```

Given here is a **version.tf** file to verify the terraform version:

```
terraform {
  required_version = ">= 0.12"
}
```

The following is the terraform script that will create S3 bucket and upload the content of the sample Angular project in it. Here, we will use S3 as the backend. It stores the Terraform state as a given key in a particular bucket on Amazon S3, as shown in *figure 9.3*. We assume that **tfstate-bucket300** is already available in Amazon S3. The Terraform state is written to the key.

Figure 9.3: *Terraform state Bucket in Amazon S3*

Let's take a look at the script:

```
terraform {
     required_providers {
          aws = {
             source = "hashicorp/aws"
             version = "3.40.0"
          }
     }
     backend "s3" {
             bucket = "tfstate-bucket0703"
             key    = "terraform.tfstate"
             region = "ap-south-1"
     }


}
```

```
provider "aws" {
  region = var.apac_region
  profile = "default"
}

#Provides an S3 object resource.
resource "aws_s3_bucket" "angular_s3_bucket" {
      bucket = var.bucket_name
      acl    = "private"
      website {
            index_document = "index.html"
      }
      tags = {
            Name = var.bucket_name
      }
}
# Attaches a policy to an S3 bucket resource.
resource "aws_s3_bucket_policy" "angular_s3_bucket_policy" {
  bucket = aws_s3_bucket.angular_s3_bucket.id
      policy = jsonencode({
            "Version": "2012-10-17",
            "Statement": [
                  {
                        "Sid": "PublicReadGetObject",
                        "Effect": "Allow",
                        "Principal": "*",
                        "Action": [
                              "s3:GetObject",
                              "s3:GetObjectVersion"
                        ],
                        "Resource": "arn:aws:s3:::${var.bucket_name}/*"
                  }
            ]
```

```
        })
}


# Provides an S3 object resource.
#content_type - Standard MIME type describing the format of the object
data, e.g., application/octet-stream. All Valid MIME Types are valid for
this input.
resource "aws_s3_bucket_object" "object" {
        for_each = fileset("browser/", "**/*.*")
        bucket = aws_s3_bucket.angular_s3_bucket.id
        key = each.value
        content_type = lookup(var.mime_types, split(".", each.value)
[length(split(".", each.value)) - 1])
# Path to a file that will be read and uploaded
        source = "browser/${each.value}"
# Triggers updates when the value changes. The only meaningful value is
filemd5("path/to/file") (Terraform 0.11.12 or later)
        etag = filemd5("browser/${each.value}")
}
```

Use the following commands for dev environment resource creation and package deployment (assuming that you already have package files to deploy in the same directory):

```
terraform init -var-file=dev/dev.tfvars

terraform workspace new dev

terraform workspace list

terraform workspace select dev

terraform plan --out=mymodule-dev.tfplan --var-file=dev/dev.tfvars
```

Use the following commands for prod environment resource creation and package deployment (assuming that you already have package files to deploy in the same directory):

```
terraform init -var-file=prod/prod.tfvars
terraform workspace new prod
```

```
terraform workspace list
terraform workspace select prod
terraform plan --out=mymodule-prod.tfplan --var-file=prod/prod.tfvars
```

> **Note: Refer to the following resources for more details on Amazon S3 and how to manage it using Terraform:**
> - **Resource: aws_s3_bucket provides a S3 bucket resource https://registry.terraform.io/providers/hashicorp/aws/latest/docs/resources/s3_bucket**
> - **Resource: aws_s3_bucket_object provides a S3 bucket object resource. https://registry.terraform.io/providers/hashicorp/aws/latest/docs/resources/s3_bucket_object**
> - **Resource: aws_s3_bucket_policy attaches a policy to an S3 bucket resource. https://registry.terraform.io/providers/hashicorp/aws/latest/docs/resources/s3_bucket_policy**
> - **Backend using S3 https://www.terraform.io/docs/language/settings/backends/s3.html**

We have Terraform scripts ready at this stage, and we also have Kubernetes cluster available as we created it in *Chapter 7, Terraform Modules.*

Let's get the details of the Kubernetes cluster created in Amazon EKS, as follows:

```
F:\1.DevOps\2022\Terraform 1.1.6\Chapter 9\cicd>kubectl cluster-info

Kubernetes master is running at https://B37843092D662BEFDA4BEFB5EAAC7324.
gr7.ap-south-1.eks.amazonaws.com

CoreDNS is running at https://B37843092D662BEFDA4BEFB5EAAC7324.gr7.ap-
south-1.eks.amazonaws.com/api/v1/namespaces/kube-system/services/kube-
dns:dns/proxy

To further debug and diagnose cluster problems, use 'kubectl cluster-info dump'.
```

Use `'kubectl cluster-info dump'` to further debug and diagnose cluster problems.

We already have Jenkins setup available. Refer to *Chapter 8: Terraform and Jenkins Integration* to integrate Kubernetes with Jenkins.

> **Note: Visit https://aws.amazon.com/blogs/storage/deploying-jenkins-on-amazon-eks-with-amazon-efs/" https://aws.amazon.com/blogs/storage/deploying-jenkins-on-amazon-eks-with-amazon-efs/ for more details about Deploying Jenkins on Amazon EKS with Amazon EFS.**

We will use Kubernetes pods for build and test execution.

1. Install Kubernetes plugin in Jenkins.

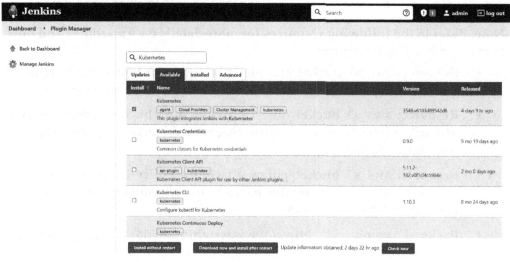

Figure 9.4: Kubernetes Plugin

2. Go to **Manage Jenkins** | **System Configuration** | **Manage Nodes and Clouds** | **Configure Clouds**. Click on **Add a new cloud** and select **Kubernetes**, as shown here:

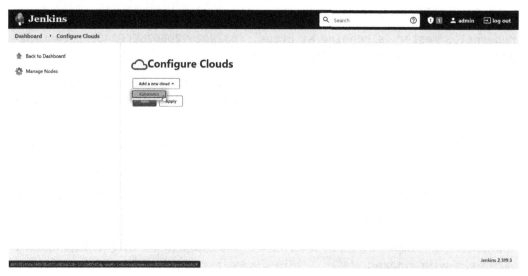

Figure 9.5: Configure Kubernetes cloud

3. Click on **Kubernetes Cloud details**:

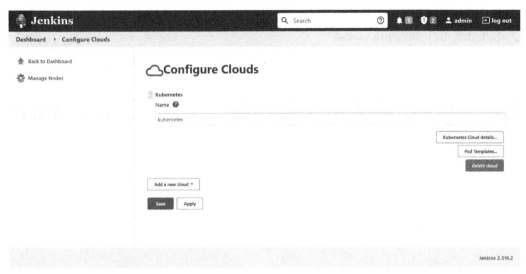

Figure 9.6: *Kubernetes Cloud details*

4. Provide the Kubernetes cluster URL that is hosted in EKS, along with the key that is configured in the config file in the **.kube** directory.

Disable the https certificate check so that communication with Kubernetes API server will rely on https but ignore ssl certificate verification. This is useful for quick setup, but it makes installation unsecure.

Figure 9.7: *Configuration of Kubernetes cloud in Jenkins*

5. Provide namespace and verify the connection.

Let's create a Jenkins agent on a laptop or virtual machine where Terraform is already installed with following steps:

1. Go to **Manage Jenkins** | **System Configuration** | **Manage Nodes and Clouds**. Give Node name and click on **OK**.

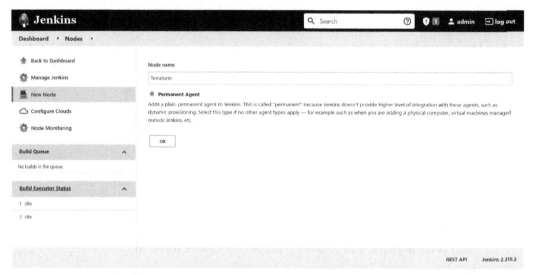

Figure 9.8: *Jenkins Agent/Node*

2. Configure a remote directory based on your operating system and give labels so that it can be utilized in **Jenkinsfile/Pipeline**.

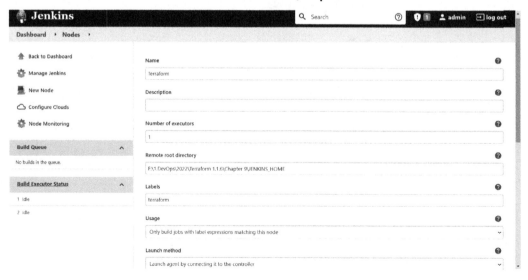

Figure 9.9: *Jenkins Agent configuration*

3. Agent is in disconnected state. Copy the command to run from command line:

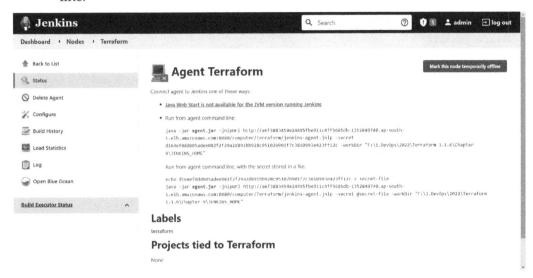

Figure 9.10: Disconnected Agent

4. Jenkins agent is connected now:

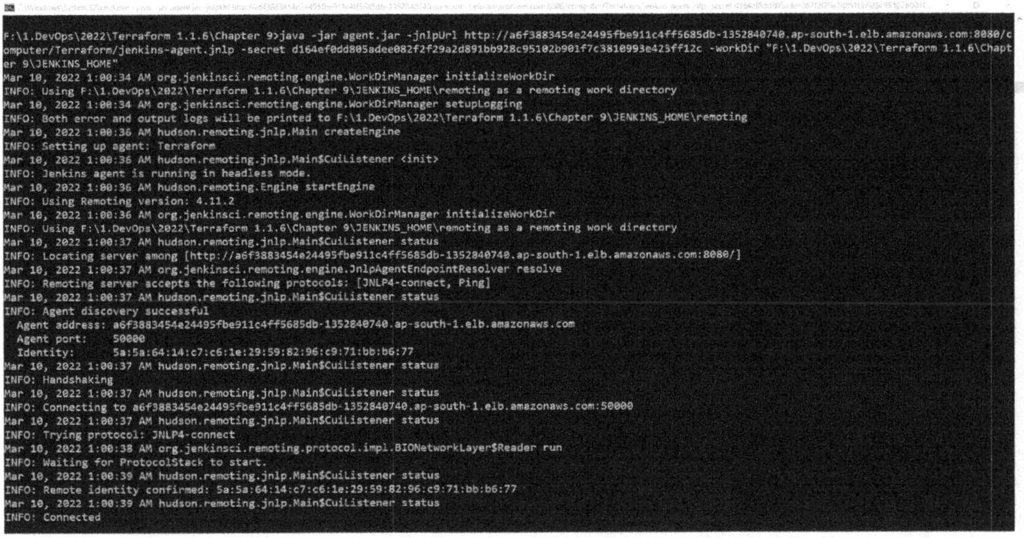

Figure 9.11: Jenkins Agent

5. Install the **Pipeline Utility Steps plugin** in Jenkins to use in the Declarative pipeline.

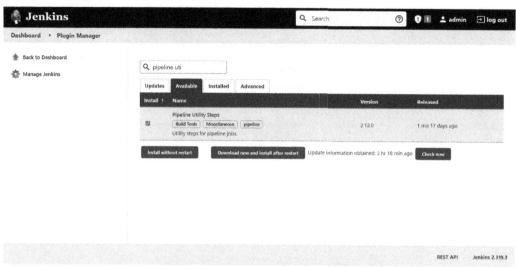

Figure 9.12: Pipeline Utility Steps plugin

We have now configured Kubernetes cluster and Terraform agent.

Let's configure SonarQube webhook.

1. We have already installed SonarQube in Kubernetes cluster; now, go to the SonarQube dashboard.

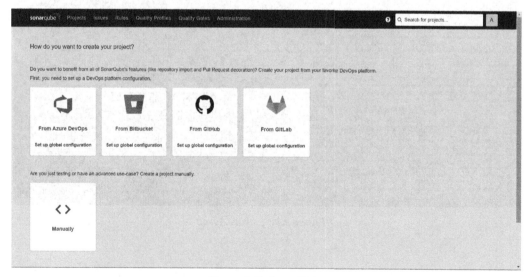

Figure 9.13: SonarQube

2. Click on **Administration**.

3. Click on **Create**.

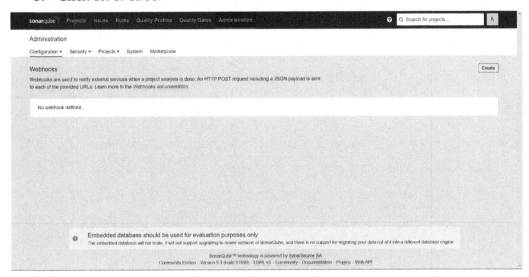

Figure 9.14: SonarQube webhook

4. Provide Jenkins URL in webhook and configure it in SonarQube.

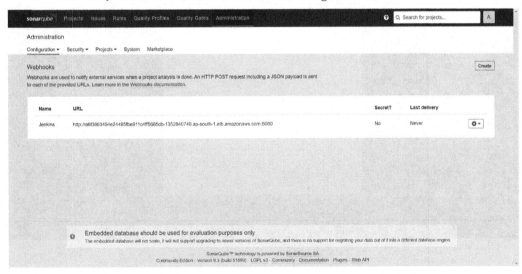

Figure 9.15: SonarQube webhook with URL

5. Let's create Sonar token. Click on **Security | Users**.

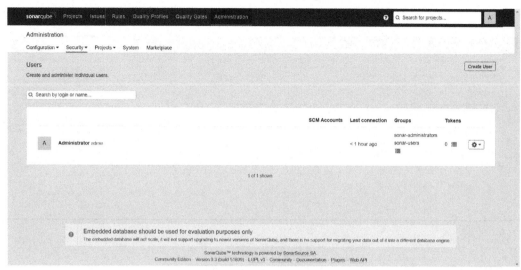

Figure 9.16: SonarQube users

6. Click on **Tokens** and create token; copy the token.

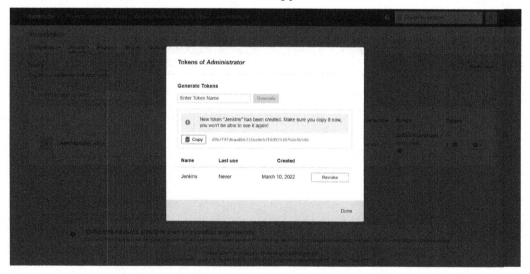

Figure 9.17: SonarQube token

7. Go to **Jenkins** | **Manage Jenkins** | **Credentials**. Add Credentials. Create a Secret text for the SonarQube token.

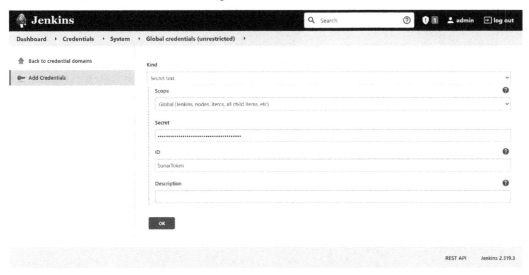

Figure 9.18: Jenkins secret of SonarQube token

8. The **build-agent-pod.yaml** will have pods definitions to execute stages. Use images such as docker:latest, node:latest, and zenika/alpine-chrome:86-with-node-12 to execute pipeline stages. The following is the skeleton script that creates the end-to-end CI/CD pipeline. It performs static code analysis and unit tests execution.

```
pipeline {
        agent {
                kubernetes {
                        idleMinutes 5  // how long the pod will live
after no jobs have run on it
                        yamlFile 'build-agent-pod.yaml'  // path to
the pod definition relative to the root of our project
                }
        }
        stages {
                stage('Static Code Analysis') {
                        steps {
                            container('node') {
                                        echo "Steps to execute SCA"
                                        sh 'wget https://binaries.
```

```
sonarsource.com/Distribution/sonar-scanner-cli/sonar-scanner-cli-
3.3.0.1492-linux.zip'
                                    sh 'unzip sonar-scanner-cli-
3.3.0.1492-linux.zip'

withSonarQubeEnv(installationName: 'SonarQube', credentialsId:
'SonarToken') {

                                  sh 'ls -l'
                                  sh 'sonar-scanner-3.3.0.1492-
linux/bin/sonar-scanner -Dsonar.projectVersion=1.0 -Dsonar.
projectKey=sample-angular-app -Dsonar.sources=src'
                                  }
                                  waitForQualityGate(abortPipeline:
true, credentialsId: 'SonarToken')
                       }
                     }
                 }
                stage('UnitTests & Coverage') {
                     steps {
                         container('chrome') {
                                 echo "Steps to execute Unit Tests"
                                 catchError(buildResult:
'SUCCESS', stageResult: 'FAILURE') {
                                     sh 'npm install &&
npm install karma-junit-reporter --save-dev && npm run test
--progress false --watch false'
                                 }
                             }
                         }
                     }
                }
                stage('Build') {
                     steps {
                         container('node') {
                                 echo "Steps to execute Build"
                             }
                         }
                     }
                }
                stage('IaC & Deploy') {
                     agent {
```

```
                        label 'terraform'
            }
            stages {
                    stage("Download Artifact") {
                            steps {
                                    echo "Steps to download
package files created in Kubernetes cluster "
                            }
                    }
                    stage('dev-plan') {
                            steps {
                                    echo "Steps to create plan
for dev environment"
                            }
                    }
                    stage('dev-build') {
                            steps {
                                    echo "Steps to create
resources for dev environment"
                            }
                    }
                    stage('Prod Deployment Approval') {
                            steps {
                                    input 'Do you want to
destroy Infrastructure?'
                            }
                    }
                    stage('prod-plan') {
                            steps {
                                    echo "Steps to create plan
for prod environment"
                            }
                    }
                    stage('prod-build') {
                            steps {
                                    echo "Steps to create
resources for prod environment"
                            }
```

```
                }
            }
        }
        post {
            always{
                echo "Post pipeline execution steps"
            }
        }
    }
```

9. This is the full stage view of pipeline:

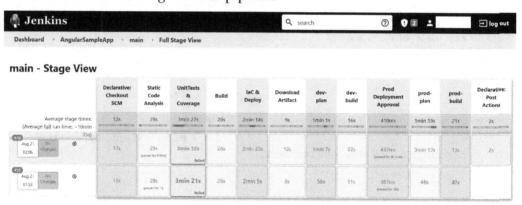

Figure 9.19: Full stage pipeline

10. Verify the SonarQube quality gate status on the Jenkins dashboard.

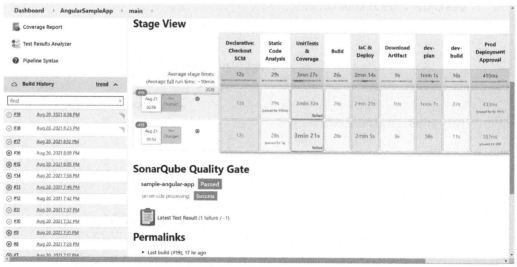

Figure 9.20: SonarQube quality gate status

11. Verify SonarQube stage on the Blue Ocean Dashboard as well.

Blue Ocean provides an easy way to create a Declarative pipeline using a new user experience available in the Blue Ocean dashboard. It is like creating a script based on selecting components or steps or tasks. Most of the automation tools and services provide similar functionality to attract beginners to adapt to new Jenkins. It is a mature and transparent representation of the end-to-end automation pipeline.

We can access the log stage-wise and access script directly into Jenkins Dashboard. It provides view, including multiple branches if branches have Jenkinsfile. We can create Jenkinsfile using Blue Ocean if it is not already available; if Jenkinsfile is already available with valid syntax, then Jenkins detects it and starts execution if a valid runtime environment is available. Blue Ocean provides a pipeline editor where we can directly enter script or add stages and steps using UI elements. Stages are represented properly, including Parallel stages execution or if the stage is skipped during execution based on condition. Stage-wise logs are available to provide quick insights in case of failures, and you don't need to scan the entire log to find an issue.

Let's understand how to start the Blue Ocean Pipeline configuration:

1. Go to **Manage Jenkins** | **Manage Plugins** | **Available** and select Blue Ocean and Install without restart.

2. After Blue Ocean plugin installation verifies the left sidebar where the new option has emerged, click on **Open Blue Ocean**.

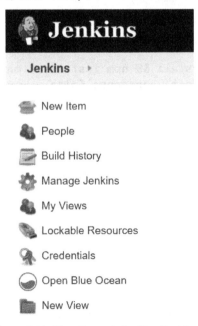

Figure 9.21: Blue Ocean in Jenkins Dashboard

3.   Verify the Blue Ocean Dashboard; it provides a new user interface.

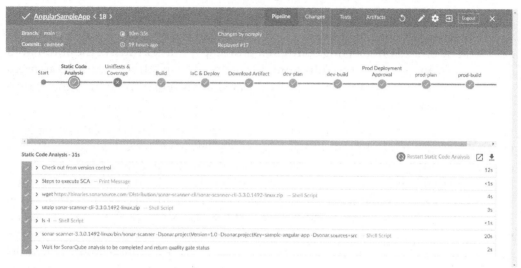

Figure 9.22: Blue Ocean Dashboard

4.   The pipeline stage to execute Unit tests is as follows:

```
stage('UnitTests & Coverage') {
    steps {
      container('chrome') {
        echo "Steps to execute Unit Tests"
        catchError(buildResult: 'SUCCESS', stageResult: 'FAILURE') {
           sh 'npm install && npm install karma-junit-reporter --save-
dev && npm run test --progress false --watch false'
        }
      }
    }
}
```

5. Verify the Test results trend on the Jenkins dashboard.

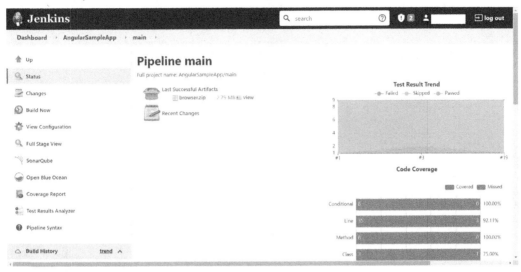

Figure 9.23: Test results trend

6. Verify code coverage.

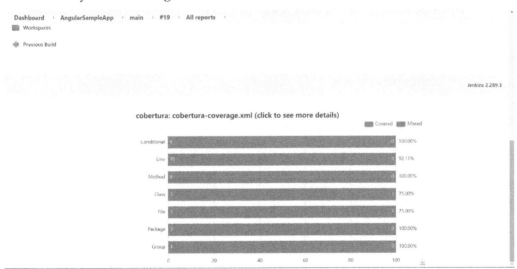

Figure 9.24: Code coverage

7. Click on the Blue Ocean link available on the Jenkins dashboard and go to **Tests** tab to get clear results of the test execution.

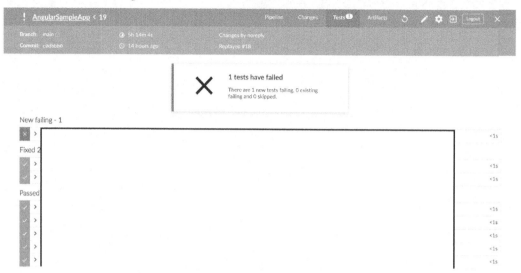

Figure 9.25: Unit tests reports in Jenkins Blue Ocean

8. The following is the pipeline stage to execute build step in **Jenkinsfile**:

```
stage('Build') {
    steps {
      container('node') {
          echo "Steps to execute Build"
          sh 'npm run build'
          zip archive: true, dir: 'dist/Demo1', glob: '', zipFile:
'browser.zip'
          stash(includes: 'browser.zip', name: 'dist')
      }


    }
}
```

9. Go to Blue Ocean and verify logs for build stage.

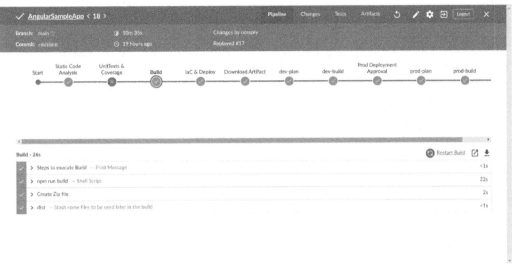

Figure 9.26: Build stage in Blue Ocean

10. Verify the pipeline execution status with build artifacts, test results, and coverage reports.

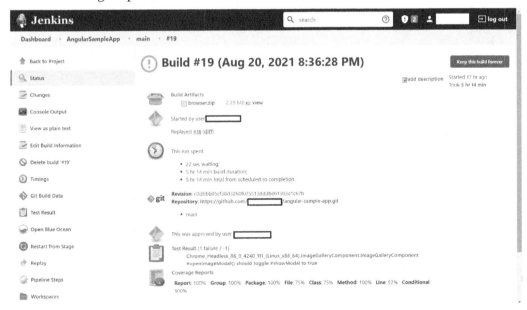

Figure 9.27: Pipeline status

The following are pipeline stages that download the artifact created at the build stage, create a new workspace for dev environment, and upload the artifact into Amazon S3 bucket that is mentioned in **dev.tfvars**.

Then, there is an approval stage for production environment creation and deployment of package. Production environment-related stages create a new workspace for production environment, and the artifact is uploaded into Amazon S3 bucket that is mentioned in **prod.tfvars**.

Following is declarative syntax for stages of Jenkinsfile.

```
stage('IaC & Deploy') {
  agent {
   label 'terraform'
  }
  stages {
   stage("Download Artifact") {
    steps {
     unstash 'dist'
     unzip dir: 'iac/dist', glob: '', zipFile: 'browser.zip'
    }
   }
   stage('dev-plan') {
    steps {
     bat '''terraform -version
     cd iac
     dir
     terraform init -var-file=dev/dev.tfvars
     terraform workspace new dev
     terraform workspace list
     terraform workspace select dev
     terraform plan --out=mymodule-dev.tfplan --var-file=dev/dev.tfvars'''
    }
   }
   stage('dev-build') {
    steps {
     bat '''terraform -version
```

```
  cd iac
  terraform workspace select dev
  terraform apply -auto-approve mymodule-dev.tfplan'''
 }
}
stage('Prod Deployment Approval') {
 steps {
  input 'Do you want to Deploy in Production environment?'
 }
}
stage('prod-plan') {
 steps {
  bat '''terraform -version
  cd iac
  dir
  terraform init -var-file=prod/prod.tfvars
  terraform workspace new prod
  terraform workspace list
  terraform workspace select prod
  terraform plan --out=mymodule-prod.tfplan --var-file=prod/prod.tfvars'''
 }
}
stage('prod-build') {
 steps {
  bat '''terraform -version
  cd iac
  terraform workspace select prod
  terraform apply -auto-approve mymodule-prod.tfplan'''
 }
}
}
}
```

The following is IaC & Deploy stage on the Blue Ocean dashboard. It contains child stages that are available after it.

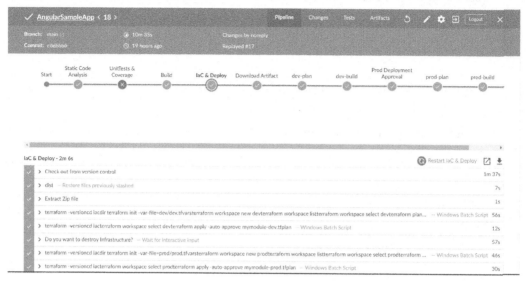

Figure 9.28: IaC & Deploy stage in Blue Ocean

The dev-build stage will create resources based on the plan created at the previous stage.

The prod-build stage will create resources based on the plan created at the previous stage.

The post block in pipeline will publish unit test results and code coverage reports after all the stages are executed or even in case of pipeline failure as we have used always block:

```
post {
  always{
    junit 'TESTS-*.xml'
    publishCoverage adapters: [coberturaAdapter(path: 'coverage/
Demo1/cobertura-coverage.xml', thresholds: [[failUnhealthy: true,
thresholdTarget: 'Line', unhealthyThreshold: 30.0, unstableThreshold:
60.0]])], failNoReports: true, failUnhealthy: true, failUnstable: true,
sourceFileResolver: sourceFiles('NEVER_STORE')
  }
}
```

Tip: The post section provides one or more additional steps that need to be executed for cleanup, or it provides notifications or other activities after the Pipeline's or stage's execution.

The following table provides details on post-section options.

Always	Execute the steps available in the post section irrespective of the completion status of the Pipeline's or stage's run.
Unstable	Execute the steps available in the post if the current Pipeline's or stage's run has an "unstable" status. The cause of unstable builds is test failures, code violations, etc.
notBuilt	Execute the steps available in the post if the build status is "Not Built".
Cleanup	Execute the steps available in the post after every other postcondition has been evaluated, irrespective of the Pipeline or stage's status.
Regression	Execute the steps available in the post if: • The current Pipeline's or stage's run's status is a failure, unstable, or aborted • The previous run was successful.
Aborted	Execute the steps available in the post if the current Pipeline's or stage's run has an aborted status.
Success	Execute the steps available in the post if the current Pipeline's or stage's run has a success status.
Failure	Execute the steps available in the post if the current Pipeline's or stage's run has a "failed" status.
Unsuccessful	Execute the steps available in the post if the current Pipeline's or stage's run has not a success status.
Fixed	Execute the steps available in the post if: • The current Pipeline's or stage's run is successful • The previous run failed or was unstable
changed	Execute the steps available in the post if the current Pipeline's or stage's run has a changed completion status from its previous execution.

Table 9.1: *Post-section options*

Syntax:

```
post {
  always {
    // One or more steps need to be included within each condition's block.
  }
  unstable {
    // One or more steps need to be included within each condition's block.
  }
  notBuilt {
    // One or more steps need to be included within each condition's block.
  }
  cleanup {
    // One or more steps need to be included within each condition's block.
  }
  regression {
    // One or more steps need to be included within each condition's block.
  }
  aborted {
    // One or more steps need to be included within each condition's block.
  }
  success {
    mail body: Pipeline Successful', subject: Pipeline Succeeded!',
           to: 'jenkinsstatus@gmail.com'  }
  failure {
       mail body: Pipeline Failed', subject: Pipeline Failed'!',
           to: 'jenkinsstatus@gmail.com'  }
  }
  unsuccessful {
    // One or more steps need to be included within each condition's block.
  }
  fixed {
     // One or more steps need to be included within each condition's
block.
  }
  changed {
     // One or more steps need to be included within each condition's
block.
  }
}
```

We have used Amazon S3 for backend. After the pipeline is executed successfully, verify Amazon S3 bucket.

Based on the workspaces that we have created, folders are created in the S3 bucket, and terraform state files are shared accordingly in the folders.

As an exercise, use the Origin Groups feature of Cloud Front to create a highly available static website in Amazon S3. The overall architecture that can be implemented using EKS, Jenkins, Amazon S3, and Amazon CloudFront is as follows:

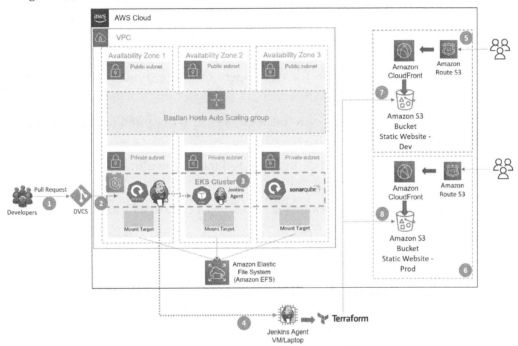

Figure 9.29: The big picture

Numbers represent the flow of pipeline in a way that allows all DevOps practices to be implemented.

Conclusion

DevOps is critical to an organization's desire to become Agile. It requires better communication and collaboration between the development and operations teams. It also creates a scenario where associates are skilled across different technologies for better alignment and implementation. DevOps practices implementation helps an organization achieve the goal of digital transformation.

In this chapter, we introduced you to Jenkins, Pipelines, Build Pipeline, Scripted Pipeline, Declarative Pipeline, and Blue Ocean. You also learnt to make Jenkins installation highly available and create a Declarative pipeline using Jenkins to perform Continuous Integration, Continuous Delivery, Resource creation and deployment using Terraform. We used a sample Angular app to showcase continuous practices implementation.

This book is the beginning of our journey in IAC and Pipeline and of understanding how different DevOps practices can be implemented.

Points to remember

- **Build Pipeline**: The traditional way to create a pipeline using upstream and downstream jobs

- **Scripted Pipeline**: Boon for developers to create dynamic pipelines using programming constructs

- **Declarative Pipeline**: Boon for beginners to write pipeline script using domain-specific language

- **Blue Ocean**: Easy way to create a declarative pipeline using a completely new user experience in Jenkins

- **Jenkinsfile**: File that contains Scripted or Declarative Pipeline by default

- **Multi-branch pipeline**: Pipeline that executes the script for all branches where Jenkinsfile is available and valid

Multiple choice questions

1. **Which of the following can be used to create a pipeline?**

   a) Build Pipeline Plugin

   b) Scripted Pipeline

   c) Declarative Pipeline

   d) Blue Ocean

   e) All of the above

2. **The following is correct in the scripted pipeline.**

   ```
   pipeline {
       /* Stages and Steps */
   }
   ```

   a) False

   b) True

3. **The following is correct in the declarative pipeline.**

```
node {
    /* Stages and Steps */
}
```

a) False

b) True

Answers

1. e
2. a
3. a

Questions

1. What is Jenkins?

2. Explain different ways to create a Pipeline.

3. Explain the difference between scripted and declarative pipelines.

4. Explain the significance of Blue Ocean.

Index

Made in the USA
Las Vegas, NV
07 December 2022

61450211R00260